Songs of the Unsung

The

Musical

and

Social

Journey of

Horace Tapscott

Songs of the Unsung

by Horace Tapscott **EDITED BY STEVEN ISOARDI**

Duke University Press Durham & London   2001

© 2001 Duke University Press   All rights reserved   Printed in the United States of America on acid-free paper ⊛   Designed by C. H. Westmoreland   Typeset by Tseng Information Systems, Inc.   Library of Congress Cataloging-in-Publication Data appear on the last printed page of this book.

This book is dedicated to the loves of my life—

Cecilia

Mary Lou, Pearline, Robbie

and the daughters, sons, grands, and great-grands.

A special thanks to my lifelong friend/brother, Wendell.

Never forget from whence we came. Keep the flame M. D.

Many thanks to those of you who support the music.

Many thanks to "Dem Folks."

—H. T.

Contents

Acknowledgments

At various stages of this book's preparation, we benefited from the reactions, suggestions, and insights of a number of excellent, involved readers. Many thanks—for their keen interest, written comments, and hours of conversation—to Robbie Tapscott Byrd, Kamau Daáood, Sylvia Jarrico, Jeannette Lindsay, Bill Madison, Mimi Melnick, Roberto Miguel Miranda, Mickey Morgan, Phil Pastras, Alyn Shipton, Cecilia Tapscott, Michael Dett Wilcots, and Renée Tapscott Wilcots.

Michael Dett Wilcots, the archivist of the Pan Afrikan Peoples Arkestra, also did a superb job in originally shooting, collecting, and then selecting and mounting most of the photographs. Without Michael's efforts, much of the history would be lost. Tamar Lando brought her artistic vision to the current scene and created some wonderful photographic images for the book's cover.

The task of preparing the discography was difficult and involved searches for a number of increasingly rare recordings. It would not have reached its current form without the assistance of Ray Avery, Self Jupiter, Ari Kleiman, Kevin Fink, and Curtis Amy, as well as Rick, Steve, and Kenn at Atomic Records in Burbank, California. A special note of thanks to Tom Albach of Nimbus West Records for his help in checking the discography's accuracy and supplying additional information not available on some recordings. Once again, Tom has played an important role in preserving the Arkestra's contribution.

The index was compiled by Mimi Melnick, who continues to be a wonderful supporter of the music in so many different ways. Eric Noble was an excellent research assistant.

We started working on this autobiography by creating a rough draft based on the lengthy transcript of the Horace Tapscott interview in the UCLA Oral History Program's Central Avenue Sounds project. Consequently, we are indebted to the program's director Dale Treleven, its organizer Alva Moore Stevenson, editors Alex Cline and Susan Douglas, and editorial assistant Peter Limbrick; their commitment to the project and exemplary professional skills led to the creation of an excellent interview transcript. That interview was made possible, in part, by the generous support of Lucille Ostrow.

Finally, a note of appreciation and respect to the wonderful staff at Duke University Press: Editor-in-Chief Ken Wissoker, Katie Courtland, Patricia Mickelberry, Laura Sell, and Cherie Westmoreland. Not only are their skills and professionalism of the highest order, but their enthusiasm for the book has made this an incredibly satisfying process.

Bright moments to all.

Foreword

Horace Tapscott, virtuoso pianist, dedicated composer and conductor, brother extraordinary, speaks of the music of his Ark-estra as music contributive toward the kind of world we want to live in, be a valuable part of, and ensure for our children. It is contributive rather than competitive. It is protective of all that has made black music endlessly fresh and stimulating, welcoming surprise and influencing all within earshot on every continent. For today, it is an alternative music, a real thing, a togetherness and belief in ourselves.

The Ark-estra came together under Horace's leadership, initially in the 1960s, to explore musically the new explosion of black self-awareness and aspiration. Black and brown musicians joined him from many parts of the United States to participate in his work of exploration. They called themselves a Society for the Preservation of Black Music and they called themselves UGMAA. They began giving performances in community centers and parks, where they handed out percussion instruments in wood, hide, metal, and shell to everyone in the audience—adults and children—who wanted to join in, who had something to say and was willing to try to say it, and who held, perhaps for the first time, an instrument with which to begin.

UGMAA meant whatever it needed to mean. As the Underground Musicians Association, and later the Union of God's Musicians and Artists Ascension, it meant the underground stream of African musical origins, and it meant the dark earth underground where roots push deep and spread, and it meant the groundswell below that ultimately restructures the surface. It was an African word, too: *ugmaa*. Like *maana,* which means "meaning"; *mbona,* "why"; *njaa,* "hunger"; and *umba,* "to create."

As a communicator, a chronicler of the times, and an actor, it is my customary way to view it all as drama, as a ceremonial procession toward the common goals that hold us together and sustain hope. Those who began the trek with us and who were felled by deprivation—dear, dear ones—we grapple them tightly to our souls and carry them gladly, to be rescued with us because remembered.

When Horace comes tipping, tapping, and finger-dancing forth on that keyboard, it isn't long before you realize that you're in the world of Tapscott, where he is master of the black and white keys to harmony and discord, where he shows us the way—in the fresh and complex unity of his Ark-estra—on our long trek together to the Ark.

The muted trumpet sings a lyrical remembrance of things rich and excellent in the high harmony of relationships. The flute and piano join in the unwonted key of peace that remembrance brings. The sounds of our black odyssey are strident, sudden, aggressive in their assault on the elements, wind and dust, dense thorny brush and pollutants, that would bar our way.

The giant awakens
Sunders his bonds
With the leverage
Of brotherhood
And moves toward home
as Dem Folks.

William Marshall
Los Angeles, 1998

Preface

It's a warm summer night in southern California in the mid-1990s. In the courtyard of the Los Angeles County Museum of Art, a standing-room-only crowd is riveted to the intense sounds coming from a jazz trio: pianist Horace Tapscott, bassist Roberto Miguel Miranda, and drummer Fritz Wise. As the last notes of "The Dark Tree" fade into the night, the audience erupts into vigorous and sustained applause. All are on their feet and many are yelling. Through the din, I hear two middle-aged suits behind me exclaim, "Who is he?!" "Where did he come from?!" No one around them seems to know.

Another Friday night, and Horace walks past KAOS and 5th Street Dick's in the Leimert Park district of South Central Los Angeles. As he turns the corner onto Degnan Boulevard and moves toward the World Stage, his presence in the village is marked by seemingly everyone he passes on the crowded street. Many say hello and some want to talk. He hasn't played a note yet.

For most of his adult life, Horace Tapscott has been one of the most creative and inspiring figures in contemporary music and his community. Yet, because of his choice to eschew the commercial mainstream of the jazz world and commit himself to the improvement of his community through music and grassroots social activism, he remains a lesser-known figure in this country, even in his own city, than his talent, accomplishments, influence, and international standing merit.

From his unique and powerful compositions, to the generations of artists who have come of age learning and working with him, to the members of the African American community of South Central Los Angeles who have benefited in so many ways from his presence and involvement, this is a life whose meaning and richness transcends a particular art form. His music was grown in neighborhood soil, and it is through his music and the projects that have formed around it that Horace has fought to transform the community. His uncompromising, lifelong commitment to a genuine and purposive music that springs from the communion of an individual soul with that of his or her community, makes him a true exemplar of a creative and contributive artist.

Before hearing a note of Horace's music, I'd heard stories of him from friends, more like whispered rumors of an underground genius in South Central Los Angeles, who, in the 1960s, defiantly turned his back on an exploitative, racist society and threw himself into the struggle to improve his community. When I picked up a copy of an early solo record, *Songs of the Unsung,* I was stunned by its originality and power. The music was so varied and the approach so clearly individual that it could not be easily labeled, a feeling reinforced not long after when I heard the assertive roar of his first album, *The Giant Is Awakened,* recorded in the late 1960s. It was clear to me that this was an artist of integrity and genius, truly beyond classification, who used and shaped many styles and techniques, from classical finesse to pounding percussiveness, to express and explore a larger vision of humanity.

Some years and many performances later, I had the opportunity to meet and interview Horace for the UCLA Oral History Program's Central Avenue Sounds project. From our first session, the quality of his engagement was the same as if he were on stage. With Horace, there are no boundaries between art and life, preparation and performance. Everything is lived in the present with commitment and intensity. In one not unusual twenty-four-hour period, he went from a gig in Leimert Park to a jam session with Don Cherry that lasted until 6:00 A.M., only to greet me in his bathrobe at 11:00 A.M. and then continue taping for the next three hours, before working on a composition for an upcoming festival, and finally, meeting with some of the members of the Pan Afrikan Peoples Arkestra and assorted friends and relatives, who randomly drifted in and out of the Tapscott home.

The two-volume transcript that resulted from those many taping sessions for UCLA during the spring and summer of 1993 served as our starting point for this book. From the summer of 1997 and into 1998, we conducted additional sessions to expand and complete the autobiography, focusing especially on the years following the formation of the Pan Afrikan Peoples Arkestra in 1961. Since much of the cultural history of the African American community in Los Angeles over the last forty years remains scarcely documented, these sessions took on an added significance and were as lengthy as the UCLA interview.

As anyone will attest who has talked to Horace or seen him perform, recordings and the written word offer an incomplete image. He lives in a world where sound and movement are intertwined, not only in performance but in conversation as well. Thoughts are only partially conveyed by words. He also communicates with his body, so much so that using corded lapel mikes in our sessions was somewhat risky. When I first interviewed him for UCLA and afterward listened to the tapes, there would be frequent pauses in his narration, but I would see the gestures and movements that amplified, developed, and at times completed his thoughts. Whenever Horace performs, there is again that motion on the bandstand—whether he is at the keyboard or dancing away from the piano as others play. In a Hollywood studio a few years ago, Dave Keller, Horace's former manager, and I sat in the control room watching Horace record "Akirfa," "Restless Nights," and "Lumumba" with his octet. When not playing, he was moving, encouraging and then dancing past each artist as they performed, possessed by the music. So much of this cannot be captured on paper.

In composing this autobiography, part of the challenge was to fill out, as much as possible, Horace's cryptic comments accompanied by gestures with fuller narration in subsequent taping sessions. I have also tried to remain close to Horace's spoken word, relying on his vocabulary and grammatical structure to convey his voice, while making the necessary modifications to create an extended prose narrative. Our earlier collaboration on Horace's chapter in *Central Avenue Sounds*,[1] drawn directly from the UCLA transcript, was edited less; instead, it was more an attempt to capture the pattern of an oral history conversational narrative. While this book is another step removed from an oral history, I hope that the literary modifications have created a more accessible text, while still allowing the reader to hear Horace. For this is a strong, committed voice, which speaks from a life spent in the middle of it, knowingly, passionately, and courageously; it is not just that of an isolated artist, but also one speaking from the heart and soul of a community and country. It is a clear, confident, and rooted voice, which gives expression to what is important and precious in life.

Steven Isoardi
Pasadena, 1998

1 Clora Bryant, Buddy Collette, William Green, Steven Isoardi, Jack Kelson, Horace Tapscott, Gerald Wilson, and Marl Young, eds., *Central Avenue Sounds: Jazz in Los Angeles* (Berkeley, Calif.: University of California Press, 1998).

Early Years in Houston

1

The beginning. In the beginning what I remember was darkness. Then, boop! It was from Robert out of Mary on April 6, 1934, at a hospital called Jefferson Davis in segregated Houston, Texas. I was locked here on this earth.

I have to set up how it was.

I was raised in Houston's Third Ward, where everyone was one family. The next-door neighbors were like my family, when I left the house. There were no locked doors. It was the kind of neighborhood where everybody knew each other. Very close. Very, very close. If you did something wrong in your class at school, the teacher would chastise you, and then come to your house and tell your parents, and—boom!—another chastisement. We had that kind of community, and I came up in this kind of environment.

In those days, people were always in the streets socializing, and there wasn't any crime to speak of. We were raised in such a way that there wasn't everyday crime against people—knocking them down, snatching purses, those kinds of things. It wasn't part of it. If you did something wrong in the community, like hurt some kid, the community would beat you up. Everybody took care of everyone else's children. They had us brainwashed to the point where we didn't think of crime. Instead, the emphasis was on trying to maintain a certain kind of quality in our race, where you can gain some respect as a whole people. And that was mostly what concerned me.

I can't remember any incidents that would cause people to get off the streets at night. Every once in a while there'd be fights over women. Cats would cut each other, but those kinds of things just involved a few people personally. If you watched yourself, kept to your business, there was no problem. What crime there was had to do with gambling, rum-running, things like that; those kinds of crimes that brought in the white police. The worst that would happen in segregated Houston was the racist attacks, the black male getting away from the white policeman, getting away from a lynch mob.

People went to the theaters for most of their entertainment, where they'd have movies and live acts. I saw all the films made by the old black producers. That's all we saw, all-black movies, like Herb Jeffries cowboy movies. They cost a nickel to get in, and everybody would leave together, walking home. I can't remember anybody getting in their car. Folks would usually go out on Friday and Saturday. On Sunday and most other nights, they'd be in some kind of church-related activity.

There was a pastor in our church named Sanders Alexander Pleasants. He would walk through the community, from his home to the church house, wearing a big ten-gallon hat and one of those coats that used to swing around him, a penguin kind of tuxedo with the tails in back. Everybody would stop what they were doing and say good morning to the reverend. The so-called prostitutes would come out of the beer joints, because he'd step into the dens of iniquity, so to speak, and talk to everybody, make them feel good. The kids would be on the porches: "Hi, Reverend Pleasants," and he'd be tipping his hat everywhere, all the way to church. Immediately after he passed, everybody would go back in, get dressed, and go right to church. I mean, the only people who weren't there were the so-called sinners, and they'd feel so bad that they'd stay off the streets, because there wasn't anybody else on the streets, you dig?

Our church was called St. John the Baptist, and everybody knew who everybody was there, all the genders from A to Z. Everything was hooked up with the community in the church, and everything happened there. It was open every day until seven or eight at night.

And children were there learning different kinds of things, always being taught about African American history. That was part of it. That's how we learned about black people. It wasn't written in the regular public school books but there were always manuscripts around that the teachers found and used. These things stayed in my head.

That's the way I still see churches today and that's why I'm not, at this moment, a part of any particular church, because I remember growing up in one that took care of the community. It made sense being at church, because the pastor would come through your home. No one starved. No one had any problems, because everybody at church was there for you. If you needed somebody to help you fix your outhouse, there was a guy there who could do it. They made sure that this person was taken care of. That's the kind of attitude that was rolling through the community, and everything was provided for the youths in the community. The church even had a great playground with swings, slides, bars, and such things for us to play on while other events were happening.

We had to be in church every night, all the kids, not two or three but twenty of us, all the ones you'd been in school with during the day. Here we were at six o'clock in the evening, sitting there, and leaving at seven, going home, going to bed, and getting up the next morning to go back before school began. I got tired of going to church every day.

The emphasis, at all times, was on study, and they made people study hard. A class at the Bible school might have 100 to 200 children. One person would go up to the pulpit and perhaps clap his or her hands, and we'd all start, in unison, singing the names of all the books of the Bible. Every one of those people who I remember liked it. Today, I'll be around a couple of those guys who I grew up with, and the books of the Bible are still in the back of their heads and they can just run them off.

Learning was so important. You got so you were just programmed. When it was time to be silent, we became silent. You could be standing up at the pulpit doing one of those numbers and you could hear a pin drop. Do you suppose you could see that today? And everybody in there was an A- plus student, because you had to be. You didn't have any choice at all. You wanted to live in this house, you wanted to be able to grow up in this community, you wanted to eat, then you had to learn how to speak and write and talk and understand. They'd have it in every house. If you wanted to see a girlfriend and her parents or older brother opened the door, they'd say, "How bad do you want to get in here?"

"Real bad."

"Well, what's nine times ninety-nine?"

If you didn't get the right answer, you didn't come in. You were always thinking, "What will they ask me now?"

I went to the Frederick Douglass Elementary School, and it was always good to be in those classes, listening to the teachers. Everybody was quiet; all you could hear was the fan. They taught us about Frederick Douglass and Countee Cullen, and other black writers, the educators of our race. As you walked down the hallway at school, you'd see these big pictures of Frederick Douglass, Booker T. Washington, Harriet Tubman, all these black people. And we just accepted it. That was the way it was supposed to be, and it was just natural to us. It was only later on, when I went to the integrated schools in California, that black people disappeared from the history being taught.

We always learned things—reading, writing, arithmetic—in unison. We had to learn things in groups. They gave us the feeling of always working together with someone, that you could do things much better with someone else, and that you could trust the person you were working with. That's the feeling we got.

In those days of segregation, in the late 1930s and early 1940s, there was a lot of activity going on all around the world, but I was surrounded only by this block that I lived on. It was like sitting on your front porch watching the whole world pass you by, all in one color. But all these people that passed here made some kind of significant contribution toward the settling of this country.

Dorie Miller was a black sailor in World War II, a cook in the navy. Blacks weren't allowed on top. They were always in the galley. But when the attack came from the Japanese at Pearl Harbor, Dorie Miller ran to a gunner's position and wiped out several of the enemy aircraft. That was hushed up for many years. He's just been written up, naturally, in the last twenty-five years into the history. But the black community in Houston knew about it. This person, Dorie Miller, once came right into my pathway, right in front of me as a kid with his white uniform on. Everyone was sitting on the porch, just talking and looking. He passed by and he was waving at the folks.

I asked my mother, "Is that Dorie Miller?"

"That's Dorie Miller."

I ran and caught him, pulled him by his coattail and asked him, "Are you Dorie Miller?"

"Yes, I'm Dorie Miller."

I spurted out something and ran back to my house. I'll always remember that.

I enjoyed those early days in our community in Houston, Texas. They more or less shaped me for what was to come, showed me how to get along with everyone, seeing people on the street and feeling safe. It looked like everything was cool.

Family

With segregation in the South, for those heroes of those days, the only place they'd be in any city was one particular village. In this case, that particular village was the Third Ward in Houston. And I had a family there. I came out of the family of the Malones and the Tapscotts. I know of one of my great-grandmothers on my mother's side, Amanda Carrington Steptoe. She was a slave and had several daughters, Pearlina Carrington, and then Jenny and Alberta, with a Mr. Steptoe. Pearlina was married at seventeen to Tommy Malone, and they had four children: Mary Lou, who became my mother, Ora, Bessie, and Willie. Pearlina then married another cat, the Reverend Richard Earl Fisher, who became my stepgrandfather.

I was raised in a house full of women, from my grandmother, Pearlina, to my two great-aunts, Aunt Jenny and Aunt Berta, my mother, and a rooming lady, Miss Chaney, who rented a room up front. As usual, the men were dead, you dig? They made babies like the black widow, I guess, because they weren't going to last. Black men were scheduled to live up to thirty. If they made forty, they were lucky. So it was mostly the women. It has a lot to do with what I think about women now. I have a lot of respect for them, because of the things they went through for us. But I also remember hearing a lot about the limitations of the male. Actually, we don't mean nothing. We drop our seed and that's it. That's all we're needed for.

My mother, Mary Lou Malone, lived to be about ninety-two. You know how men are about their moms. They're the queen and there's nothing like them, especially when you think of what they had to go through. She was pregnant when she was a teenager, but didn't let it bother her; she just kept on stepping. When she was carrying me, at first she thought she was sick, but even the doctors in the hospitals didn't know what was the matter with her. Then the local voodoo lady came by, pointed to her, and said, "That's a boy inside you."

Voodoo was a part of the community, sprinkled throughout. There were old houses, Madame so-and-so's place, for those who wanted it. Sometimes, the old soothsayers would be sitting out front, sewing or whatever. It was that strong, was respected, and I grew up in it. I've always had respect for it. I didn't bother with it, but I believed in it. A lot of the families had some beliefs or customs that probably went back to African tribal beliefs, as well as the Christian teachings.

Mary Lou was very attractive, and there were a lot of cats trying to get to her. I remember one person always coming back and that's the cat she married, because he treated her children all right. His name was Leon Jackson and he liked us for real; he wasn't just trying to get to my mom. So he took me on. He was the father who I remember as my father. I always introduced him as my stepfather and I called him "Mr. Leon" all his life. That's how I was raised.

My stepfather was a real dynamite kind of a person, half Native American and half African American. He had a great look and could run fast, and I loved to run. When I used to have a problem, I'd just take off running, because I felt like I was the wind. And this guy could run fast, because I remember him running from the police, who were shooting at him. He had this gambling house next to the railroad tracks, and every now and then the police would break up those places. I'd see these guys busting out, running all different ways, and my stepfather was whippin'. I used to love to see him run. Yeah, he'd be doing it and he never took a bullet. I liked him, and we used to run a lot.

Mr. Leon would always take me places to make sure that I would be a part of what was happening. He was somewhat of a pool shark, and when we later moved to Los Angeles, he'd take me to a pool hall on Central Avenue and Twenty-first Street. He was teaching me how to socialize with all sorts of people. He wanted us to know.

Even after he and my mother separated some years later, he'd come by the pad all the time to visit me and my sister, Robbie Tapscott Byrd. He lived down the street and was always there taking care of me, showing me how to drive and things like that. He was still the cat who was showing me around, showing me the man's side of life. Later on, he'd be at all my concerts and really get into it. He and my mother never talked against each other, and they always encouraged us to respect the other. Mr. Leon never hit my mama, and I was aware of that. She wasn't angry with him and he wasn't with her. They just couldn't get along and so they split. But he was a good old cat. He lived until I was in my thirties and was always there for me. He was my father.

I had an uncle whose name was Willie Malone and who was a heavyweight in the community. He was a gangster and he taught me how to use firearms. Uncle Willie was never without anything and was probably in on most of the organized crime rackets. If there was any crime there, it would have been him, being the head criminal. Willie Malone was the cat. One year, he brought thousands of dollars to my mama's house, and they refused to let him in, because they knew it was gambling money and had to do with the mob in the black community. Even the white policemen respected him, and white judges used to cut him loose all the time. I guess he was probably working with them, too.

Uncle Willie was a tough guy, kind of like a bull, a real huge black man. The white people even had him wrestling bears. One day, my mother grabbed a baseball bat and went after him: "You wrestle that bear and you're going to wrestle me!" It seemed that he always had to prove something. My grandmother Pearl was crippled as a child. Because of a burn, one leg was shorter than the other. One day, she was walking through the neighborhood. Some person made a statement about this crippled lady, and man, Uncle Willie was in there. He hit this guy so hard, he went through the plate-glass window at the Blue Sky Cafe on Dowling Street.

My family could walk the streets. Everybody would be tipping their hats to the women, because they knew they belonged to the Malone clan.

Men at that time had different families on the same block, two or three houses from each other. Everybody knew it, and these cats stayed in none of the places, but could go in to eat. It was accepted in church that these were their children and their children's brothers lived down the street. The women wouldn't get that friction, because they had to sit together and be together for the sake of the children, for the sake of keeping everything tolerable. I could go to some cat's house, see his daddy, go three or four houses down, and his daddy would also be down there. It wasn't anything that was hidden. Maybe it was necessary to save a race of people. It could have been a holdover from the days of early Africa, when cats had so many wives. And the reason why they had them was because they could take care of them. There was also a shortage of males, and that probably carried on until maybe the early 1950s.

My father, the Reverend Robert Tapscott, had two or three ladies in his church. They all went to the same church and they all had his babies. I met him once. I was on the street in Houston one day when I was about six, standing on this corner, and this real tall guy reached down to pat me. He said, "Hello, son," and gave me twenty cents. That's all I can remember about him. He was in the area, but I only had communications with him that one time. The next time I saw him was a picture of him in a casket. I was told that the guy died jumping off a truck, helping his seventh wife move. He was in his sixties or seventies at the time, and I guess he was still pumping them. Steve Lacy reminds me of him. He has that kind of complexion. The first time I met Steve, I said, "Wow! Man, you look just like my dad."

Since Mr. Leon came on the scene when I was about four years old, I didn't really have to deal with my father not being there. I didn't have any bitterness and I never thought about it. But when I got older, I hit on my mom one time: "Mother, where is my father, Robert Tapscott?" And she told me not to ever mention his name. She got angry, and I backed off.

My father's lifestyle did lead to some strange situations later on in my life. When I was seventeen and living in Los Angeles, I went back to Houston with my mom and my sister to visit the rest of our people. One day, I was just walking around the streets, visiting the old places, and I went to Emancipation Park on Dowling Street. The park was full of all these young folks, and I spotted this one lady who really attracted me out of all the women there. I walked over to her and introduced myself, told her my name was Horace, and she said she was Benny. We started talking, and as we were walking, someone called out, "Tapscott!" I turned around and thought to myself, "Who knows I'm here?"

Meanwhile, Benny turned her head and said, "What?"

I stared at her and said, "My name's Horace Tapscott."

"I'm Benny Marie Tapscott."

"What's your father's name, Benny?"

"Robert."

"Hello, sister!"

She was my half sister.

The following Sunday, we went to the old church we grew up in, St. John's. All of a sudden, one of the deacons announced from the pulpit that a solo was going to be performed by Reverend Tapscott's son. I had my trombone with me, so I got up and started toward the front when I noticed across the aisle another guy walking toward the pulpit. Both of us kept walking and looking sideways until we got to the front, where we turned and faced each other.

"Hello, I'm Horace."

"Hello, I'm Robert."

"You go first."

"No, you go first."

Just like Benny, we didn't know anything. It was the first time I'd met this cat. He was a singer and Reverend Tapscott's son.

That visit to Houston was an experience for me. But somehow it all worked out, because family was so important then and when I was growing up in Houston. And they've passed along all the family history to their kids and grandkids. Not long ago, I was playing a gig in New York at the Music Center, and during a rehearsal or sound check, this girl walked up and introduced herself as Vanessa Tapscott, my half brother's granddaughter and my great-niece. I even found out later that my father's father, my grandfather Tapscott, was a white cat with a black woman up in Montana, or someplace like that, and that there's a whole set of white cousins out there.

I didn't have anything against my old man, because I knew where he was coming from in that day and age. Black men in that time had few opportunities, were always pushed to the back, told they had no brains. These attitudes and the way society was just belittled these men, and probably forced them to be a certain kind of person. As I got older, I began to understand what they went through and why they were like they were. The ones who survived were there, and they were wise men who talked to us about the world and the way things were.

Everybody was supportive of the family. That's the way it was. Everything that I remember had to do with family, and everybody had that. Family values were actually valuable things that people passed on from one to another, from one family to another, and from one person within that family to another. School functions were always a family thing. You'd get off from your job early so you could make your son's or your daughter's little recital at school. And everybody was there. You could walk down the street the next day, and the iceman might pull his truck over and say, "That was a good recital you had, son."

There were bad times, as far as the economy and having food were concerned. We used to get food from a barbecue place, Avalon's, where my stepgrandfather would pay a nickel for a bag of garbage food they were throwing out. But I don't remember ever starving. We always had a garden, and you could go out in your yard and get some food. And people always made things for you. Grandparents would be sewing the soles on your shoes, so you could go to church.

I'll always remember one time with my sister, Robbie. I was hungry, and my mother had been sitting on the couch, thinking about how to get some food. Somehow we got a meal. A neighbor might have brought us a plate. My mother halved it between me and my sister, and Robbie said, "No, I don't want it. Give it to Horace. He's hungry." I never forgot that. She went without eating so I wouldn't be hungry. That's why I love her so much. When I'd be out in the streets, begging for money like the kids do in Haiti, I'd always ask for double what people would give me. I'd tell them that I've got a sister. She's a grandmother now and used to live within walking distance from us. She just moved back to Texas. But that's how Mary Lou raised us: always take care of each other in some kind of way.

As a kid, I played out in the streets a lot; all the kids did. Most of the time it wasn't dangerous, as far as traffic was concerned. But when I was four or five, still just so close to the ground, I was playing with this litter of young puppies. One day I was going across the street, and they followed me, as they usually did. But when I had to get out of the way of something coming, they didn't move. Whatever it was, a truck or a carriage, ran over them, and they were all dead, five of them. It just took me out, all these dogs dying. I was pretty sad about that, and it has stayed with me. When I was in the service, I'd have dreams about it and wake up sweating. I never wanted to hurt anything. This was the first hard thing I had to deal with in my young life. The second involved my mother.

Racism

I have a vision that stays in my head. Even today, I might have a dream and all of a sudden it's back to that evening in Houston, Texas. I was about five or six years old and laying in bed with my mother. It was late at night and it was dark. I remember this white guy, with a coat and hat on, breaking my window with his fist and then pushing through with this gun in his hand. He put it to my mother's head, yelling, "Where's your brother? I'm going to kill that nigger tonight!" It was the police and that's all I remember. I was crying, I guess. Years later, I found out that they were looking for my Uncle Willie.

I had a real thing about racism as a little child, and that vision stayed with me a long time. It stayed with me for so long that I was afraid of and didn't like anybody I saw who was white, because of what they did to my mother. All I saw was this white guy putting his gun to her head, talking about how he's "going to kill that nigger tonight." That soaked in and went on through the years. That was my first experience with racism, and I had never seen a white person before. That was the first time.

The only time I saw white people was when I went to town. The first time, all these things were fascinating to me, because I hadn't been out of the neighborhood. Afterward, we always went somewhere and not because we were living in a bad environment. Everybody, every house, was intent, so to speak, on their children learning, and part of that was traveling, seeing new things. They dominated your mind, and I appreciated all that. But during the travels you'd also be reminded, once again, of that pain of segregation, that pain of prejudice.

Every now and then you had to go downtown in Houston, and that meant you had to ride in the back of the bus. One time, me and my mother got on this bus, and I sat down in the middle, because there wasn't anybody else there. I'm a kid. I don't know I'm supposed to sit in the back, so I sit down in front of the colored sign. The bus driver was looking in the mirror, and I remember my mother saying to me, "Come back here. Come on."

"Why?"

And she wouldn't tell me I wasn't good enough to sit up there. I'll never forget that. She never said I wasn't good enough. She said, "Well, I want you to sit back here," because of this, because of that, but never because I was black. I put her through a whole lot of things, because I can remember the pain in her eyes having to tell me where to sit.

My Uncle Willie had a number of people who were legally under his particular command. He was also a painter, and would go out and paint these mansions in the white neighborhoods. They had two cars, and I would travel with these cats. I'd never seen mansions with long staircases and bathrooms, with toilets and tubs, blocks of those kinds of structures and neighborhoods with no one on the streets. I didn't have any idea what was happening. I'd never experienced this kind of activity or nonactivity. There were all these great, southern homes, and there was nobody around, not one kid in the streets playing. Coming from my neighborhood, this was strange and kind of frightening.

I was only about five or six years old, but I was learning about the kinds of problems that black men were having in those times, and how we had to always get out of the way for some reason. I learned quickly that during those days it was really dangerous for us to be alone on the highway, because you might get pulled over, killed, or something like that. As I got older and looked back, I'd see why it was what it was. I could imagine the Native American villages being that way, because that's what it was. None of this dawned on me for many years, but I remember seeing so many things happen growing up in that community.

Music from Day One

Music started at home with my mother. She had her own small group, maybe a quartet, in the early part of the century, playing jazz in the segregated black areas of Texas and Louisiana, what used to be called the chitlin' circuit. Yeah, a woman jazz lady, Mary Lou Malone. My grandmother, Pearlina, was always humming, but she never did anything musically.

We had this home at 2719 Dowling Street and this house was a shotgun type of a house. You'd come through the front and you'd see the back. She had a big old stand-up piano in those days. It was very large and it took up part of the doorway. So when you came in my house, you had to play the piano to get to the couch. And the seat, if you had the bench out, took up all the room. You couldn't even walk down the hall. You had to wait. My mother's friends would play things as they came in. You had to play something or you wouldn't be let in the house.

From day one it was music. All I remember when I came into being, all I saw and heard around me, was music. All these blues cats—Floyd Dixon and Amos Milburn—would be coming by my house. And they lived in the neighborhood. My sister and Floyd Dixon were girlfriend and boyfriend, and they know each other today. In 1939, I was in kindergarten with Johnny "Guitar" Watson and Edwin Pleasants—a cousin of the preacher. To this day, Edwin still plays flute with me in our Pan Afrikan Peoples Arkestra. When he moved to Los Angeles in the 1960s, he joined us and has been with us ever since. There were just all kinds of people around in those days because of segregation. Whoever you were, whatever class you were in, you still had to live in this area.

In those days blues singing was everywhere. You've got to have the music all the time; it was part of the fabric of the community. And on Sunday that same blues became the spiritual. All of it to me was blues, because I could hear the blues running through every phase of all the music that came out of the community. It was all based on that "hmmm." Out of that came the spiritual and the blues, rock and roll, and rhythm and blues, all of that. All the artists were trained the same way. Every woman singing the blues came out of the church choir. It all began in church. The church was our thing.

I remember listening to Marian Anderson. She had that look, that classy look of my grandmother and my aunt, those high cheekbones, that stare, that open stare like an evergreen forest. We would all sit in our homes and listen to her sing on the radio. Once, she came through the community and sang at church. We got to see and hear all those people up close. There was the Hall Johnson Choir, and some of the early musicians who have made such a contribution even to European classical music, like Roland Hayes. We used to listen to him.

On Sundays, most parents might take their youngsters to some kind of sports activity. In my case the activity was a musical activity, some kind of concert somewhere in the community at some church, anywhere that featured orchestras. My mother loved it, and she'd always take me and my sister to these concerts. We had two bands at our church, two full orchestras, twenty and thirty people. Sitting on this side was the junior band, about thirty people. On the other side was the senior band, and my mother played in that. Lawrence "Tricky" Lofton was a trombonist in the junior band. I was about to get into that orchestra when we cut out and went to California.

When I was six or seven years old, I had my first band. I always used to have a gang of cats who would follow me. We got some old furnaces, buckets, tin pans, skillets, and some sticks, and I'd play these like they were drums, setting the rhythm. The other cats would be up front blowing into some things or whatever instruments they had. It seemed like everybody had instruments or wanted to. We thought we were playing music. And we always had an audience, because the whole family would sit down and listen sometime during the day.

I had to spend a lot of time with music and I was exposed to every type of music. I had to play all of it and I took it all. There was one particular concert we went to, and one of the pieces was the *William Tell* Overture by Rossini. There's a part in it that features the brass, and it's real majestic and real macho. I was watching and saw the instrument for me. I wanted that instrument. My mother saved her money from the jobs she had in those days, and one day, came down to the area where I was playing and gave me my signal, which was a whistle. Wherever I was, I'd hear it and I'd know it was her. That particular whistle is in one of my compositions, a suite called *Ancestral Echoes*. I wrote a whole line of that sound. So she gave me that whistle, and I came running.

"What do you think I've got behind my back?"

"I don't know."

She gave me my first instrument, a trombone. I was about eight or nine.

We already had a piano in the house, and Mary Lou started teaching me when I was six, but I wanted a horn. Growing up in those days, if you played the piano and the violin, you'd go outside and the cats would want to beat up on you. That was just for girls, playing the piano. If you're going to play an instrument, you're going to play a horn or something. The first time I blew on it, my neighbor yelled, "Oh, my God, the boy got a horn!"

And every day they'd hear me.

My mother was my first teacher. What she laid on me was discipline, getting to it and working at it, and listening and learning from what she was doing. She'd play a tune at the piano, and then she'd have me get up and try to play it on the piano. And then my sister would try. Then she'd be back at me. So there's no reading yet, no notes. It's all in the head. When she bought me that trombone, then she got me a teacher. I had to learn to read now. My teacher was Professor Hogan, and the first thing he did was put a sheet of music in front of me. I'll never forget, the first tune was the "Blue Bells of Scotland" in the key of E-flat.

I'd spend at least four hours practicing every day—two hours on one instrument and two on the other. I was learning fast. I had long arms and I was going to seventh position on the trombone. I got to the point where instead of just practicing scales and such, I started taking one position, trying to see how many notes were in there. And I started trying to hum while I was playing—all kinds of crazy things at the time. The attitude was always, "Let's search." There were no boundaries, and I've always felt that.

California

2

We came to Los Angeles in 1943 so my stepfather could work in nearby San Pedro at the shipyards. During the war, jobs were opening up. The best job that black men had in those days was being a chauffeur or working on a train as a porter. Those were the two highest paying, outside of the preachers in the community. When the wartime boom in the defense industries happened, that's when most of the people left Texas and Louisiana for California.

On the train heading toward Los Angeles, it was segregated all the way, but nobody even thought about it. "Okay, so they ride up there; we ride back here." We had our things back there, and cats would be meeting and singing. It was cool. I saw my first sexual act on the train. Some soldier got on and met this woman. By the time we got to Arizona, they were humping. I was sitting right behind them and I was supposed to be asleep. I was a little kid, about nine or ten years old. I remember them getting off at Union Station in Los Angeles, saying good-bye to each other. That was out.

Union Station was beautiful. It was busy and you'd see movie stars coming through. I was really taken: "All these white cats, man. Where am I?" My first scene getting off at Union Station was that city hall building, at the time the tallest building in the city. And, man, it was another kind of city. All of a sudden you'd start seeing palm trees and all these fruit trees right on the street. And it was cool for you to pick and eat them, as you're walking along; they didn't belong to anybody. All that was colorful. We got into this car and started driving down Central Avenue.

I got down on Central and I started seeing the street life unfold in front of me. Before we got to our house, my mother told the driver to stop the car. Our suitcase was still in the trunk.

I said, "This is where we live?"

"No, this is not where we live. I want to introduce you to your music teacher."

Somehow she'd already picked him out. It's the first time I'd ever been in California in my life. We hadn't gotten to the house yet. I don't know where I live. And before we get there, I'm introduced to my music teacher. That's the first person I met in Los Angeles— Harry Southard, a barber on Fifty-second Street and Central, but a trombonist as well, and years earlier one of the first jazz band leaders in Los Angeles. I got out and met this guy. He said, "I'll be seeing you, son." The next day I was at music lessons.

We went to 1964 Naomi Avenue, about a block east of Central Avenue between Washington Boulevard and Twentieth Street. It was a two-story house, and we lived upstairs. Me and my sister were in one room, and my mother and my stepfather were in the room up front. An older lady, Mrs. Young, who was the landlady, lived downstairs. She was a soothsayer, had to be a voodoo lady, and I used to be scared of her. I didn't like to come in the house by myself when she was there. She was out—a real short lady with that Maria Ouspenskaya look, that actress who played in the werewolf movies with Lon Chaney Jr. She had that thing about her and she'd be sliding down the hall . . . put chills on me. But like in Houston, voodoo was a part of the community. Some people refused it and some accepted it.

The neighborhood was packed with people and was lovely. It was all single family homes with a lot of land around the houses to grow things. The doors were still unlocked and the windows were open. You didn't have to look behind your back. Everybody would walk to the movies and, at night, would walk home together. Everyone knew everyone, and everyone spoke to everyone. It was peaceful. Some cats might be fighting every now and then, but it was between them and didn't have anything to do with you and yours. It was a good community, and we took all these things for granted.

My school, the Twentieth Street Elementary School at Twentieth and Naomi, was right across the street from my house, which meant that I walked to school every day. There were a lot of people on that street who were musicians. My neighbor was Etta James, and we used to go to school together. We'd wake up, and then run and play. She was living with her grandparents, and they kept a close watch on her. She was a pretty little thing and would sit up on their porch with that blond hair, opening her legs and shit, and we'd be on the other side of the street waving. After a while, the old man would be on her case and wouldn't let none of us get next to her.

She was Jamesetta Rogers then and the highlight of the community. She used to sing at the Saint Paul Baptist Church every Sunday and started breaking people up when she was about twelve years old. For a little girl to have such heavy, strong lungs, they'd have people coming to that church just to hear her. A few years later, about the time we were going to junior high school, she moved to San Francisco to live with her mother.

Country Years

I only stayed there a few months, because it got really crowded. My sister and I were getting to that age, and we needed different rooms. Until the family got their money together for a bigger pad, I had to go somewhere else to live. I was sent to Fresno, California, a few hundred miles north of Los Angeles in the central valley, and stayed about two years with my great-uncle, Lawyer Lusk, and great-aunt, Jenny Lusk, my grandmother Pearlina's sister.

Fresno was country. I would get up at four o'clock every morning to pick cotton. When grape time came, it was up at four to cut grapes. This went on every day. Going to the outhouse was the biggest problem with living in the country. That was a terrible experience, especially at nighttime. It was about forty yards from the back door, and you'd always have to watch for spiders or snakes in those things. Then you'd have a long walk back to the house, and your imagination would start working on you. You'd start seeing spirits dancing and jumping all over the backyard. That would be a trip. There was a cesspool back there, and I had to help my uncle clean it out. Finally, they got a toilet in the house, and that was a big deal on the block when the people started getting the inside toilets. Up until then, everybody had an outhouse. I guess that's why all the food grew like it did.

In the evenings, everybody would be on their front porches, watching the sunset, kids out on the road playing, people singing, talking, dancing. All the way down the street, activity was going on family wise. Everybody knew each other, worked together out in the fields, and at night, would be out visiting and talking with each other up and down the street. They'd turn the radio on every once in a while, but most of the time communication was one to the other. I grew up in that atmosphere and I got turned on by it.

During my few years there I'd go for walks with my uncle. As we walked through some meadows, he'd be explaining why this or that was happening, and how nature and you were one thing together, and how to treat people with respect. He believed you could be in harmony with every living thing. Everything that's breathing is helping everything else that's breathing. There were many things he passed on that I couldn't understand then, but they stayed with me. I remember one time, years later when I was in the air force, waking up at two in the morning and yelling, "That's what he meant!" He and my aunt had traveled around the country for years before they settled in Fresno, and he had that aura of wisdom. As time passed we got closer. That's when life started opening up to me, because of this uncle.

I went to my first mixed school in Fresno—the Kirk Elementary School—the first time I'd ever gone to school with anybody white. The Twentieth Street Elementary School in Los Angeles had some Mexican and maybe Native American students, but no whites. I walked to school with these other black cats who lived on the street. The first time I got on the school grounds, there were two white guys fighting. This big old blond cat was beating up on this brown-haired cat. I ran over, pushed them aside, and looked at the big one.

"Try that on me, man!"

This cat said, "What?"

"Do it! Do it! Hit me!"

I didn't know this guy. He had blue eyes, and I caught myself looking right at him. I had never seen anybody who looked like him.

"Aw, go away."

I'm really mean, now. I'm in a mean stage, prejudiced, and I want to fight him. He didn't hit me, so I hit him. That was my first day at this school. I hadn't even registered yet.

When I finally went to class, I looked across the room and there was this beautiful blond girl with blue eyes. I'd never seen anyone who looked like that. I started looking at her, and she looked at me. I can see her face now. She was so beautiful. That turned me around, and she became my girlfriend. Her name was Barbra, and I fell in love with her. We'd talk about race. She was trying to cool me down, because I was fighting white cats all day, every day. Many years later, when I wrote that tune, "Dial 'B' for Barbra," it was for her. I don't remember her last name and I don't know what in the world ever happened to her.

Kirk was a colorful school and it was beautiful. They had this Indian girl there named Carmen. I'll never forget her. She had long black hair, and some of the things she made me do, I don't even want to mention. My first Mexican friend was a cat I had a fight with. We fought all day. He wasn't giving up; he was macho. And I wasn't giving up; I'd started the fight. We were kept after school, and the teacher wasn't going to let us go home unless one of us apologized. We made a deal, although he said, "You're going to have to apologize first." So I was learning. Me and this cat became great friends after that, and I started trying to get along with the rest of the people.

But I never could get along with most of the guys. I had just come out of Texas and I was reacting. I was ten or eleven years old and I was big. The white cats weren't even bothering me. If they saw me coming, they'd move to the side, because I had gotten that rep by then—"It's that crazy kid from the South." They had passed the word on to stay out of my way, until I started getting used to the fact that there were other people in the world. Parents started talking to me. Miss Ayres, my teacher, sent a note home to my aunt and uncle, telling them that I was very racially prejudiced against the boys: "He has to learn how to get along, how to live with other people." She took time with me, and tried to teach me about being gentle and loving, and that not everyone was mean. I suppose they were trying, but I didn't know what to think. I was confused and I felt ashamed for disrupting classes, for being so crazy and mean.

I remember when Roosevelt died in 1945, I turned on this little white girl just to be mean, just to make her cry. I was at school, and this nice kid who was riding her bicycle around came up to me.

"Horace, President Roosevelt's dead."

I said, "So!"

"Why aren't you crying?"

"Why should I cry? What do I got to cry about? So, he's dead. So what! Where's Eleanor?"

All the black folks used to talk about Eleanor. The black women enjoyed her. Some of them claimed that because she was so ugly, nobody liked her for the right reason. But her name was all around the black homes, because of what she did for Marian Anderson, who was our queen. The Daughters of the American Revolution, or some group like that, refused to allow Marian Anderson to sing at some event in Washington, D.C. Eleanor Roosevelt then arranged for her to sing at another place. That move made her a heroine in the black community, and they were all in her corner, but not the cat, President Roosevelt. People in the community felt that Eleanor was closer to them, to minority people, and whatever progress was coming out of Washington was due to her, not the president.

I do remember demanding how come the history course wasn't talking about black people. I'd mention somebody like Frederick Douglass, who I had learned about in Houston. I wanted to know how come the history I was reading didn't have me in it, except as a slave. And I had some teachers, some white teachers that I'll never forget, who sat down and explained to me why. They told me the truth, why things were like they were. Then I began to understand more. I still had that prejudice, but I wasn't as crazy as I was at first. Then I made a friend, a white guy, who came up to me and said, "Hey, man, let's talk, just talk." He took time with me, and I'd never talked with a white cat before, at least on the basis of friendship.

I was learning very slowly, because each time I saw a white male, all I saw was a guy with the gun at my mama's head. I didn't get past that almost until I got into the air force in 1953. And when I got into the service, there was a new set of rules. There was a whole new racial thing there right after Truman had integrated the armed services, and it was hard for both sides to get used to each other.

Musically, I had my horn with me and was practicing all the time in the backyard by myself. I knew I'd have to face Mary Lou. She'd want to hear a tune and she'd want to hear it right away. So I played all the time. But there was no music at this school. I did a lot of stage work, dancing and acting, and I was the star of the school play one year. My mother and my sister were there; they'd come up to visit and see me in this show. There were only two black families in this theater, but everyone had been feeling nice, and we'd been rehearsing a lot for this night. At one point, I was sitting in this chair in the middle of the stage and all the kids were dancing around me. It wasn't until years later that I found out the play was about old black Joe, some Uncle Tom slave cat! In another part of the play, I was dancing in an Indian outfit and this guy next to me stepped on my foot. I stopped dancing and punched him in the face, right on stage. I popped him. My mama and my sister just slid down in their seats.

But during that time in Fresno, I realized I should try to take it easy and smell the flowers, and listen and look, and check out different things. Open up your ears to what is and what isn't, and how you should guide yourself and your seed. Those kinds of things were coming to me, those small things that can't be taught to you technically or through a book on how to act. I enjoyed those two years in Fresno. I fell in love with it. But all parts of California at the time were just beautiful, and living in that country atmosphere was different for me.

When the money got a little better, I came back to Los Angeles, and my family moved across Central Avenue to 1154 East Twenty-first Street and a bigger house. I was different when I came back, really different. I started thinking about compositions, about dance, about plays I wanted to write. And I did start writing a play in high school.

I went to Lafayette Junior High, just off Central and Fourteenth Street, and got right into the music program, where you were encouraged to write your own music. We had a band session every day to play our music after we wrote it and that helped quite a bit. Mr. Samuel Browne used to come over to listen to us from nearby Jefferson High School, where he was teaching music. I wrote a tune then, the first song I ever wrote, called "Bongo Bill." I remember playing it with Mr. Browne listening and critiquing it. He wouldn't let me know that he dug it but he encouraged me to keep it up. When I saw him smiling at me, at the arrangement, I knew it was cool.

My thought pattern started stretching out. I wanted to play different music. I remember the *Peer Gynt* Suite, which I used to play a lot, those kinds of things that had to do with composers. I started listening to cats who were looked on as the revolutionaries or the outcast cats. All their music was great, even the Beethoven and Haydn cats. I started listening to the other side of the coin as well.

I met my wife, Cecilia, during those days. We were fourteen years old and in the eighth grade. There was another girl with her, who was the sweetheart of the campus. There are certain people you never forget, I don't care how long you live, and I remember this girl from when we were in grammar school on Twentieth Street. She would stand at the gate every day after school, when we were in sixth grade, and kiss all the boys good-bye until tomorrow. Her name was Dorothy and she lived in a house where two other girls lived, one of whom was Cecilia. All three of these families were in this pad. When we were at Lafayette, I saw this girl in the auditorium who turned around with all these eyes. I said,

"Who is that?" I wanted to meet her. So Dorothy, being who she was, introduced us.

After that things started happening. Every time I'd play, Cecilia would hide her face. I'd be playing Tommy Dorsey's "Marie" all through school. Me and a couple of cats on drums and such used to entertain the people at lunchtime. I became the student body president, and Cecilia became the vice president of the junior high. Roy Brewster, one of the musicians I grew up with here, was the main cat who got me elected president. He and a couple of other cats in the band walked around the school with placards, "Vote for Horace! Vote for Horace!"

At that time, there were kids who didn't have enough money to eat in the cafeteria, and so they brought their lunches. Since there were more of them than anybody else, they'd all have to eat in the auditorium. Well, I was also on the stage crew and would be in the auditorium, so we'd put on these old Billy Eckstine records and would do a show mimicking Eckstine for all these races of kids. It was a rainbow looking out there, and they'd be clapping. When it was voting time, they remembered Horace.

We were running things and changed the rules at the school. They went for it, and we had concerts there. We decided that there would be music at the noon hour all the time. It was a lot of fun. I had all the ladies running after me. That was nice.

Cecilia and I used to walk the streets together, and we got to see all these people. We used to listen to Art Tatum, Red Callender, and Bill Douglass at the Clark Annex near the Clark Hotel, right on the corner of Washington Boulevard and Central Avenue. Being so young, we weren't able to go into the club part but we stood at the window. We'd just watch Tatum play, and he'd be looking out the window at us. He had that blind eye, and that's all I used to look at. I'd also see him daily up and down Central. Then you'd go across the street and Billie Holiday would be there. Down the street there'd be big bands—Lunceford, Henderson—all of them playing up and down Central Avenue. And Dorothy Donegan was on the scene. I loved her. I love her today, too, but when I was a teenager, I loved Dorothy. I didn't even bother about her playing, she looked so good. And that's what we used to walk through.

We'd see all these people, all the time, on the avenue, some going into stores, just shopping. Red Callender lived on Newton Street, next to the police station. We used to go around to his house, as he was leaving for a gig. Me and his stepson, Ronald Sibley, were close in school, and that's how I met Red. I'd be over at his house all the time when he was on his way to work around the corner at the Clark Hotel.

Central Avenue is heartbreaking now. I hate to go down there, because when I came here, it was just live. Houston was live, too, because I was in that part of Houston that was a main part of town, where you saw a lot of activity. The only difference compared to Houston was that in Los Angeles, there were so many musicians at one time, playing all the time and listening, getting a chance to listen to each other doing a job. During intermissions, they'd come across the street or go next door to hear the other cats, and those in turn would do the same thing, all night long.

Lafayette Junior High School was my second time with colorful, mixed ethnic groups. I also got a chance to hear different kinds of music and started to play different music. The band there was led by Percy McDavid, who taught Illinois Jacquet and all the cats in Houston, Texas. That's how I got hooked up with Illinois and Russell Jacquet, and Arnett Cobb, and all those guys. Mr. McDavid also had a band that played in different parks around the city every Sunday. He had Charlie Mingus, Britt Woodman, Eric Dolphy, Buddy Collette, Red Callender, and John "Streamline" Ewing. All the cats were in it. On a certain night every week there was a rehearsal at the junior high school. I met the composer William Grant Still and Mr. Browne there. William Grant Still gave me a critique of one of my compositions, "The Golden Pearl," which the orchestra played. He told me that he liked the line and the under-current, but he wanted the sound corrected. He was there listening and was approachable. He lived in the area, and he and Dr. Browne were really tight.

I played with this band from junior high school until we were all adults. I just grew up playing in the parks with that band. We played every Sunday at a different park all around Los Angeles, and everybody would come. You'd have your family there. The union was supporting the band, so I'd get paid $20.75. That band was a great service, and that experience opened the doors for a lot of opportunities. You had a chance to realize what part of music you were born to be in, now that you'd been a part of it. This was the roots of cats.

My trombone teacher, Mr. Southard, once took me down to the black musicians' union. The musicians' union was segregated then, with the black Local 767 on Central Avenue and the white Local 47 downtown. He said, "You'll be here a lot." The union building was just an old, two-story house with offices down below and space upstairs for rehearsals. I couldn't join yet, since I was just twelve years old, not even a teenager. So I spent my time sitting on the stoop, and every cat touched me on my head, my shoulder, and my back and told me something. Every black musician in the world would pass by there, slap you upside the head, and say something smart to you: "What's happening, young blood?" POW! And that shit hurt, but I kept sitting there. Me, Eric Dolphy, Don Cherry, Frank Morgan, Hadley Caliman, Leroy "Sweet Pea" Robinson, Clyde Dunn, and the other young guys were sitting there all the time, during all those years. That's where I met Larance Marable, the drummer. It was just rich, very rich.

Naturally, I didn't realize it until afterward but I was taking advantage of it, because you didn't have any choice but to take advantage of it. One teacher knew the other teacher. "I teach you something, and then what I taught you, you're teaching this other person, and it's coming back around to me with another flavor to it." In other words, they were putting things to you and pulling it out of you. How many mentors you'd have in a day was impossible to count. They'd all be telling us about being musicians, about life, about dealing with segregation and racism. Most of the knowledge I got came from these cats laying things on me, and telling me that while a lot of the stuff was written down, some of it wasn't and was passed along by word of mouth. They kept passing information onto us, the young cats, one on one, and we knew it was important.

I learned how to write from those cats: Melba Liston, Gerald Wilson. Gerald was the first guy that got me into arranging and composing for a big orchestra. I met him on Central one day when I was walking home from Percy McDavid's rehearsal at Lafayette Junior High. I had my trombone with me, and as I passed the union, Gerald walked out and said, "Hey, young blood, can you play that instrument?"

I said, "Yeeeaaahhh." Well, I was fourteen years old.

"Well, come on upstairs, then."

I went upstairs and there was his band, with Melba Liston playing first trombone and all these cats in the trombone section. Melba said sweetly, "Sit down, young baby, sit here."

I thought, "This woman is playing trombone?"

Then she gave me the music, and it had her name on it, a tune called "Delusions." They hit the first note and that was the end of it. I didn't see nothing after that. I didn't know where the hell these people were. But they said, "That's okay, young blood, it's all right, next time." Melba knew my heart was broken, so she gave me the chart.

And, man, that really got me started. I went home with that chart and I learned it. It brought me to another level of thinking about myself and playing. They gave me the attitude that "You can do it. You can do it." They were always pushing me. When I saw Gerald's writing, I had never seen anything like that in my life. I was supposed to be able to read music. I read it well, but I couldn't follow any of those charts. So I kept coming until I got it. I was still cocky, but not to the point of not having anything to show for it.

A few years later, around 1951, I played my first gig in Gerald's band and I was still going to Jefferson High School. Me, Larance Marable, and Frank Morgan were the youngsters in the band. I was in a learning process with all those cats.

I used to hang with Gerald and John Anderson, another one of the great writers around here. So many cats were writing and they'd always turn you on. You had to learn how. I didn't go to a class to learn to write. I went to the action to learn to write, looking and listening, and asking questions, and hearing it right away, so you could know where you were from that point. That way of passing on teaching was very good for me, because I could handle that—all different kinds of people telling you different things about the same thing, and their approaches to it, and how many ways it can be done.

I refused to go to the Juilliard School of Music because of that. My mother had saved up some money, and my sister had given up the money that was saved for her college, so I could go to Juilliard. I said, "No thank you. I appreciate it. I love you. But I have the best right here. You already put me in the best atmosphere, and I can't leave." It was SWU, "Sidewalk University," because these cats would be on your case all the time.

Of course, I did go through music and college classes, so that I could learn the European approach, but I made sure that everything that happened to me musically, happened from the heart with the feeling first. Know the solution and then deal with the formula. That's how I worked it out. When I had students, they'd ask, "When are we going to get to so-and-so?"

"We're already in it."

"But when are we getting into eurythmics?"

"You're already playing a different kind of rhythm. That's your eurythmic period."

What turned them around was the work itself. They'd begin to understand that it's all one kind of sound going on. It's how you apply it. That's the way it was shown to me. The music wasn't so stiffly passed on. I had an understanding of it from the jump, from hearing it all around me, all of my life.

I've been looking at Duke Ellington's writing since I was thirteen. When his band rehearsed at the union, I'd walk right through the sections and look at the music, ask a question if I wanted. And they let me sit in during the rehearsals. It was cool. I did that with all the cats who came by the union: Ellington, the Basie band, the Fletcher and Horace Henderson band, and Lionel Hampton's band. You were expected to be there; you were expected to ask questions. They knew who you were. They'd seen you, and you were welcome. All the cats were welcome. If you didn't understand what had just happened with the flow of the music, you'd ask, "What was that?" Then you'd look at the score and they'd say, "That's the . . . You can do that with the so-and-so-and-so."

Gerald Wilson used to come to my house and pick me up for rehearsal. My mother saw to that. Red Kelly, a trumpet player, used to come to my house to pick me up. All the musicians would come pick you up, the young cats, take you to rehearsal, and bring you back home. Yeah, it was something, wasn't it, man? You'd come out of the house and there was a well-known, world-renowned trumpet player waiting to take you to a rehearsal. They were always looking out for you and they were serious; they wanted you to learn. All the time you were riding with them, they're talking and they're jamming you.

That was most of my tutoring and all the mentors that I had. There was a main one all the time that you would report to, like Samuel Browne or Lloyd Reese, an important private teacher, but then you'd also be with Gerald Wilson, Buddy Collette, John "Streamline" Ewing, Red Callender, Wardell Gray, and so-and-so. You'd always have somebody to ask questions: "How far could I write this for a trombone?" You could turn to Britt Woodman, who'd be interested in that kind of thing. That's how I learned most of it. And Gerald Wilson later paid twenty-five dollars for me to join the union.

I had so many mentors up and down the avenue at the black musicians' union, I couldn't have gone wrong if I tried. They were telling me about everything: the music, the dope that's coming in, and what to do and what not to mess with.

"Don't get the impression that because certain cats—the dope addicts—play so well, that you have to shoot dope to play like them."

You don't learn to play by shooting dope.

"If you're going to shoot dope, you'd better learn how to play first. And if you're going to deal with it, don't deal with anything that's going to cripple you."

They were talking about it then.

Setting the Pace

3

I was looking forward to going to Jefferson High School, because I was already scheduled to be in the band with Mr. Browne. When I was in junior high school, Mr. Browne would come over and recruit for his band at Jefferson. "You're going to play in my orchestra. You're playing second horn." He'd be getting you ready for high school, getting you in and getting you started even before you graduated from Lafayette. The same way they do in sports, they did with music. There was "You're going to run the 440 when you get to Jeff" as well as "You're going to be playing first trombone when you get to Jeff." And the cats, naturally, would be practicing, because they wanted to do it.

In 1949, I went to Jeff and it was something. There was a lot of activity. Anything you wanted to get into was available to you. There were no gates, no fences, no locks, no graffiti, but everybody stayed on campus. The only thing you went off school grounds for was to get some hamburgers. Right across the street, you could get the best hamburgers in the city at Kilgores. People still talk about it now. But the cafeteria was full of good food and my mother worked there. Everywhere I was, she worked. She was on my case.

During that time, Jesse Belvin was going there along with Ernie Andrews and O. C. Smith, the guy who sang "Little Green Apples." There were a lot of opera singers that later went over to Europe to work who were under Samuel Browne. We had a choir under Mr. Moon, the school marching band directed by Stewart Aspen, and then the swing band, Mr. Browne's function. There were two harmony classes, a counterpoint class, a music reading class, and a solfège class. They had art for artists; I even did a class in ceramics. You had the chance to do other things, to stretch out your abilities, as much as you could. And they had libraries in the school and in the community. Within a few blocks of your home would be a good library that was open until eight o'clock. Families would go there and study together, and read all the books that were written by black writers, which had to be distributed by hand to the people.

There were opportunities that weren't available to me. When I enrolled in drafting, one of the white teachers told me, "Horace, there isn't any point in you taking drafting. Black people aren't going to be architects."

"Well, weren't black people architects thousands of years ago?"

He didn't care for that. Some of the teachers were discouraging. They thought they were just "telling you what was happening." But they could have been pissed off because it wasn't available for me. And my drafting teacher was right; it wasn't for me at that time. So what if I learned to be a draftsman or architect? I couldn't get the gig to do it, because I was black. In 1950, that's what he was telling me. But that's one of the things I would like to have been a part of as well. Now I've got a niece, Robin Byrd, who is a professional architect. I guess it must have run through the blood to her. I also used to fantasize about being a truck driver, going out in the wide open spaces for many, many, many days alone. I liked thinking about that as a job. But that wasn't open to me at the time either.

Music was my thing, and I was listening to Tommy Dorsey and J. C. Higginbotham and Kid Ory and Dicky Wells. I got to see many of them on Central Avenue. But I really got turned around on trombone by Dizzy Gillespie. I tried to play the trombone like he played the trumpet. I had the jowls and all, and I used to play all his tunes.

At Jefferson, sixth period every day, about two o'clock in the afternoon, we had the big band class for an hour. Sometimes we'd also give concerts at other schools, like Fairfax High, or out in the

San Fernando Valley at Taft High. We might go to one of Stan Kenton's early rehearsals in Hollywood. Dr. Browne would introduce us to the legends. That's how I first met Shelly Manne, when Shelly was in Kenton's band. He also took us to listen to the Henderson band. And the cats would come over to the school to talk to you. Lionel Hampton always came over and brought his big band. Once I told Lionel, "Man, I'm going to get in your band one day."

He said, "Okay, baby, I'll look for you."

That was in 1950, or something like that. They'd come over and play, and the whole school would be screaming and hollering and dancing up and down the aisles.

Some of the cats, the former students, used to come back to Jeff, like Sonny Criss, who might be playing upstairs. All the players around the city would come back. The band rehearsed at the end of the day and they might have some arrangements they wanted to hear. Cats would be playing on the avenue or up and down the West Coast, but when they were home, they'd come back to the school and sit in, and might say something to the cats, tell them where they're playing and all that. There was always some kind of hookup.

All the high school bands that were around got some attention from the older musicians, who made sure that the bands had a stockpile of original music by these people, all from Central Avenue. Jordan High School in Watts had a band, and then there was Santa Fe Avenue High School, which was supposedly the bad guys' school. When you got too rough for Jefferson or Jordan, they'd send you to Santa Fe, where they'd guard you all the time. They had a hell of a band over there.

Dr. Browne was one of my influences on piano. When the big band rehearsed after school, sometimes we'd get a chance to hear him. He played like Teddy Wilson, Duke Ellington, always into chord changes and putting new sounds together. But he also was an influence because he stayed in the community totally. When he drove down the street, everybody would say, "Hello, Dr. Browne." He would come to certain musicians' houses to see that they were taking care of business, and was at my house and Frank Morgan's house all the time. He'd stop by all the cats' pads and he knew your family. They knew him. He knew that the family was important in inspiring the youngsters and he was making sure the foundation was being correctly set from the family on up. He was able to come in and teach or inspire, just come and talk with you. He made sure he kept an eye on you and he really dug you.

"I dig you, man."

That's what he'd tell you.

"You don't understand that yet. But I dig you."

Dr. Browne was also telling us how to survive.

"I don't care how good you are, because of the racist society you live in, you have to be much better than the guys who go to Hollywood High. You can play, but you've got to learn how to read and write and count and comprehend what's going on. You've got to learn what words mean when people are talking to you. You just can't go for the 'okeydoke.'"

That's what Dr. Sam Browne always said.

"You've got to think, man. Think. I've been there."

We knew what he was talking about.

"You can fool around if you like, but those guys out at Hollywood High, they're going to be the ones who take care of business. And you're going to be hip. All you're going to be is a hipster. That's all you want to be, is that it? Okay, you're going the right direction, if that's all you want. But if you want more, you'll try to do more. You'll try to study and learn more."

That was the thought of the day all the time: try to do better. Jefferson was a proud school, a very proud school. Everybody wanted to do his or her best for it.

Then you'd go home and you'd get that same kind of atmosphere: try to do better. Your parents went so far, and they'd say, "Now, I'd like to see you go further." In those days, they wanted you to go to college. That was one of your main objectives. We didn't know the difference between the city college, the community college, or whatever college, as long as you went to college. They wanted to be able to say, "My child goes to college."

Another thing I was active in was track. I loved to run, ever since my days in Houston with my stepfather. My best race was the 440, because I could take those long steps and push, and I could run a long time before I got tired. I had strong lungs; I could stay under-water for a long time. Track in those days was something. People would take off from their jobs early for the track meet on Fridays at Jefferson High. The whole area closed up, and everybody came to the track meet. *Everybody.* And they were all betting on who was going to take second in the meet, because everyone knew Jeff was going to take first. In each race, we always took first, second, and third places. The next fastest school was in fourth. Three cats from the same school hitting the tape. We'd be racing against each other in practice and in the meets against each other, because nobody could outrun us. It was out.

In both track and music there was that attitude. I mean, it was so inspiring seeing people take off work to see you run at the meet or play in the band. You're going to be proud, run or play. That's long gone now. It would have been nice to be able to keep that going with the talent the youngsters have today.

I also studied with Lloyd Reese, who was the highest paid private teacher in the area, and was with him all the time. I was there be-cause Samuel Browne and Lloyd Reese were real tight. Whenever Dr. Browne got someone at school who he thought was promis-ing, he'd send him to Reese. All the cats would go to him; he never left his pad at Jefferson Boulevard and Maple Avenue. I met Duke Ellington and a lot of the guys at Lloyd's. And down the street from him was Professor Gray's Conservatory of Music. We were surrounded by it. You'd walk down the street and all kinds of cats would be walking around with instruments. It was something.

Lloyd looked like Duke, was a chain-smoker, and could party his ass off. These cats would start Thursday night and party until Saturday morning. It would be really fucked-up around his pad by Saturday. There was shit everywhere—beer cans, rubbers, and all that. But that's how we got our music lessons. Eric Dolphy was there, too, and we couldn't pay any money, so we'd clean his pad. There were five of us: Eric, Troy Brown, Arthone Elster, myself, and one other cat. Eric cleaned inside the house, and the rest of us would be outside doing it. Eric would tell us, "Y'all the field niggers. I'm the house nigger." That was Eric. He'd do that shit. He was the oldest, so he had the edge.

When we finished, we'd get our lessons Saturday afternoon and Reese would be on our ass. As long as I knew him, he'd never say my name correctly.

"Come here, Tapshack! Sit on the piano!"

He really focused on how to make sounds and his ear was incredible. He had one of those terrible ears that would hear everything. One time, he told me to sit on the piano and put my hands, my ass, all over the keyboard. Then he called all the notes. He was that kind of cat. Reese would give me something to work on for maybe two weeks, like getting some kinds of sounds. He wouldn't tell me how to work on this, but for me to find a way to do it. He knew there was more than one way to do something, more than one way to play, and he wanted me to find my way to get a sound, to find a way that physically suited me to make these sounds. That approach was so important and opened up a lot of creativity. I studied trombone and piano with Lloyd Reese until he died in the late 1950s, early 1960s. He was my last teacher. I never studied with anyone else after he died.

Eric was about four years older than me, but musically we were tight. Whenever we could, we hung out with Gerald Wilson's band when they were rehearsing. Eric also had his own group by this time with Lester Robertson and a few of the cats, and I had a band, also. Eric was looking outside even then, but he wasn't the only one. Before him there was a cat named George Newman, a saxophonist, who used to be with Don Cherry a lot. He was the first cat who Mr. Browne called, "This guy's out." Don and Lester Robertson weren't from the Eastside area but they'd leave their school early and come up to Jeff to sit in on the band class, which was cool with Mr. Browne. There were several cats who were reaching out, and then Ornette Coleman was around, too. Eric, however, was able to do a lot of things because, musically, he had a broad background. While most guys were just playing changes, straight ahead, he was stretching the music.

Ornette was different. He was living in the mountains and had about four or five cats with him. He had these long dreads that went down to his ass. One day he came by Jefferson. Mr. Browne looked out at him and said, "Ah! Here come black Jesus!" Ornette had hooked up with Don Cherry, who was at Jeff rehearsing with us, and had come by to hear some music. But before Ornette, Don and George Newman had a great group with Billy Higgins and Bill Pickens, until George went out of his mind and out of music.

There were just so many cats around here then and everybody was working on their own thing, bringing their own shot at the music. Everybody played different and there was always somebody trying to do something different. And most of them came from under the tutelage of Samuel Browne and Lloyd Reese.

I had a band while I was at Jeff. Charles Pendergraff played drums. Guido Sinclair, whose name then was Sinclair Greenwell, was also in the band, and Roy Brewster, who later played with me in the Pan Afrikan Peoples Arkestra. Guido was one of the founding members of the Arkestra in 1961 and stayed with us until the mid-1980s, when he moved to the Midwest. We met in junior high at Lafayette, and he was always on his instrument. He was a "Bird" person; anything Charlie Parker played, he wanted to play. He'd be practicing eight hours a day. I'd have to go and get him out of the house.

"Man, let's go hang out."

"Oh, okay, okay."

He just didn't want to leave his instrument.

We'd always come together and play, all day and all night, especially blues, like "Decision," I think it was called. We'd learn our charts and then go try for the talent shows. Racehorse Williams was one of the MCs at these things. At the theaters, there would be maybe a show, a comedian, a few acts, maybe tap dancers or singers, and then the movies would start. They also had talent contests, and I won one when I was seventeen years old in 1950, $200 at the Rosebud Theatre for playing "Marie" on the trombone, me and Charles. We ran back to my house and threw the money on the table. My mother was so surprised, she said, "Boy, where'd you get this money?" She went off. That was a lot of money.

Just a week or two before graduation from Jeff in 1952, I was in an accident. Since then, every time I explain this story, the cats say, "Yeah, sure." What happened was, I had asked Cecilia to go to the beach with me one night, and she couldn't go for some reason, which pissed me off. So I got my friend Willie Cawthorne, and his future wife, Barbara, and a girlfriend I had at Jeff named Marita, and we went out to the beach.

On the way back along Washington Boulevard, everybody went to sleep and the girl up front laid on my lap as I was driving. I was going about thirty-five miles an hour, and there wasn't anybody on the street. It was cool and I had the windows down, so I reached past her feet for a blanket to cover her. As I came up, I hit one of those high curbs; the car shot up and went right into the light pole. It fell on the car, and the people in the back were thrown into the front seat. I'm thinking I'm in a dream. I looked over and saw the girl who'd been with me on the front of the car, and then realized that we were in a wreck. It took me that long to figure out what had happened. Then I saw blood on my suit and almost panicked. I opened the door and pulled out the rest of the people. By that time some people had come by. I remember them looking at me and saying, "We'd better lay this guy down; he's going." They laid me down and that was it. I don't remember anything else.

When I came to in the hospital, I was dizzy and my mouth was covered in blood; my front teeth had been loosened, and all I could think about was the trombone solo I had to play for graduation in a week or two. Mr. Browne was going to accompany me. Somehow these doctors fixed my teeth, and I played that solo. It came off pretty nice. Mr. Browne smiled; he was happy. The girl made it to graduation, too, on crutches. But it cost me $270 for that light post, and I had one hell of a time explaining what happened. After my stepfather, Leon, brought me home from the hospital, Cecilia's mother and my mother talked about me like a dog. And it took forty-five years before anybody would even think about believing me.

A Terrible Taste of College

When I graduated from Jeff in the summer of 1952, I didn't have any real plans. All we knew was that we were trying to stay out of the service. The Korean War was happening and that was on our minds. We kept hoping that they wouldn't take us but we knew they were going to get us. And I got a notice a few months after graduation that I was going to be drafted in six months: "You will be called."

I started talking with the cats about the military bands. All my mentors—Buddy Collette, Red Callender, Streamline Ewing, Red Kelly, and Gerald Wilson—had been in the military bands during World War II. And they were saying that they had gotten us ready to play in those bands. We could read anything now. But things had changed and college experience was important. So these same cats from the "University of the Streets" told me to go to college, because that's what they were going to ask for when you go in the service: "Did you have college music?"

So I went to Los Angeles City College. That was a big thing for black folks in the 1940s and 1950s. It didn't matter what college, just as long as you went to college. Everybody in the community was celebrating. You'd get free bread at the store. "This boy is going to college. And a male, at that!" It was more common with females, but a black male going to college, and he wasn't an athlete, that was news. Most people went because they dug their parents and they wanted to make them feel good, but many didn't care for it. I went because of the draft, and I didn't have anything else to do during the day but hang around Central Avenue and try to get a gig playing, which was easy to do since I was young and out of high school. There were still plenty of clubs, even though many were shutting down in the early 1950s.

I was satisfied with my knowledge of what I had playing wise. I did take music at the college and got in the European orchestra, so I could see what was happening there and conduct one of those European symphonies. That's all I wanted to do; I wasn't going after any particular degree.

I was in the college band. That was the band that Stan Kenton and Woody Herman would hire their people out of. It was that kind of band, and I think every one of them is now living on mountains or near lakes with four or five Rolls Royces. One cat, Jules Chaykin, stopped playing altogether and started managing. It was a good band, but there were still these culture problems going on, you

dig? I was a young, cocky black musician with an older white instructor, Mr. McDonald. We were playing a tune called "My Silent
Love," and I was playing the trombone with him. There was a written solo. The cat who usually played it, the Tijuana Brass cat—I
can't think of his name—he would play it just like that, note for
note, with a great sound. I played it one time with funny styles
and shit.

McDonald said, "Wait a minute. Wait a minute."

I said, "What?"

"Why don't you play it like it's written."

"Well, I don't hear it like that."

"All you guys from Jefferson, you're not God's gift to music."

I laughed with all the rest of the white cats in there.

"Well, maybe I'm not *the* God's gift but I'm one of them."

"Get out."

He put me out of the band. I was the only black cat in there, and
he threw me out.

I did meet some other out cats—one a white guy, Jack Millman.
Mr. McDonald had problems with him, too. McDonald's best man
was Bob Florence, the blind piano player who's making so many
records now. He was one of those talented cats and he was a favorite of McDonald. Jack could write and play as well, but he had his
own thing going. I got to meet a lot of the white musicians at City
College, and many of them became famous in the bands. There
were only four other black cats at the school: Jimmy Woods, an
excellent saxophonist; Lester Robertson, who took my place in the
band when McDonald threw me out; Leroy Brooks, a drummer
from Kansas City; and Bobby Gross, also a drummer, who later got
me into some studio work.

There was one instructor there, Dominic DiSarro, who I had an
open line to. He was the conductor of the symphony orchestra of
the college and was really into it heavy. But he gave me time, asked
what I was doing, listened to my work, and we got a thing going.
He let me conduct the orchestra. He dug me and stayed on my
case. The reason I lasted as many months as I did was because of
Dominic DiSarro. Even though he was a European master, and he

knew all of it, he allowed: "But there are no boundaries." When he said things like that, I knew that this was the cat to be with.

I was in another class where one of these harmony teachers didn't like the way I was taught solfège at Jefferson High by Samuel Browne, hearing the notes and writing them without playing them. Once I was at the blackboard, and he was playing a tape. I had a few minutes to write down what I'd heard. Of course, with my training, I wrote it all down, which seemed to surprise and upset him. A little while later, something else pissed him off, and he told us that music was supposed to be controlled and that's why we were studying Bach's method. I didn't have anything against studying Bach. We were taught that at Jefferson, also. He wasn't telling me something I didn't know. But he was also telling me that it had to be played a certain way. I didn't like it but to pass the test I did that.

Then he had the gall to stand up in front of the class and say, "Duke Ellington's music is wrong. It's written wrong." He said that in harmony, you're not supposed to double thirds and have parallel fifths going.

"Well, why not?" is what I wanted to know, and he really couldn't explain.

"Because it's incorrect. You're playing the wrong notes."

"Okay."

We finally got to that day. He played a little bit, just a tiny bit, of Duke's *Black, Brown, and Beige* and said it was written wrong. That did it for me, man. It was a personal insult, as well as a standard one. I said, "That's it," then got up and left. This school was a waste of my time. I left City College before I got into trouble, because I wanted to hit him. He had pissed me off actually to the point where I wanted to just jump on this cat. The best thing for me to do was to leave. I went back to the U of S, University of the Streets, on Central Avenue.

4

There were all kinds of young players around, seeing each other all the time: Billy Higgins, Frank Morgan, Hadley Caliman, Walter Benton, Don Cherry, and many others. Even in high school, we'd hit the clubs on Central on the weekends. The guys from Jefferson were large guys, tall for our age, so we could get into the clubs at the age of seventeen, maybe, and play. All they wanted to hear was you playing anyway. They didn't care how old you were. A lot of the young cats would meet these dancers, these chorus ladies who'd be dancing at the clubs. They'd be jamming the young cats. That was always a plus.

A lot of the cats, like Gerald and Buddy, would invite us into the clubs to sit in with them. I might be hanging on the outside with Troy Brown and Guido. We'd all have our instruments with us. During their breaks, the cats would come out on the streets, see us, and invite us to come in and play. Buddy worked quite a bit at the Downbeat and brought us in a few times. Jack's Basket Room was another place like that. The cats were always looking for us and they wanted us to play.

"Hey, come on over here young blood. You want to get in on this tune?"

I didn't think much about it at the time but it was really something.

Every now and then, and usually on the weekends, we'd play with bands. When I was fifteen, I played a weekend date with a guy named Monroe Tucker somewhere on Central Avenue. That was my first professional gig. He came through and needed a trombone player. I sat right in there and got it. Cecilia was there with me and she remembers that gig. Monroe played piano, and they had to carry him in, because he didn't have any legs.

Not long after I got out of Jeff in 1952, I was playing in some club with Guido and this cat, Chuck Higgins, a black saxophonist, came along. He listened to us for a while, liked what he heard, and then came up and told us that he had this record he wanted to make. It seemed cool so we met him a while later at the 5–4 Ballroom on Fifty-fourth Street and Broadway, and recorded "Pachuko Hop" there. I even arranged it. It became a big hit, although somebody dropped our horn parts, or maybe recorded it again using my arrangement. But we never saw any money and we never saw Chuck Higgins after that. I don't know who that masked man was.

Eventually all the cats would be playing. I know Clifford Solomon, Hadley Caliman, Sweetpea Robinson, Frank Morgan, and those cats were doing it. And a lot of the music that cats were playing was called too out for anybody to listen to, because they were really creating. I mean creativity was the call of the day, every day and every night, a "Let's create something" kind of attitude. And the drugs were just a by-product. They didn't go there to get the drugs to create. They went to create and then got some of whatever they wanted.

Before they got started on drugs, these people were coming together. Two cats or three, but always some people were trying to put something together, using all kinds of different instruments. Maybe it wouldn't even be a formal kind of organization—piano, bass, and drums. It might be a flute player and a tuba player and a violinist. But they had something they wanted to try. That kind of thing was going on all the time. Someone might say, "Come by my pad. I've got some music I did for so-and-so."

"Yeah, I'll be by."

They'd get together.

"Hey, why don't we add this or do it this way?"

"There's four or five of us in here and we're here to make music. We're not here to compete. We're here to contribute."

They were all open, regardless of how out their ideas. If someone showed you how to do it, you'd try it. All of a sudden you'd hear what he was talking about. It was that kind of a closeness that brought about the creativity during those early years of the music.

There was so much music created because of the feeling that people had with each other. And I mean all the music—blues, jazz, and pop—not only in the music that I was part of. Richard Rogers and Lorenz Hart, and all those cats, would be writing good music. There was a separation between the races, but everyone had respect for the music that was coming together. White musicians and black musicians had an understanding of what was going on, and were able to communicate. That's one time it didn't have anything to do with race.

It had to do with a feeling and a hookup to creativity and understanding, and how people can come together regardless of what's happening around them, because of the creativity, because of the naturalness. That kind of attitude, that kind of thought pattern, was always shown to me when I was growing up. Because of this racist society, I had to understand that not everyone was a racist in its worst sense. And I was able to understand this, because there was certain music that I would hear by European composers that was beautiful to me. It was totally European and that told me, "Okay, now I have to erase this other part of me and open up to something else."

Central Avenue brought a lot of people together musically, artistically. I think Central Avenue is just as legendary a place as the Great White Way that they speak about. It had all of the musicians, all of the artists, who helped make the music of this country what it is today. That's what Central Avenue gave to this community, all these people, and they'd be right there on Central Avenue gathering together every night. It was like a bonanza. There was gold coming out of Central Avenue.

To walk down Central, by the time you got to the end of a block, you'd have heard a whole new melody, because so many things were happening. To me, it was colorful and it was educational. It was an experience that I can't ever forget, because it raised me. It was more or less like musicians raised me on the avenue. It came about in my real formative years, when I wanted to know different things. I was twelve or thirteen years old when I started to come to the avenue, and I got the bulk of it, the last good four or five years of it. I saw it, I was in the middle of it, and I saw the end of it.

A few years ago, me and Don Cherry were saying that was a good time. We came up in real good times. There isn't anything to do now but give it back in some kind of way. I can think of all the cats who passed things onto me and I'll never forget those people. Sometimes the names might leave, but their faces I remember—like Roy Porter, who was here for years and who died just recently. He was around then with his band. I mean we were just surrounded by music, just surrounded by it.

Central Avenue declined in the 1950s as a result of politics. It was a city hall crackdown and that was because of the racial harmony that was happening. People of all races would come to the avenue at night, although it was mostly white celebrities who brought attention to the place. Even the bands that played in Hollywood, the white bands, during the after hours they'd come to Central, so they could play in all-night sessions. And that wasn't too sweet to the powers that be. Yeah, it was integrated, and the white ladies were coming down, especially the blonds, like Lana Turner, and Ava Gardner was also there. There's an old black magazine, *Ebony* or *Sepia,* by John H. Johnson that Ava Gardner is in with Dizzy Gillespie and Charlie Parker. The item says, "Diz and Bird show Ava Gardner how to eat a banana." I'll never forget that. I can't recall what date or edition that was but it was in there. All the cats at the union made a big joke out of it.

One year, around 1958, I was gigging at the Troubadour on La Cienega Boulevard. It was a little place with a piano and seats right next to it. One night, I looked up and Ava Gardner was sitting there. Long, pretty, with some jeans on, and with some old cat. He was trying to kiss her all over. It was dark in the club, just a little candlelight. She was trying to listen to the music, and he's hitting on her. Man, I used to have fantasies about her! I looked up and said, "Wow!" She stayed the whole set, and my mind kept going back to that advertisement. I cracked myself up, but also thought, "This cat is with her."

That kind of thing is what started closing down the avenue. Integration raised its head and racism snapped it off, as usual.

The Amalgamation of Locals 767 and 47

To top it off that's when Local 767 was dissolved. By that time, in the early fifties, Central Avenue was closing down. It was on its way and, as a matter of fact, it didn't have but a few more feet to go before it was over. Jazz clubs had started opening up in Hollywood and throughout Los Angeles, so there was more work outside of Central for black musicians.

I had joined the union when I was fifteen, and with the amalgamation, we were looking forward to making a little more money, having more gigs. It was supposed to get us better pay. It was supposed to get us jobs in the studios. Buddy Collette, Gerald Wilson, Bill Douglass, Marl Young, and Benny Carter were the vanguard of the movement. They figured it would be better for us. They had proven that they could write and read the music, as well as play it.

When they said, "Well, we're going to have better jobs, Tapscott. You'll be doing movie studios, and when television gets straight, we'll be doing that."

I said, "Oh. Let's do it."

I didn't think about it too much until after the fact. Some black musicians did well, like Bill Green, the cat who played all instruments, played them as if they were all one. Each instrument he picked up, he mastered. He made it in the studios, as did Buddy Collette with his versatility and Britt Woodman, when he was living here and not with Duke Ellington.

So what was the problem?

The problem was that when they did have the amalgamation, some of the white musicians got called for jobs—and they were used to being called—some of the black musicians came, and then the cliques started forming all of a sudden. Some of the white cats

46

who were working would hire different black cats and then they'd have their little old clique. And that particular, small, black group of guys would work all the time, because they were in that particular clique with these particular guys who ran the studios. It wasn't a racial thing. It was run by cliques.

There was a positive aspect, because it all added to the music. It was always nice after a gig. Everyone was glad to be with each other, because we came to a center and we had to play the music. That was the most important thing. If I was playing with some cats who lived out in the San Fernando Valley and we'd never seen each other before, we'd come right in. So it was easy for cats to get along, white or black, because the cats who were really into the music had another thinking pattern going. And that's how I started working with some of the white cats. They'd call me, cats like Jack Millman, all the out cats. You would be together all the time, because you had a hookup.

So the work was getting better, seemed to have gotten better for certain people, after the old Local 767 closed up, but a lot of the older players I didn't see anymore. They used to be around all the time on Central at one gig or another. All of them used to hang around the union; they'd just be there. When that closed down, they didn't have anyplace to go.

Drugs in the Community

Until the early 1950s, the only thing in our neighborhood was marijuana, and that was almost legal, because nobody was imposing any laws on it at that time. Most of the people who were smoking it were the African Americans, the Indians, and the Mexicans who were in the community. It wasn't rushed into the white community, so it wasn't a problem. When the dope came along, a whole other scene started happening with a lot of the young cats.

It was about 1951 that hard drugs started coming onto Central Avenue. I got through it because of the mentors I had: Dr. Browne, Gerald Wilson, Buddy Collette. They kept us posted on what was going on and talked to us about the temptations that would be coming our way. Their influence was very important. And I never had the desire to use any drugs, because when I was coming up I saw what was happening to the drug users, many of whom were friends of mine. A couple of times the cats asked me to try it. But after a while, they saw that it just pissed me off whenever they'd bring it up.

I'd say, "Man, you're already a prisoner, already in jail, so why do you want to be *in jail* in jail? Why do you want the powers that be to control even more of your life? Every time you use dope, they just get more control of you."

"Ah, man, you're square," they'd say.

I used marijuana, but never any hard drugs, and I never have until this day. The only problem I've ever had was when I got strung out in the air force in the mid-1950s. I was in the base hospital for kidney stones, and in those days, whenever you had a pain, the nurse would come running with a shot of Demerol. Junkies used kidney stones as an excuse to get dope, and the people in this hospital thought I was another dope addict. That really pissed me off. After a week of that, twice a day, they released me, and on my way home I started feeling funny. My stomach was upset and I was just in a daze. Then I realized I was strung out. I laid up for about three days and sweated it out of me.

When hard drugs hit the community in Los Angeles, it was a big deal. I mean, it was like being in a clique. If you didn't shoot smack, it wouldn't matter how good you played, because the other cats wouldn't feel comfortable playing with you. I did get shut out at first, or shut myself out, but I always showed them respect. And they learned to show me respect by keeping clean whenever they played with me, or at least showing up on the bandstand in a condition to play.

Each individual has to know his or her limitations, and they're different for every person. A lot of cats were able to handle it and made it. A lot of real gifted players couldn't handle it and just stopped playing or killed themselves. I saw a lot of cats die early from not being able to handle narcotics. When the hard drugs came in, it was really a monster, because you'd start seeing cats changing personalities. All of a sudden you didn't want them to come to your house anymore. A cat might have been able to run through your whole pad. You didn't have to worry about him until he got a jones. He might love you, but he's got to take care of it. He might be able to get a dime or two for your television. Then he'd come back and tell you he did it. He didn't want to do it but he did it. That's when you knew that they'd become zombies. Nothing else mattered. That's when it really hit bottom.

All they wanted to do was just get high and nod. And they had too much talent for that, and that was whipping them. The cats who were doing it didn't want to do anything but feel good. "Well, I can at least feel a little better for a few moments." But you don't really feel good, because you know.

I've seen a lot of cats come out of it on their own, cold turkey. There were those who went through those desolate times and came through it, getting out of it, never to return. It did happen, mostly because they had the support of a family, people who really dug them, knew what they had to offer, and said, "You can get off it." And they just stopped, because what was around them was so well put together that they felt out of place themselves. Once they realized that they meant something, how important they were to the whole scheme, the "If you're out of the thing, the thing ain't going to work" kind of attitude, then they understood that they had a part. They didn't have to try to kill themselves for no reason at all.

I spent a lot of time with some of these older pianists who were supposedly hooked on drugs. They took so much time to show me what they knew in case they wouldn't be able to do it anymore. "I'm hooked, you take it"—that kind of attitude. Later on in the 1960s, Elmo Hope was one of these people. He'd always show me how to play different tunes. By this time his hands were all shot up and he couldn't play. He said, "I won't be able to finish all this. So I want to pass this onto you." It was always lovely music, but very rigid and very hard to play. You had to be on it. The thing of his I liked most was *The Fox* album that he did with Harold Land. I recorded his composition "Something for Kenny"—which he wrote for an island drummer, Kenny Shurland, who lives here now—on my first solo album, *Songs of the Unsung*.

For me it was an advantage, because most of these people were good people in the first place. They wanted to build something. They wanted to be part of a movement, so to speak. They wanted to be recognized for their contributions to this whole thing and got detoured into a whole other area that was strange to them, and they didn't know how to deal with it.

It didn't have to do with just narcotics. It had to do with living every day under the cloak in the kind of society that it was in the early 1950s for black people and the black male in particular. Today, he still has that kind of cloak over him. However, he had to think of all those other things that had to be done. Maybe he had a family. Maybe he couldn't work the way he wanted to. Maybe he was worried about getting drafted, being sent to the front line, where they were putting all the black soldiers at the time, and dying. They had a lot of things on their minds. They knew it wasn't right. They couldn't raise their families because of this or that. And then they got the attitude, and got the jacket on them about not being black men, that they "weren't good fathers." That whole kind of down-trodden man started after the Korean War.

Military Service

5

After I left Los Angeles City College, I knew I'd be called into the army unless I enlisted in another branch of the service. My first choice was to join the navy. Most of my mentors had been in navy bands, and Dorie Miller was still in my head. I was going to the navy, man. Me and a couple of other guys went down to the recruiting office together. It was at a place called Mode O'Day on Washington Boulevard.

A lot of the cats got turned down. The man asked them, "Has anybody here ever smoked any marijuana?" Some cats raised their hands! They put them to the side and wouldn't take them. We were on the other side in another line cracking up. They told me I could join the navy. At the time, I couldn't swim but I felt I could rectify that by finding a way to avoid having to do it. I figured that I'd be in the band and wouldn't be on one of those ships. But they told me, "The first thing you've got to do is jump off a twenty-foot tower into the water." I backed out and walked around the corner to join the air force.

Race and Music in the Air Force

I went to the air force because I didn't have to worry about flying no airplane. I figured I'd be on the ground in the air force band and that's what happened. After basic training, I was sent to the band barracks in Pleasanton, California. You had to go to band school for about a month and then it was time for the test. If you passed, then you'd go to a band. If you failed, you'd be assigned something else.

By this time, I was pretty cocky about my music. The services had also just been integrated, but in my mind I was still at war and some of the white cats were still thinking like the Ku Klux Klan. I knew this. I walked into the testing area and registered. I had a baritone horn and the trombone with me. And I'm so cocky that the white cats and even some of the black cats were glad to see me go into that test room.

"This sucker, man, he makes me sick. He's so cocky."

They were waiting for me to be taken down.

I walked into the room and there were these two guys, a warrant officer and a sergeant. They had a music stand with an exercise on it that all the trombone players were supposed to play. I played it. They gave me another thing to play, and I played it.

They said, "You read that pretty well."

"Yeah."

"Are you a jazz player? It's always a treat to see a jazz player who can read music. Most of them don't read music."

"I came in here under those kinds of thought patterns, knowing that's what you were thinking."

That came from my attitude. But I played it, so they couldn't get me that way.

The cats who were heading the band school, a couple of white sergeants who played trumpet and saxophone, didn't like my ass. They were pissed off at me; they didn't like my attitude. When they started passing out the base assignments, I wanted to stay near Los Angeles, because that meant that I could come here and play in town. I had it all set in my head. Clifford Brown and those cats were arriving in Los Angeles then. I was anxious. "Let me get my thing where I'm going." All these cats were getting places like Honolulu, New York, San Francisco, all the good places. I thought, "Oh, man, I'm in!"

"Tapscott, Fort Warren Air Force Base, Cheyenne, Wyoming."

Dig this. Fort Warren was where they sent all the cats who they couldn't make into soldiers, regardless of whether you're a musician or a medic, the Santa Fe Avenue High School of the air force. And there I am, snowed in for months.

They had a full band there. We had a barracks on one end of the base, which was about four miles long, in a giant building with a big basement, all equipped with music things. It must have been 200 feet across. Upstairs, the main room was full of bunk beds, and there were five or six private rooms that two cats could share.

At first, I was the only black cat in the band. They had one black sergeant, William McCoy, a vibraphonist and percussionist, but he lived off base. So the rest of the guys in the barracks were white cats. I met a couple of them quickly.

They had one guy named Sergeant Paul Moriarty. He was a short guy, wore glasses, had one cockeye, and real black, wavy, Italian hair. He was an old soldier and a sergeant with four stripes who played trombone, the kind of cat that could only make it in the service and that was his home. So I came into this secluded part of the country, Cheyenne, Wyoming, and my first impression was, "Man, where am I?" One of the first things I heard Sergeant Moriarty say was: "If we get any more of these guys in, we're going to have to use these white sheets as covers."

Immediately that shadow came back on me again. He was talking to the other white guys downstairs, and I'm on the stairway, you dig? But then I thought, "No, I'm not going to relate to this. I'm going to leave it alone this time." I first wanted to know where I was. Then one of the white guys from Arizona, a tuba player, big guy, came up to me and said, "My name is Bill Smith. Did you hear what this guy said? Not all of us think like that."

I said, "Thank you." Then he went upstairs.

Not long after that, I noticed something else. We all had to take turns shoveling coal in the boiler room down in the basement. I was being assigned twice as many days down there as anybody else. They might have had three days a month, and I was getting six. So I said, "Man, I'm not going to shovel anymore." The sergeant reported me to the captain. With the sergeant there, this captain, a big, long, Texas white cat—big, mean cat—was trying to straighten me out. Then he told the sergeant to leave, because I was going off on the sergeant. He told me to settle down and warned me that I could get busted.

"You can take these stripes, sir. I'm not shoveling any more coal."

He didn't scare me by talking about taking my stripes and losing the allotment for my family.

"I understand what you're talking about. This guy is an old soldier and he's a prejudiced so-and-so."

"I don't care about that, captain. You're not going to mess me over. You understand what I mean? I'm not going to shovel no more coal. I'll go to prison; I'll do anything, but I ain't shoveling any more coal, period."

And this cat said, "Okay, I'll straighten it out."

I didn't shovel any more coal, and that pissed the sergeant off.

Moriarty and I had problems even in the band room, and especially when he couldn't read something. During rehearsal when he'd miss a note, I'd say, "Let a real trombone player show you how this is supposed to sound." He'd turn red in the face. It wasn't that I hated this guy; he was just prejudiced. I was also getting promoted real fast. In a couple of years I had four stripes, and he couldn't stand that. "It took me thirteen years to make this stripe, and you've been in here two and a half. What's happening?"

Later on there was a party that brought all this stuff to a head. Moriarty was having a good time, laughing and talking. Our wives were there. His old lady was drunk and wanted my pants. That's just the way it was. I had no idea that this was going to happen. She was so loaded, talking loud, and he was trying to shut her up. She said, "I'll go sit over there," and walked over to me, sat on my lap, put her arm around me, and kissed me on the neck. I looked over at this cat. Whew! His face was flushed and he was trying to smile. He would rather I had hit him than what his woman did. Not long after that we were alone, and this cat started crying and apologized to me for that statement about the sheets. And that had been much earlier.

His turnaround was so unique that I began to realize that anything could happen. Because when we first met, this guy was a

At Jefferson High School, early 1950s. (All photos courtesy of Horace Tapscott unless otherwise indicated.)

(Above) Soloing with the Jefferson High School big band in the school auditorium, early 1950s. Alto saxophonist Earl Anderza is to the left. "Earl Anderza was bad. He was one of the cats when Frank Morgan and Ornette Coleman were in Los Angeles playing alto sax. But Earl was the outest, the one everyone said played that 'crazy sound'" (Horace Tapscott).

(Right) Displaying the winning prize from the talent show at the Rosebud Theatre.

Air force band, Fort Warren, mid-1950s. Robbie Robertson (front row, left), Paul Morlidge (front row, fifth from left), Horace (middle row, left), Leroy Riley (middle row, second from left), Coen Dale Mix (back row, left), Luke McCaleb (back row, third from left), Gene Miller (drums), "Schwimmer" (bass), and Mr. Hayes (leader).

With Gene Miller's daughter at Fort Warren Air Force Base, Cheyenne, Wyoming, mid-1950s.

Soloing in front of the air force band, mid-1950s.

On leave in Los Angeles, mid-1950s. Mother-in-law, Carrie Payne (left), and Cecilia Tapscott (right).

Gigging at a club in Cheyenne, mid-1950s, and playing one of the first electric pianos; Robbie Robertson (tenor saxophone).

staunch racist against me. There was something about him that I kind of liked. I enjoyed talking to this cat about race, because he would give me exactly what he was thinking. One thing about Moriarty was that his racist attitude was out-front and he told me why. He wasn't used to being around black cats and he had taken the attitudes that were around him. But in Cheyenne, he was confined with black cats for the first time and he started seeing other things after a while. This cat started seeing things from a human point of view. So when he broke down in front of us, I knew this was the real thing. When he started crying, that's when I knew that he had cut loose a lot of that racist stuff.

There were a lot of women, mostly white, who came to see the band. One time we were in the city, where most of the cats probably came from the South, and everyone was carrying rifles. They got upset because these chicks were with the black cats in the band. The situation in Cheyenne was serious. It was serious, man. Shootings were going on. Our cars and barracks were being shot at, and we were shooting back, whenever we could.

So I got called down again to the captain's office. I was told that there was trouble on the base, that there were some guys from the South who were really upset. The captain said, "I'm not blaming you and I'm not saying to stop. What do you think we can do?"

"Captain, you can send in some black airwomen."

Two weeks later at the train station in Cheyenne, Wyoming, there were three carloads of black WAFs (Women's Air Force). There was a white woman, Mary Cantor, who went and picked them up, because she used to hang with the band. She married one of the cats, Donald Dean, the drummer who lives down the street from me. They had kids, and she used to babysit Renée, my oldest daughter. Mary took all the chicks to where they had to go. I thought, "Wow! Two weeks later and three carloads of black women . . . on my call."

I got my third stripe in about a year and a half and that was fast; it drove most of the old sergeants crazy. Then I got the fourth one a year or so later. I became a staff sergeant, and they couldn't believe it. I wound up running the base. Anything that had to do with race, they came to me. I'm the most radical cat on the base, but I was the one they talked to and the one who had some solutions. Just before my hitch was up, they offered me six stripes to sign up for another hitch. But I was a musician and didn't want to be a warrant officer. So I decided not to stay and I'm very glad I didn't.

I got married while I was in the service. I joined the air force on March 27, 1953, and got married on July 5. Cecilia and I had known each other for five years, and she got pregnant finally. I was nineteen years old, going into the service, and it was time to be a man. I asked Cecilia to marry me, but I didn't know nothing, not one thing. I didn't know what love was, didn't know what commitment was. All I knew was that I was going to be a daddy.

When I was sent to Wyoming, I went alone. Cecilia was having our first child, Renée, and stayed in Los Angeles. She would come every now and then, but she could only last so long. Then her attitude changed, as she got to know people. Cecilia stayed my last two years, but I didn't go anywhere else.

Playing in the air force band, we traveled around that part of the country quite a bit. There was a time we had a concert somewhere in Montana. And Montana is even more empty than Wyoming. The water is great and the air is great, but you don't see anything. It's like looking into another dimension. You're just looking. And it's out, man. So the gig was over. Our percussionist, Sergeant William McCoy, and I were driving back to Cheyenne in his car on this two-lane highway. It was a barren area. We had a lot of gas, hoping we'd never run out, because there weren't any gas stations. We kept moving and moving and moving, and we didn't even have tapes in those days. It was like being in an airplane. You look out the window and it seems you're just standing still. That's how the car got. We started feeling like we weren't going anywhere and nothing was changing. It started getting dark when I looked out of the windshield to my right and saw a whole posse of Indians on horses. They came up on us and went right over the top of the car without looking at us. I didn't say a word but thought to myself, "I'm hallucinating." Then McCoy looked over at me and said, "Did you see that?" From then on, we just drove in silence, no sound but the car's motor.

I believe anything can happen. If you can think of it, it can happen. But the effect of that land out there, it has something beautiful and eerie and spiritual about it. That was something. I'd never had that happen, but it's a vivid thing that remains in my mind and I'll never forget it.

I also had a group at the base called the Nu-Tones with Billy James, the drummer who played with Shirley Scott, the female organist for Bill Cosby on the remake of the old Groucho Marx show. Herbert Baker was our bassist and Robbie Robertson played saxophone. We used to travel from that base in Wyoming to all the other bases. They even had a band contest, called Tops in Blue. We rehearsed for it and went all the way to the finals in Las Vegas. We knew we were going to lose in Vegas. This white cat had a Dixieland band, and the judges gave it to those cats. We played "Blue Room" and it went over, but the judges still voted for this other cat. They gave you what looked like an Oscar and called them Rogers. We got the silver Roger for second place.

Vegas was still segregated then, and we had to stay across the tracks. But after the contest, this white guy said, "You guys played so well, you can come and play in the bar here, and I'll give you so much for drinks when the people come in." Not long after we started playing, here comes six couples. There was a blond in the group and she spotted me. We finally took an intermission and were standing at the bar talking about what we were going to play next. Here comes this blond, who looked at me as she walked past and then went into the bathroom. We continued talking until she came out of the bathroom, walked straight up to my mouth, and stuck her tongue in it. Man, the guy behind the bar went into a state of shock. I'll never forget my drummer, Billy, saying, "Time to tear down, Tap!" He started tearing down the drums to get away, because those cats were pissed off and she was with them. I don't know why she did it. They didn't bother us but they wanted to. We were ready for them. My man said, "I've got my drum rack here." But we had to leave. The bartender said, "I guess you guys had better get on out of here right now, while you can."

That kind of experience was a trip. It wasn't too long after Wardell Gray had been killed up there. We figured it was either Wardell fooling around with a white girl or it had something to do with narcotics. It might also have been a case of mistaken identity. Wardell wasn't by himself. There was another cat the mob was after, a dancer named Teddy Hale or something, and Wardell just happened to be in the wrong place at the wrong time. It wasn't just a random thing, because they made sure. They cut his head off and left it in one place and the body in another. That's why we knew it was one of the mobs up there. They don't fool around and nobody gets blamed for the murder, if the victim's black. The dancer got away and never went back to Vegas.

The best time I had in that city was a few years later in the late 1950s, when I was at the Flamingo with Gerald Wilson's band. One night Gerald said, "Tonight, we're going to break the color line." And I was ready for that. The whole band just got up from the stage and walked into the casino. I went toward some slots and noticed this gangster nodding me toward one of the machines. I won a $500 jackpot off that thing. I guess they felt it was time, too.

My air force adventures, musically, were going to all these towns. Once, our air force band went to a town in Wyoming to do a concert and march in a parade. Cecilia and Renée, who was just a little baby, were with me. After the parade was over, I was just walking around with them and all these kids started following us. They hadn't seen any black people and had never been around them.

"Please, can I see her?"

"Please, can I touch her?"

"She's so pretty."

We let them do that, because they were kids, and I knew they were doing this for real. They didn't mean Renée any harm, so I let them rub on her.

"It doesn't come off."

They thought all the people in the world were white. Like when I was a kid, I thought all the people in the world were black. When we went into a restaurant, they were all at the windows staring in at us. They stayed with us until we left town. Those kids really didn't know about racism. They had no idea it existed. It was invisible to them.

My years in the air force were good, learning years. Ever since that scene in Houston with my mother, I had all this hate for white men. In the air force, I started seeing other things happening. We had a southern bass player in the band from Mississippi, the deepest part of the South. I can't remember his name; it was something like "Schwimmer." He had been in the service a few months when he was transferred to our band. At that time, there were four black guys in the band out of thirty-five to forty pieces. The rest were white and they were from all different parts of the states. After he'd been with us for a while, this bass player came up to us, while we were just standing around in the dayroom talking. He was real short, and all the black cats were six feet and over—big, mean, and nasty. He just walked up to us.

"Can I talk to you guys for a minute?"

"Yeah, yeah."

"When I was a kid, I was raised in Mississippi and was raised to think of black people as being monkeys, having tails; everyone carried razors and had big dicks; you were lazy and didn't have any intelligence. My parents, all my relatives, all my people who I grew up around taught me to think of you as being nothing. My people lied to me. I've been here a year with you guys and my people lied to me. And I wanted to tell you this, because I'm apologizing for being brought up to think that way."

He loved my wife. We played a gig once at the officers' club, and he danced with her. Some cat said something to him about it, and he went off on him. They finally got rid of us; we couldn't play there anymore. We had a white pianist, Dick Shreve, who lives in Los Angeles now. His wife danced with one of the blacks at one of the clubs, and a sergeant said, "What are you doing dancing with that nigger?" She just hit the guy. And when she hit him, all of us on the bandstand jumped down on the floor and started fighting these cats. It went on until the military police stopped it, and we were out of another job.

Those kinds of experiences were something. Many of the white guys in the band were there because they were against all that racism. Gene Miller was a drummer with the Airmen of Note, the top air force band, until he turned up in Wyoming. I asked him why, and he said, "The Airmen of Note are so prejudiced; it's terrible. There are no black players in the band; they don't even want them. What really did it for me was one night at a party following a concert. They wanted to swap wives." There was no way Gene was going to do that with any of those fools, so he put in a complaint about the prejudices and left the band. They wouldn't allow any Jewish cats in there, either. Naturally, they wanted to get rid of him quietly, so nothing would appear in the newspapers, and they just transferred him . . . to that base in Wyoming, where they sent all the cats that they didn't want. That's why we're friends today.

Billy James started playing drums in the air force thanks to Gene. Billy had been in another part of the air force and not connected to the band. But he'd come over to the band barracks and play bongos and congas with us. When Gene heard him, he said, "Man, this guy's got impeccable rhythm. How come you aren't in the band?" Billy told him that he couldn't read and didn't have any instrument. Gene said he'd take care of it and he wrote or called back to Washington, D.C. Next thing we knew, Billy James was in the band and Gene taught him to read.

This cat, Gene Miller, now lives in Denver, Colorado, and is a wrought iron maker. He's a good cat, the kind of guy you don't forget. And he had one of those faces that you don't forget: round, blond hair, glasses, and always intense. He said what he felt and he gained your confidence. Our daughters grew up together, because he was a family person, and he had a sweet woman. I could see why he told those colonels or generals, "You come near her and I'll cut your throat." Dick Shreve and Gene Miller, and some of the other Caucasian guys I met in the service, were the real deal, real human beings, and I still know them today.

I also had a friend in the service who was an artist and a saxophonist—a black guy named Merton D. Simpson. He's now a big-time artist in Paris and New York with galleries in both places. He got out of the service for painting a general's portrait so uniquely and convincingly that the general asked him what he wanted. Merton said he'd like to get out six months early to enroll in a particular college and he got out with all the benefits. When I first went to New York with Lionel Hampton's band after the service, I stayed in his gallery and ate his food. Now he's stretched on out. He's also a musician; plays tenor sax. When I was at the Village Vanguard in New York in 1991, he came by. Whenever I'm there, we get together.

During the time I was in the air force, most of the music seemed to be coming out of New York. Everybody was there. We followed it, but we were also in a kind of vacuum between 1953 and 1957, because the music wasn't around us, not in Wyoming. So a lot of music was in the garage, coming out of the garage. And that was happening in the service, too, with certain cats. We would play different kinds of music, and somebody would say, "What's that? What's that out shit you're all playing?" Then someone answered, "Avant-garde," and everyone started using that word. It sounded nice to the brothers, because it was a French word—you might as well call it like it is. They had no idea what it really meant at the time.

But all this music was also coming out of the civil rights movement, out of all the crud that was happening. Even in Wyoming we read about it, heard about it, and we knew what it was about. We had been fighting those battles in Wyoming, on that air force base. And that affected us and our music. The anger would come out when we played. Cats would just be screaming through their horns, portraying what was happening to black people through their art.

So the air force was a lot of good experiences and good friends, most of whom I've kept up with. I had my own band within the air force band, and I was writing and putting things together, the odd concert. I had a radio show in Wyoming called "Beyond the Blue Horizon." It was in town and came on every Wednesday at twelve in the afternoon for fifteen minutes.

The service experience got me ready to come out into the world. The discipline helped, being able to set your mind to something and carry it through. The service is a kind of microcosm of the world. It helps you understand, up to a point, how to go about surviving in this world, to get your piece of the action. You learn that, and you learn that it isn't going to be easy. But beyond that point, it destroys. Everything in the service has to do with keeping things in order. Everything they do has to do with keeping you in order, to the point where you won't be able to advance yourself on your own initiative. Everything is there for you; you just have to go through all the red tape and so much bureaucracy. You have to follow the orders. Under that kind of an organization, they try to psychologically gain control of your thought processes, to dampen or corrupt your creative capabilities. It's just like the situation that the black male faces. Society just throws up one hurdle after another. After a while your patience will run out: "Well, I'm going to go down to the Bank of America." Eventually, the only option is to be a criminal.

In some cases the service created criminals, like when they turned out the black cats during the Korean conflict. In case they were shot, the soldiers on the front line had bags of Demerol that they could shoot anytime. Well, if you started using the stuff, and if you survived the war, as soon as you got discharged, your name was sent to the nearest police station. All the black cats that I knew who came out of my neighborhood started going to jail for being junkies, because by the time they got out of the service, they were junkies. There was no medical help for them, nothing. They were just thrown out in the cold. Meanwhile, the service was telling the police, "Make sure you watch this guy. He's a dope addict. He's still trigger-happy and he's liable to do anything." I saw it happen to so many guys, some very good friends. I saw the changes in these guys. Cats who used to be real factual minded would just go off and not remember anything. It wasn't until years later that I understood that it was all a plan, a genocidal plan. Start with the men, of course. It was similar to the syphilis tests that went on in the 1940s with black men.

We were trying to raise our children in this kind of crud and tried to give them hope. They'd say, "But daddy . . ." and you had to be ready to deal with that "but" part, because they'd seen something else and something else had been said to them. It was confusing and caused a lot of problems when you're trying to raise a family. You wanted to see them raised a certain way and give a contribution to society. You wanted to be able to give them the means to do this. You wanted a good job, but you weren't allowed to get one. The only job you could get then was a janitor down at the bus station.

All these kinds of things were on a lot of black cats' minds and they were the topic of the day during my years in the service. Music was our way of dealing with it. We'd just create something that expressed the way we were feeling about whatever had just happened. I've never thought of myself as having a lock on what's happening. But I do think I'm able to catch on to how it's happening. I have no verbal explanation for it, but I know the feeling I have. If I want to let someone else know how I'm feeling, I can do it through creating music.

6

When I came out of the service and returned to Los Angeles, it was real strenuous during those days with my growing family. Cecilia and I had four children now: Renée, Laurence Tremayne, Vincent Marcell, and Darion Lamont. But I was gigging and making some money, maybe ten dollars a night on Friday and Saturday at the Bucket o' Blood down on Vernon Avenue and Main Street. It was enough to get by. In those days, ten dollars would buy you four or five bags of groceries. We didn't go hungry and even had a little change left over. And this all came from playing in the community, in the bars at night. This was a little while after the Central Avenue period. It didn't have the flourish, the kind of feeling that was there in the earlier days. It was dying in the 1950s, but there were still places where you could make a little money. After a while I got a regular gig at the Troubadour on La Cienega Boulevard, outside the community.

There were a lot of the out cats in town. Ornette Coleman was giggin' with his band at the Hillcrest Club on Washington Boulevard. All the out cats came by there. The It Club and the Black Orchid also opened nearby. The It Club had John T. McClain running it and all kinds of shit went on there. McClain had a house behind the club for Phineas Newborn, so he could keep him in tow. It was out. And all the cats played there. I remember people walking out on John Coltrane, but a lot of cats appreciated what he was doing and how he was stretching out.

Between Washington Boulevard in the midcity area and Hollywood above it, that's where most of the clubs were and a lot of cats were working. The tenor saxophonist Charles Brackeen was out here. His wife, Joanne, was with him, but she never played piano then, just took care of her two babies. All these out cats were here, a lot of them from Central Avenue days, but nobody followed anyone in particular. Everyone had an individual approach with a lot of people doing different things, but all of it helping the music to grow. It was happening out here, even if all people ever heard about the West Coast was tiptoe-through-the-tulips music. Cannonball Adderley once said in an interview, "Wait a minute, man, have you been out on the West Coast? Have you been to the bush? You've got to go to the bush. Not downtown. They've got a lot of cats out there playing." That was a time when the music was popping out here, and nobody was paying any attention to it.

During this time I also got to sit in one night with Ben Webster at the Milomó club on Western Avenue. He invited me up to the bandstand, and I spent the evening playing the blues, listening to him play, grinning and just enjoying it. And Big Ben was teaching all the time. I was doing my Dizzy Gillespie shit on trombone, just firing away, and he'd say, "Take your time. Take your time." I'll never forget that scene.

I also started working with the bigger bands in the community. The established bands that were around at the time were getting gigs. I worked with Horace Henderson's band every now and then, the Peppy Prince band, the Chick Touchstone orchestra, the Jeep Smith band, Sammy Franklin's band—bassist Henry Franklin's father. And I still worked Sunday afternoons in the parks with Percy McDavid's concert orchestra. These kinds of things enabled us to survive.

We didn't have a pad and were living with my parents in this house on Fifty-sixth Street. Then we lived with Cecilia's parents on Eighty-fourth until we finally got our own place near Sixty-sixth Street and Avalon Boulevard. We were getting by, and the weekend gigs were enough to pay the rent and cover expenses. Cecilia also started working by this time as an administrator at the county hospital, and I'd be home with the kids during the week, raising and disciplining them, changing the diapers and teaching them, taking them to school and picking them up.

Although people knew me as a trombonist, I had been playing piano all along. In fact, I had almost given trombone up when trombonist Lester Robertson, my partner, called me up in the last part of 1958 and asked if I wanted to go to New York with Lionel Hampton. I wasn't working much here at the time and the gig paid $125 a week. That was the starting pay; I started and finished with that pay, but $125 was pretty cool at the time. I joined Hamp's band and stayed until the first part of 1961.

In Hamp's band, there were times when the pianist might not show up and he'd say to me, "You play piano." Certain folks knew that I played piano. In Los Angeles, I'd often get together with musicians like David Bryant and Alan Hines, and play piano in these groups. When we got the Arkestra together in the early 1960s, I started playing piano exclusively. It was easier on me physically. By then I had lost my front teeth anyway and had totally given up the trombone. I gave my horn to my partner, Lester, because he had lost his through the years.

I was first influenced on piano by my mother, and then by Samuel Browne and Lloyd Reese. As far as regular players, I loved listening to Art Tatum, Erroll Garner, and Earl "Fatha" Hines. They didn't influence my wanting to play piano but I recognized what they were doing right away. I liked the way they played. With Tatum, there were no rules for him; he made his own rules. No matter what song, when you heard him play, it was like the first time you were hearing it. He'd just dig into the music.

Earl "Fatha" Hines and Erroll Garner: I loved those two cats, just like I loved Art Tatum. It was a great feeling being up around all those people. I met Earl Hines at the black musicians' union on Central Avenue and Erroll Garner later on, when I was giggin' in the early 1960s with my trio at the Sea Witch on the corner of Sunset and La Cienega Boulevards. He was playing next door and on his break came by with his lady. Erroll sat behind me, and the cats didn't tell me he was there. Then he came up, grabbed me by my shoulders, and said, "Just keep doing that, man. It has its own definition."

I said, "Man, I've loved you ever since I was a kid. And I'm going to keep on loving you, baby."

He could never read, and I'm glad he never did. How could any music come out more pure than it came out of Erroll Garner? If he had started reading, it would have ruined everything. He was an amazing cat, just one of those special players with a whole orchestra in his fingers. The cat's hands, when he stretched them out on the box . . . whew! He had small hands, but when he got them on that piano, they just seemed to grow. He was playing tenths and that's where he got that sound. Yeah, I loved his playing. He was a hell of a player, just an exciting person.

But probably the most influential was Duke Ellington. I loved the way he played with that strong, masterful sound that said, "Listen. I have something to tell you." And he used the piano like it was an orchestra. Every note meant something. His whole approach to the band was also important to me. It's like Duke said in his book: the best part of having a band is that you can write anything you want and you can hear it right away to see if it's cool. That's why, later on, I always had the Pan Afrikan Peoples Arkestra. I could write something and I could hear it the next day. And I tried to make my relationships with other musicians on that kind of level. They are artists themselves, and I had them in mind when I was writing, because you want to get all you can out of the person's creativity to put into this music.

When I was in the air force, I used to follow the Ellington band. One time they played Cheyenne, Wyoming. When Duke walked by me, he grabbed my shoulder, showing that he remembered me from Central Avenue. Then I followed him to Denver and brought this girl with me, a WAF (Women's Air Force) named Mary Saliveria. She was real tall, probably a mixture of black and Italian, and had the kind of face that just made you look at her. We were near the stage at the concert, and Duke looked over and saw this chick. While the band was playing, he started gesturing to me, asking if she was my woman, would I introduce him. Mary didn't come back to the base for days, traveling with Ellington's band through the Rocky Mountains. Duke and I got closer after that.

Whenever I could, I'd follow the band. I knew all the charts and

I'd be out on the dance floor conducting the band every gig. One night, I was out on the floor dancing and went to cut off the band, but it didn't cut off. Clark Terry, who was in the band, pointed at me and cracked up: "We got you that time!"

Ellington took three of the charts that I'd arranged while I was in the air force. I gave him "Rhapsody in Blues," "Bongo Bill," my first chart, and an old standard that I arranged called "Street of Dreams." They're probably still in the book.

That's the list in terms of influences. There were certain players whose music I would buy, other pianists, because I respected their playing, as well as their creativity and the way they approached music. Among classical artists I liked Glenn Gould. His interpretations were different. Andre Watts. And, of course, I always dug the old man, Vladimir Horowitz. I loved him, the way he took command. He'd sit down and play the motherfucker, just play. But there wasn't anyone who I'd just follow or totally wanted to be like. In a way, everyone and no one has influenced me. But these people I've named are the ones who I paid more attention to, who brought me to the light of what was going on musically. The way they approached the piano allows me the freedom to know that it's cool for me to approach it the way I do, to see what I can pull out of it.

From early on, I was always trying to do things differently. When I was a kid in Houston, I had that gang that used to follow me and I had my first band when I was very young. We were always trying different ways of playing tunes. That was in my mind at all times. "Let's go here. Let's take this mountain." It may have been someone else's music, but always my interpretation of it. By the early 1960s, when I was in my late twenties, I was trying to use the piano in different ways, trying for different sounds by using the pedals to expand and color the music, getting the tone rising up and down. I even used them to tune the Arkestra, holding one down without hitting a note on the piano. The sound would collide with the string sound if it wasn't in tune. It wouldn't be that extreme but you could hear the difference. I was also playing the piano strings like a harp and even tapping on the wood, especially on a good piano. Later on I wrote a piece, "Stringeurisms," that treats the piano like a harp. Everyone was trying to do something different with sound. Lester would be playing his trombone and trying to hum at the same time.

I played both instruments so much and was always doing something musically. During the day, a friend would come by and bring his duet books. Then we'd go rehearse with the big band and make a couple of record dates. In Hamp's band we recorded quite a bit. On one of the sessions, I finally got a solo on a piece called "Blue Bone." All three bones were soloing. That was my first solo with Hamp.

Life on the road with Hamp was never dull. When we got to New York on that first trip, Hamp took a small group for some gigs elsewhere and left the rest of us. For a week or two in New York, we didn't work and didn't have any money. Finally, Lester and I got put out of the Flanders Hotel. He went to stay with Eric Dolphy, and I put up at Merton Simpson's pad. For food, we'd share hot dogs and cups of coffee.

It wasn't Hamp's fault; he thought we were getting paid. It was his wife, Gladys, who wouldn't pay us. When Hamp got back and found out what was happening, he put us back in the hotel and paid us. But this was just the beginning. I was working hard for what I was after and I wasn't just playing trombone. I arranged a lot for the band, and Hamp played my arrangements all the time, especially one I'd done for "I Remember Clifford." It's probably still in the book. But I was always hassling with Gladys Hampton about money for arrangements. And I needed it. I had to send money back home to my growing family. Gladys and I never got along too well. There's only a few women in the world, in my life, who I've never really cared for and she's one of them. The other was one of the musicians' wives. They're the only two I can remember. One of them is still alive, but I don't have to see her.

New York was happening then. Everybody was there. One night a bunch of us, including John Coltrane, were in this place talking. Ornette Coleman, who had just arrived, walked in, and Trane jumped away from the conversation, saying, "I gotta go meet this cat." It was flourishing.

When I was on the road with Hamp it was rough in those segregated times. There were so many times that Lionel Hampton had to go through the back door of places to get something to eat. But one evening we had been on the road a long time, traveling from Philadelphia down South. It was raining, and we were tired and hungry by the time we got to this little restaurant somewhere in Alabama. There were about twenty of us on the bus, and Hamp was going to send in this guy who could pass for white, just like he always did. We had this trumpet player, a big dude, who said, "Fuck that! We're going in there now to eat and they're going to serve us!"

I said, "Right on! That's what we're gonna do!"

All the cats jumped off the bus and poured into that place, just looking for trouble. We were hungry, tired, mad, pissed off— Gladys was probably behind in the band's money, too. There were two white cats and a waitress in there, and their eyes just bugged open.

"Can we help you guys?"

And they served us . . . at the front counter.

Whenever we went anywhere, we traveled in groups. We knew what was going on and we were angry. And we knew we had to stick together and cover each other's back.

But the biggest problem always came when white women were involved, no matter what part of the country. Once we were in Buffalo, New York, playing this gig. Afterward, the cops just poured into the backstage area, because all the little, white, blond girls were back there. They saw all these black cats and they just went off. But the girls were all they could handle. These girls were jumping through the windows of the bus to get at us. Then they invited the band to this party and it was a scene. All of a sudden seventeen young, strong black cats came walking through the front door of this house. The thing that broke everything up was when this white lady got so drunk and wanted Virgil Jones, one of our trumpeters, so bad that she pulled him on her lap and went after him in the middle of this party.

We said, "Okay! Time to go!"

Man, it was trippin'. Buffalo, New York. There were so many

nights like that. Chicks were all over—backstage, under the tables —doing everything you can think of. It was out. It was so out.

One night, Hamp took a chick away from Lester and me in this hotel where the band was staying. He had come downstairs in his shorts to get a soda or something and saw us with this redhead. He asked her, "How much are they paying, honey?"

"Ten dollars."

"I'll give you twenty. Sorry guys."

And he headed upstairs with the babe, where he already had two young girls waiting in his room. The next morning, he came down with three babes running out of the hotel.

The old man was something. He was a bad dude. On some nights, like in Las Vegas, after the crowd had left the gig, he'd get to playing and that shit would come out of him, just tear the band up. We'd just say, "Ah, man, this crazy, little motherfucker can play his ass off!"

Traveling with Hamp, I also got to meet Louis Armstrong. He had just come back from Africa and was in Las Vegas when we were there.

Louis called Hamp, "Hey, Gates, come on over, man."

"Okay, Satch, and I'm gonna bring a young blood with me who I want you to meet"—meaning me.

"Bring him along, man."

They took me outside, and Louis offered us some of his reefer.

"Hey, Gates, you got to try some of this. I just brought it back and you got to watch out for it."

Lionel said, "Yeah, all right. Give it to young blood, too. But don't hit it too hard, young blood."

We were out there for about an hour, and I was just listening to these two cats. They'd be passing the joints back and forth, and they were smoking, man, but it didn't even faze them. Louis was also telling me how marijuana helped him, kept his blood pressure down. Then Louis told us that they had stopped fighting in this one area when he was in Africa.

"That's the best thing that happened to me. They stopped fighting to hear me play. Then they gave me this reefer. I've been smoking reefer since I came out of the womb. And I'm gonna smoke reefer all the way to the tomb. Till they throw the dirt on me, I'm gonna be smoking. I love this stuff."

"I love it, too," Hamp said.

And I said I loved it.

"Well, here you go, young blood, try it again."

I got so loaded that all I could say was that I'd had enough. Then we had to go back in and play. When Lester Robertson saw us, he said, "Oh, man!" Gates and Satch were just smiling at me, because I was so loaded and just grinning the whole time I was on stage. Louis turned me on good.

Hamp was funny. The band would usually open with a number while he was in the dressing room. Then the announcer would call his name, and Hamp would make his first appearance on stage. One night, I kicked the band off with my arrangement of "I Remember Clifford," and he came running out there with his shirt all fucked up, saying, "I got to get me some of that." He played his ass off, then ran backstage, finished dressing, and waited until they announced him to come out again. Too much.

That's what I remember about Gates, and how he never knew Lester Robertson's name. All those years in the band and he'd always call him John. "Hey, John! John!" And Lester had a way of ignoring your ass. A few years later, we had a guy in the Arkestra like that, Everett Brown, who didn't know anybody's name. All he knew was Arthur Blythe, me, and David Bryant. The rest of the cats were, "Hey, man, hey!" He'd see the cats every day, but he never knew their names.

Hamp's showmanship was an issue for me when I was younger. I thought all the grinning and clowning was like that Stepin Fetchit, Uncle Tom shit, and I didn't like it. I always made sure I never did anything like that. When I got older and started seeing things, I began to understand what was really happening. One day, Stepin Fetchit's son was over at my place and crying about the way his father was treated by black people, and how his father really didn't feel that way, and was just trying to work and take care of his family. As I got older and had moved through all the levels of segregation, and had started to think about it, I could see what it did to people. And I learned to understand that everyone was human and that, at times, you just have to take small steps to make progress. By the time I got into Hamp's band, I understood that he would do the same thing with a black audience that he did with a white audience, do the same thing before any audience in the world. I saw that it was just showmanship, that's all it came down to.

Then after two years with Hamp, one day when we were traveling through the South, I said, "What is the point of all this? Why did I get into music in the first place? Did I get into it to become this or become that? Or did I get into it because I love the sounds and trying to make the best music I can, and being part of that kind of scene?" I questioned myself. Was it just for another record, another tour? It just wasn't making any sense to me anymore.

With Hamp, we played mostly in the South and New York. Those were two racist places and still are. I thought, "Well, there's no point. What's the point of playing this music here? These people don't pay any attention to it and don't have any idea what we're playing. If it was a European orchestra, they'd be sitting there listening and trying to hear." And the band was playing great music. There were a lot of great writers and great players in the band, cats like Skinny Bergen on bass, Virgil Jones on trumpet, and Mike Romero on drums. But the way it was approached by most people, I just didn't want to deal with that kind of attitude. I just felt, "What is the point of me traveling the road playing with the band?" which I enjoyed. We made a pretty good living, and I'd send money back home to raise my family. But it still wasn't doing what one would expect it to do to a person who had a job with a professional bandleader, a real great bandleader. It would seem that a person in my position would be pretty much satisfied, but I wasn't satisfied. And the reason I wasn't satisfied was because I didn't feel the music was making any point.

Then the band came to Los Angeles for a gig out on Sunset Boulevard. I'll never forget. After the last performance, we were getting ready to head back to New York. At four o'clock that morning, I got off the bus. Oliver Jackson, the drummer, said, "Where you going, Horace?"

"This is it, brother. I've had it."

I wanted to do something else. I wanted my own thing; I wanted to write it and I wanted to help preserve the music. The music was just going off, and nobody knew who wrote the music or cared. I had been in school at Jeff with Richard Berry when he wrote "Louie, Louie," and no one knew Richard Berry. And that's why my feelings got to the point where these people, these men and women who really were in the music, like Melba Liston and all those folks, should be recognized and their contribution to this whole scheme of things should be recognized.

This is when I first started thinking about putting the Arkestra together and that's why I got off the road to start my band, to preserve black music. I wanted to preserve and teach and show and perform the music of black Americans and Pan-African music, to preserve it by playing it and writing it and taking it to the community. That was what it was about, being part of the community, and that's the reason I left Hamp's band that night. I decided that what my family had gone through for me to get into the music was for this particular reason, to make a point, to say something with it, for it to be accepted as good music and to be accepted as part of the fabric of the whole society that we all dream of having. And that meant being home.

At the same time, I was also thinking about raising my family. I had babies and another son, Niles, our fifth child, was born on August 16, 1961. Not long after that I was back in New York and that's when I first met Randy Weston. He offered me his house in Brooklyn, because he was leaving the country. I could have stayed there and settled into the New York scene, but I said, "I can't do this. I'm not going to bring my kids up into this kind of society. I can't stand it. I don't want them to be in it. I'm at least going to tell them the truth." I remember Don Cherry saying, when he was living on Washington Square in New York, "I can't grow my kids up, man, in the streets, on the sidewalks, in New York."

I said, "That's right, man. I can't do that."

I knew I wouldn't have lasted there with the racial attitudes. Don stayed as long as he could, but I cut on out, came back here, and started making that endeavor. I wanted to raise my children in the kind of society where they could feel free to walk the streets of their neighborhood. And the only way that was going to happen was if I started working to help build that kind of a community. When I left Hamp's band early in 1961, I started slowly putting the pieces together for a community orchestra. After the trip to New York, I threw myself into it.

Going through the South with Hamp and remembering the air force days also made me realize how people hadn't changed. And things like that wouldn't change if you weren't there trying to instigate it. I said, "Man, if you don't like it, then change it, or else shut up. Stop talking so much about it. Stop beefing and screaming and hollering. Get out there and make a motion."

Cats said, "Man, you made a big decision; that took a lot of guts."

It's not even over yet. It's still happening.

All of these thoughts were going through my head when I got off Hamp's bus that morning. That was the end of it, man, and I've been in it since then, up till now, until the dirt is thrown in my face.

7

During the 1950s, there wasn't much cultural activity going on in the African American community of Los Angeles. Segregation had ended, and people were getting better jobs and moving away from the Central Avenue area. They were now concerned with issues like where their kids would go to school. Communication was missing; the social contact that people used to have on Central Avenue was gone. So there was a sense of searching for something better, resetting things now that segregation was over.

I've always thought that music gets people's attention and brings people together. It's a focal point. And I felt that having the Arkestra—which had a message to give, playing original music, dances, and poetry—would give us an opportunity to open up all the areas in our culture that had been stopped. That was the chore that we took off on. The Arkestra would allow the creativity in the community to come together, would allow people to recognize each other as one people and ask, "Now what can we do to make this community better? What can we do for this community together?" So I figured that would be the best move to make, while realizing that it was going to take some time. It's going to take a little time to do anything, but you can plant the seed and nurture it and watch it.

That's how the Pan Afrikan Peoples Arkestra—the Ark—began, with the knowledge that we wanted to preserve the black arts in the community. We wanted an aggregation that put all this music, this music that came from the blues and from the churches—but even then from the same source, from the same scales—into one place, one chart, for the one Arkestra, and to play it all for the people all the time. I wanted to say, "This is your music. This is black music, and I want to present a panorama of the entire thing right here." So we'd play only music by black composers, unknown mostly.

That's what I had in mind in starting the Pan Afrikan Peoples Arkestra: "Pan Afrikan," because the music would be drawn from African peoples around the world, and "Arkestra," building off the word *ark* and Noah using it to save different parts of the world, as told in the Bible. We would preserve the music on our ark, the mothership, and it will be around for people to listen to and enjoy. We would preserve all this music, show the differences within it, and even go into the small details, as educators or scholars would do. We'd provide the information for scholars to work with. That was my gig.

Of course, I was aware of Sun Ra's Arkestra, always respected what he was doing, and got my spelling of that word from him, but that was as far as the hookup went. While he was thinking in terms of space, of an ark traveling through space, I was thinking in terms of a cultural safe house for the music.

What I remember real hard and real reddish-like is how the band itself came about. I started by looking for different kinds of personalities who were involved in the music. And every person I brought in was an outsider, so to speak. They leaned a little bit, you dig? They didn't walk a straight line; they leaned as they walked. And I ran into a lot of people, different people, some I had known before, who wanted to play something else. They didn't like what they were doing, or were trying to find something different in the music. There were players around, perhaps working in bands across town, who approached the music in an out way for the bands they were in. They'd end up with no solos and not being used very much. So I sought out those kinds of people, those who weren't a part of the studio cliques, a part of the group of people who worked a particular area all the time. I looked for these people, because I figured that they had much more to offer and that was something very precious.

I would also check out what kind of person they were and if they had families. All those things were going through my mind, because I figured that had a lot to do with what we had to do in the community, and that kind of approach to the music would have to have some support from people who were very close. Otherwise, it was not going to do very well. So most of the guys were married or living with some ladies and had children.

When I got seven or eight people together, we started. In 1961, me and Linda Hill, Lester Robertson, David Bryant, Alan Hines, Jimmy Woods, and Guido Sinclair put the Arkestra together. Jimmy Woods I'd known since Los Angeles City College and he was real talented. He recorded two albums—*Awakening* and *Conflict*—for Les Koenig's Contemporary Records in the early 1960s. Jimmy was an inspiration to all the modern players around. I'll never forget an incident one Sunday at Larry Hearns's club off Central Avenue at Avalon and Forty-second, across from the old Wrigley ballpark. Sunday was the day of the fast gun, seeing who could play the fastest. There were the junkies, the nonjunkies, the weed heads— everyone there was categorized. But Jimmy was off on the side by himself, in his old blue suit and glasses. When he got on stage, the cats looked at each other and said, "Man, who is this guy?"

"I don't know, man. I ain't never seen him."

"Okay, 'Cherokee' . . . up! One, two . . . One-two-three-four!"

One of them looked at Jimmy and said, "Okay, man, you take the bridge."

They figured they'd just blow him off. But when they got to the bridge, Jimmy Woods just blew through it. He *ate* the bridge up!

"Who the fuck is this?"

"Where'd he come from?"

They had to come out of their act and from then on the cats gave him respect. You had to pay attention.

David Bryant and Alan Hines were our first bassists. I've known David through the years. He's a little older, but I was aware of him playing around Central Avenue with everybody and backing all these singers. I met Alan Hines in the late 1950s at a club one Sunday afternoon. I walked in this place on Long Beach Boulevard and 55th, and there was this guy on stage playing bass with a drummer named Edgar Jones. I heard this cat say, "You put your ax down, I'll kick your ass!" I was at the bar, and the next thing I know the bassist put his instrument down and the drummer jumped up, and they were going at it on the stage. One was screaming at the other, "You broke the time!" I cracked up. We jumped off the stools and pulled the cats apart. That's when I first met Al Hines.

I met Linda in the General Hospital, where she was a nurse and was taking care of me. I still had the kidney stones and they'd become awfully painful. It started happening in the air force and continued flaring up every year in the month of June for the next ten years. Then it finally disappeared. But it got so bad this time, I had to go to the hospital, because I hadn't experienced that kind of pain before. Cecilia had given a party for us, some kind of anniversary, and that's when I'd gotten ill. I started having convulsions and experiencing this intense pain. They took me to the hospital, but all they did was go through this terrible investigation of my lower body area. I didn't know what was happening with this mystery pain, and it was a kind of pain that I'd never like to have again.

When I woke up, there was this big, tall, beautiful woman standing over me. She was a nurse, but she told me how much she wanted to play music and was interested in the community. After I got out, Linda stayed on my case, because she knew I was into the music and she wanted to do it. Linda had never studied music, but she always had that feeling and she was talented. She learned to play the piano and write, and became a very important person in the community, though people were afraid of her at first. She'd walk around with a bald head, big earrings, and dashikis. Then they got used to it. I saw her grow so much, and she became the most talented woman I ever met. She became the Ark's matriarch. I gave her the nickname "Lino," and later wrote a tune about her and her place called "Lino's Pad."

We started rehearsing in that small place, at Linda's house on Seventy-fifth Street between Central Avenue and Hooper. The first thing we did was just start playing. That's all we did; sat around and played and played and played. We rehearsed there twenty-four hours, if necessary. People started bringing in their own music. We added that to the pot and then it was left up to me to arrange it correctly. "Okay, here it is, Horace. Now what?" Boom! And I'd put something together. We started real, real lightweight. "You two play this and you two play this. On my signal, we'll do this and then we'll do that." There wasn't anything heavy about it.

One day, I brought some music and they were just looking at it. Some of the cats couldn't read that well. So I gave a class in reading. I wanted the cats to be able to read the music and to write it down. Most of the guys were in that situation, but we had a few who had the abilities and they were able to help teach the others. That's how we got started, and a lot of the guys learned to write from those early days.

In a few months, we'd built up from seven or eight to about eighteen cats, regular cats who you'd see all the time, men and women. Musicians started living there. The girls would bring their children with them. Linda would provide for the children, so the women and the mothers would have a room where they could sit with their babies or leave them, while they were in the other rooms doing their dancing or singing or rehearsing.

Leroy Brooks, a drummer and another friend from college days, joined us in 1962. He was a very studious guy and hated the social situation. When he joined the Ark, he became a major part of the group, both for his philosophy and his playing. In later years he started getting ill, brain wise, and he stopped talking. He used to come over here and babysit my kids. They loved him. But he was crazy as a loon and ended up killing himself. The night he did it, he called my place at three in the morning. I wasn't home but he talked to Cecilia, told her what he was going to do and not to feel bad, because he knew what he was doing. Then he went in the garage and asphyxiated himself. He left a note telling the Ark to keep going, but that he was "going to the high level now."

Arthur Blythe also joined us early on and he was one of the main cats who was serious about playing. He was a stone wall, this brother. I always dug him, because he'd make up his mind to do something and he'd do it, whatever it took. Whatever they'd throw at him, he'd go through it to get it. I met him at Linda Hill's. He'd come up from San Diego and was playing in a blues band. The word had started to go around the neighborhood about us, and he just showed up at Linda's one day. When Arthur first came, he would always play in the corner, but he was there every day. I think he was in his early twenties, had his own big sound, and was known as "Black Arthur."

Initially I was doing all of the music, preparing and rehearsing it. Then we got a bandleader, Ernest Straughter, in the mid-1960s. When Ernest left a while later, Jesse Sharps became the bandleader. Jesse would rehearse the band and go through the intricate parts. We first got him during this early period, while he was in high school, and he grew up in the Ark. All of them did, but he later took on a leadership part. He became the Ark leader, the band rehearsal man; he was hard-core. They'd all be quiet and listen to him when he talked. He's in his forties now and working in Europe, but he's still got that same attitude toward music.

People got involved with the Arkestra like it was their life's work. They got serious about it. Having a group of people who were trying to preserve, develop, teach, and enlighten was very important. And it was important that the group got together so everyone could speak their minds, and that they put something down on paper, made some kind of sound together, made some kind of point. So with that kind of activity going on inside, it attracted quite a few people, an intense group of people committed to our goal, people with personalities who didn't want to just complain but wanted to find solutions to problems around us, wanted to cut through the shit. These were the kind of people I wanted to be around.

The Underground Musicians Association

We were moving beyond being just an Arkestra, so we formed a larger group called the Underground Musicians Association (UGMA). Because the music we played wasn't accepted on top of the ground, we just separated ourselves. People said, "Y'all are playing that underground music." That's what they called it and we went with it. "We're the underground musicians."

We were starting to develop a reputation. At first people weren't sure about us. We were "the wild band," "that crazy band," "that gang," "that posse." The other musicians in the community would say, "Here come those guys, man, that wild band over there on the Eastside, those cats who play that outside music, all that race music and that weird stuff." I wanted to preserve black music, and none of the cats who were out in the studios in Hollywood would touch that phrase, because that was "those racist cats' idea of music." Because we played and talked about being black, about Africa, about preserving our culture, it scared them. In the early 1960s, no one was talking about these things. So we were called "those racist cats playing hate music." Well, I used that phrase because that's the way I saw it. It was called preserving black music by playing it and writing it and taking it to the community. This had nothing to do with hate.

In these early days, UGMA became a very dangerous commodity to the community, because of our comradeship and because of what we were saying about what was happening in the community. People started caring about each other and that was dangerous. We watched each other's back and took care of each other as a group. That became intimidating, to the point where we were called a gang or a "perversion against the country." Everywhere we went, the whole group would be with me. We'd all be in cars, four or five of us, all the time, and we'd go to places together, not only to play but also to listen. "Oh, here comes that guy and the posse." They'd get shook up. "Here come them cats with them dashikis on and them long naturals." At that time, we weren't wearing dreadlocks but it was the naturals and dashikis, and not many people were doing that.

We were also talking against the things that were happening to the community, like police brutality. We were onto that early, and that scared a lot of people in the community. We'd be standing out in the street rapping with the police, protesting this and that. People weren't used to standing up against the police and talking about respect. But after a while it came to a point where they understood, because they knew we were right and they saw us there, in the community, over time. They got to know us, and their children started coming around.

UGMA was the whole organization, and the Ark was only a part of UGMA. We had other things happening. Early on we had a class for children in reading, writing, and spelling, that Linda organized with some of the ladies of UGMA. They had remedial classes for kids who were supposedly slow in school. She'd also have them doing art and singing, learning the tunes of the band. Some of these kids grew up and became part of the Ark. That's how the band really started stretching by the early 1970s, because some of the kids from the early 1960s had started expanding their thought patterns and even taking it outside to their schools.

Other people started coming by, like the actor William Marshall, who taught acting. He would come down all the time just to help out. The first time I heard of William was in 1952, seeing him in the movie *Lydia Bailey,* where he played the part of a Haitian rebel who was fighting against slavery. I was in my teens and that really impressed me, because he didn't have one of those low roles that black actors and actresses would always get. William had been a protégé of Paul Robeson, had hung with him through the years, and it showed. He was a real strong-sounding brother. When he started coming around UGMA, that's when I met him. Jayne Cortez, the poet, also started coming by. She had been married to Ornette Coleman, but moved to Los Angeles to raise her son and got hooked up with us. Queen Emanon, a lady from the community, was also there teaching dance.

The people on the block became so accustomed to the music that when they didn't hear it, they thought something was wrong. Serious, man, and the people got the vibe. The kids and the old folks would come by and just say, "That was nice." The community wasn't calling the police on the band for playing after ten o'clock. One day, the band wasn't rehearsing or playing and one of the winos on Central Avenue said, "Hey, man, where's our band?" Where's *our* band. He'd never seen it; he'd just heard it all the time. Others would say, "How come our band ain't playing today? I can't do my work around the house."

Soon, kids in the neighborhood would come up to us: "I might want to play a horn. Where can I go to get some instructions?" Now they knew where, and that's how a lot of guys started playing. So we stayed in that community. There was a lot of fun in doing it and in working with different people, and talking about getting people off drugs and getting off their habits of hitting, stealing, or shooting.

That was what it was about, being a part of the community. I was raised in simple segregation. We were forced apart. But we didn't think less of ourselves because we were segregated, and we built a community. I'm used to speaking to everybody: "Hello." I'm used to communicating and not being afraid or feeling strange walking down my street in my community. And we didn't have this in Los Angeles when we started the Ark in the early 1960s. We still don't have it to the degree that it should be. But we didn't have it at all during those times. So we had to deal with it. All of this was a part of the idea of us being in the community, playing and practicing. We just couldn't live, play, and say, "Everything is okay, and if the police harass us, we'll just demand black policemen."

We were always up on what was going on in the world that had to do with any person, black or not, who was subjected to being a work hog. Newspapers from around the world were always around the UGMA house. Our concern was our particular area and black people, but we sympathized with peoples' struggles around the world. And we'd have visitors from many of these places, people who were under the gun, and they would inform us about what was going on elsewhere. We had to bring all these other things to light, because at first a lot of our listeners were saying, "You guys are talking that hate talk."

I told them, "I never talk hate. We're not talking hate. We're talking about love of yourself. This has to do with you loving who you are. And how you do that is to be involved, to be a part of it."

Becoming Visible

We played for about six or seven months at Linda's pad—what had become the first UGMA house—until some of the cats said, "Hey, why don't we do something with this?" And that's what I was waiting for. Then we moved outside; we started playing in South Park over on Fifty-first Street and Avalon Boulevard. We picked South Park because it was beautiful. It already had a stage and the whole setup. Everything was there and people would just be laying around; a lot of families were there all the time. One day, we just showed up and got on the bandstand. And after a while people accepted us. Even the guy who was supervising the park would help us in any way he could. There was a little old lightweight piano they had locked up. They'd start taking it out for us and then tuning it after they knew we were coming. We started playing every weekend at South Park.

By the early to mid-1960s, the community bands, like Percy McDavid's, weren't happening in a place like South Park in South Central Los Angeles. It wasn't happening in Latino East Los Angeles. It was still happening in the white communities. All the concerts by these municipal park bands were now only in the white communities. But all kinds of people would still come from all over, from all the different communities, to those white areas to hear the bands. Whenever I played with Percy's band, everybody would be listening as we played different composers, black as well as European.

They had some meetings at Local 47 about the locations for the concerts. One day I got up and said, "You've got money for musicians. Why don't we have some of that sent down to South Park at Fifty-first Street and Avalon Boulevard? They've got a great stage there, and I'll get the band." We were playing in South Park already for free every weekend. People would come by and they'd fill up the seats to listen to that *bad* band. We weren't getting paid for it, because we weren't certified on the union list. That's what my argument was about. I called it racist and told that to the president of the union, John Tranchitella—we used to call him "Tarantula." That's when they put a little mark by your name. I was in and out of a few board meetings, calling them the same thing, because they wouldn't support music at South Park and in East Los Angeles. Some of the black cats were drugged, because they were in the studio cliques and were going the other way. But I was talking about the mass, not about the few. I was talking about music *for* the black people over in the community, as well as having black and Latino cats playing.

At first, there were more people in the Ark than there were in the audience. But we'd play to an audience of two or three people like they were two or three thousand. That was the kind of spirit the band had. We kept playing and people accepted us. It became something they could look forward to and bring their children to hear. And we didn't just have the music; we had dancers and poets and many different kinds of things that had to do with communication and giving it to people. All that was done free. The gas money was coming out of our own pockets. I'd usually have a little pocket money, because if you're the bandleader and your drummer needs some gas, you have to come up with it.

There was never any notice about us playing in the park; nothing in the papers, nothing on the radio about a concert. But on Saturdays and Sundays, they'd be piled in there looking at the stage and swaying with the music. One of the children might have just been killed by a policeman, but here they all came together. We'd be remembering this kid and swinging, just trying to bring it out, get all the frustrations out.

But it was when those four little girls died in that church bombing in Birmingham, Alabama, that we almost went crazy. Everybody was going off, crying, and the music changed immediately. It had that low "hmmmm," that channeled anger, and seemed to immediately affect the performance of all the cats. Some would be standing in corners just pouring their efforts into their instruments, and then coming together as the Ark and making those sounds that expressed what we were all feeling. This was when the band really changed, and the people were ready for it. Those four little girls changed everybody.

We played mostly original music, including compositions of mine such as "Thoughts of Dar es Salaam," "The Giant Is Awakened," "Nyja's Theme," and "The Dark Tree," music that I was composing during that time. These were pieces that everyone seemed to know after a while. The audience would be clapping and dancing to the music. Afterward, you'd hear the people humming the tunes as they left. That's when you knew you had made a point, when you'd look out at that South Park audience and everybody would be on their feet, swaying, crying, yelling, and singing.

One time, there were some cats running around drunk while we were playing. They were loud, and all the people were sitting there knowing. One of them came up to the bandstand, turned around, pointed, grabbed my ankles, and said, "This is our band! This is our band! This is our band!" Then he just walked away. That was really uplifting, and the people, who had been pissed off at him, started applauding.

All of the moves that I made, that would put me in another bracket, all came from my own people, from people in my community, which I was happy about. Many didn't have any knowledge about what was going on musically but the music was very important to them. Cats would come and sit by themselves, or with their women and their kids, and cry at certain songs that we played. That's how we knew that we were doing the correct thing; all those rehearsals, those painful things, and people were finally listening to our music. At first, it was that "racist music" or that "free music," that "out music," and they didn't want to hear it. Then all of a sudden, you'd hear them saying, "I listened to you the other day." These things were important to me, these small things. The cats who worked at the grocery store would say, "I heard the band the other day and I'd never heard them play like that before." They'd say that to you. "What was the name of that song that girl sang?" These were the small things that reassured us we were doing it correctly, even though monetarily it was a disaster.

And it was so bad, such a disaster, that we didn't even think about it. We didn't worry about it, because we knew there wasn't any money in it. You're just going to do it. If there wasn't any money, so what? We had a whole bunch of people who would offer us meals. We could go to any house and get served, or get a ride on any street in the community. It all said we were starting to make an impact.

By being so staunch in our beliefs and by sticking with it every day, other people started to say, "Well, what is this? Let me check this out. I've got things I want to do." It became an open place for all kinds of artists. We had poets, young poets, coming on. They started making up poems about the community and what's going on in the community—police arrests and activities of that sort that affected us every day. This was long before popular groups started recording these kinds of things.

After a while, the police started coming around to see what was going on at the park. They hadn't bothered us yet. Then one time they came up to us and asked for a permit. We just packed up and left. We didn't want to deal with them, and we had other places to go. They weren't going to get to us mentally. Soon, they started busting guys for parking tickets or warrants of some kind, and they'd come after them. We'd go get them out as quick as we could. And it wasn't just the band; the police were doing this throughout the neighborhood. They'd ride through and just try to mess the people over.

Into the Community . . . Real Deep

Around 1963, two years or so after we started the Ark, we moved from Linda's place to a house on Fifty-sixth Street and Figueroa, the second UGMA house. It was a big, giant house that belonged to a very serious artist, Brother Percy Smith, and we needed it. By this time the band had grown to thirty people. As the band grew, I'd write more. Every time a new person would come into the band, I'd add them to the music, write another part for them. It got to the point where I could give it to Linda or Guido or Jimmy, and they'd write the new parts. They were also starting to write their own charts.

Some of the members had jobs in the schools around the city and some got jobs as substitute teachers. They'd bring the music into the schools, wherever they taught and whenever they'd sub. We'd sneak it in. We knew it was important to get into the community, deep, real deep, and we wanted to have the schools as our launching pad. Some of the principals were schoolmates of mine.

"Oh, Horace, you want to bring the band in? That would be wonderful."

The kids would look for us on certain days, because we were

the underground. They called us "the musicians." "Here come the musicians!" They'd be ready for music. We played our music, and they just went for it, because they knew we weren't jiving. We had music, man.

Linda Hill had written a song called "Children" and outlined a whole program that she wanted to do with children at the schools. One of our bass players, Eddie Mathias, would have a thing called the Flute Society. At that time, we had access to a lot of wooden flutes, two boxes full, and we'd pass them out to the kids. We'd say "Let's play" to the kids, and they'd all play with us. That was thick. It wasn't in vogue then and it was very necessary. We had kids as young as four and five years old coming around. Some of those cats are in their thirties and forties now, and come up and say how they remember this and that. Parents would bring their kids with them. Everybody became a part of it.

We wanted to get to the children as early as possible and start playing black music, and telling them stories about black folks in history, so they could have something to hook up with, because there was so little for them. Without this, they'd always see the white world as the better world. Straight hair would be seen as good; nappy would be bad hair. Lighter skin would be more beautiful than darker. That's how many in my generation and before grew up, and that's the poison, the dangerous poison, that UGMA wanted to attack. We wanted the children to care about themselves.

We even had cats going around teaching older people how to read and write. We started a program called Medimusic to take our program to the senior citizens and to mentally sick patients, using our music and our coloring schemes. We'd play at senior homes and mental health facilities during the day, and you could see the effect on the people. We'd play differently, try to find different ways where the music would just creep up on them. The next thing you'd know, they'd be smiling and feeling better. We weren't the first to think about this but not many people have followed through with this approach. Medimusic lasted for several months. It was a very good experiment and it worked for people.

One time, we were playing on a street corner and we saw this flatbed truck parked nearby. The guy who owned it said we could use it, so we put the band on the back of it and drove through the different neighborhoods, stopping at corners where the people were and playing. And they'd be dancing out there. Yeah. And then we'd drive on to the next street or intersection with the people waving at us.

The Ark got so busy. There was always something going on every morning. I'd wake up, go to the UGMA house, and wake the brothers for rehearsal. I used to have a lot of problems with the wives coming to get their old men early in the morning and that kind of stuff.

By this time we were having some internal problems. Drugs were an issue for maybe every one person out of four or five in the Ark. But we quickly got it to the point where there were no dope problems at all. We had to, because I was aware of what it could do to a person, and what it could do to an organization like ours that was trying to be a positive force in the community and trying to reach the children. We were developing a routine, and if anyone started disrupting this, we'd approach them nicely, with a loving and caring attitude, and try to straighten them out, get them to see themselves and what they were doing to those around them and our program. If they didn't respond, if they got in the way of us achieving our goals, we'd ask them to leave. If they were going to continue destroying themselves in front of us, we wouldn't allow it. They had to make the choice.

When crack came in later, it posed another set of problems. Cats using that would smoke it for a while before it began to show, and by then it was usually too late. All of a sudden there'd be this roar from the guy, and we'd say, "Oh, no. What you smoking, man?" All we could do was get rid of those cats. They were worse than junkies.

Most of the internal problems we had were male/female issues. We had a few women in the Ark, a trombonist and a trumpet player. Adele Sebastian played flute. We had a couple of female drummers and a couple of female bass players. Linda Hill played piano. By this time, we also had an UGMA choir—the Voices of UGMA—that was mostly women and dancers and singers. And all these females were great looking. Those internal problems had to do with a lot of jealousies. You might lay up with this lady, and if she's in the band and some other lady dancer starts hitting on you, it could be disruptive, and it was. Sometimes we'd have to split up a rehearsal, because someone's crying that someone else isn't paying them more attention. We had some chicks who came to me and said, "I'm going to break up this band." And this had nothing to do with anything else except their own little thing.

So I said, "We've got a group here and the only way this group will be destroyed is by all this tension inside. If you're going to lay up with this lady, or lady if you're going to lay up with this guy, go on and do that and get it over with. But don't expect him or her to be a certain way. If you get strung out over this and start messing up our group, we'll get rid of you. If it's going to be a hassle, you can't come anymore. You're either here to help or you're not here. Whatever you do, it better not bother the group."

We had to work through those situations. In some cases, people put their grief into writing. I'd say, "Why don't you just write a song, or write a poem about it, or do a choreography about how you feel?"

"Okay."

Every time you'd hear the poem, you'd know who it was for. Then people got more relaxed with each other. We got much closer and became more family. That's when we started flourishing. The music really started coming in. Guys had learned to write and were trying different ways of writing music, and we would be rehearsing every night. Cats were always meeting together, always doing something and learning and teaching. We had a schedule now, and someone had to take care of the building. There would be regular cleanup crews.

We made most decisions collectively and decided on things as they came up. Sometimes we might vote, and whichever way it went, we supported whoever won that particular time. A couple of times we had disagreements like, "Man, I don't want to keep playing down there. Those people don't appreciate it and we ain't getting no money." We had a lot of those arguments within the group. It never got to the point of busting up; just getting pissed off and calling each other a couple of names before getting back to it. They'd never leave. Some guys would go away for a while, play with a group, make a little money, then come on back. They'd go right back to their seat and be pissed off if someone else was sitting there. When it got to the point where everyone felt it was their Arkestra, then it became something.

When it came to the music, I'd usually decide on which pieces to play. After a while, other members of the band would make suggestions. But we had so much time that we were rehearsing most days and got a chance to work on all the music we had. And what cats couldn't play, we'd form a class to deal with it.

We developed a book of music, but I'd always forget it, you dig? On the morning of a concert, I'd forget all the music we rehearsed. Then they got used to that routine. One morning, one of the girls in the band, Adele Sebastian, asked, "Are you going to forget the music this time, Papa?" They called me "Papa," because of our name, the P[an]A[frican]P[eoples]A[rkestra].

"Yeah, I might forget it this time. I'm not sure."

The band was supposed to know what they were playing and they did. That really made me proud. I'd just give signals to the band, never talked, never had any music on the bandstand, but they knew what I meant.

During rehearsals I'd give them the signals. "This is what I'm going to do when I want you to play this part. Maybe I'll want you to repeat it again right behind so-and-so's solo. This is once. This is twice. This is around again. This is a halfbar. Watch out for the cutoff." We didn't need the music. Just the signals would be enough. Halfway through one chorus, I could set up the next one with just a few motions. And when that chorus ended—Pow!— the band was into the next one. It was a gas. It gave them more freedom and it gave me more freedom, because I liked to dance and I could do that while giving the signals.

We spent those first few years actually underground, because we were doing things with music, with bands, with big bands, that weren't very popular. We were learning our music by memory, learning everything about the music, and then trying to perform it in such a way that it was like you were choreographing somebody's mind in sound. When we had rehearsals, we would approach music from the angle of the writer's point of view, regardless of whether a piece called for this or that. The band would even move around while on stage according to the sound. Probably the only stable people were the trap drummer and the bass player.

After we had developed a piece of music, somebody would create a dance to it, or we'd have some words or some poems written for the tune. Everyone had a shot at creating something around this particular composition. A poet might write a beautiful line for a certain spot in the composition, and we'd add it. A dancer might develop a nice step for it, and we'd utilize that in presenting the tune. We'd try to present all the facets of the composition.

Some years later, Cecil Rhodes wrote a play in the community that had to do with the mind-set of the people in the community. It's called *Three Brothers* and has to do with three brothers being each other's keeper during the days of the early 1960s. One is like Martin Luther King Jr.; one is like Malcolm X; one is like Medgar Evers. They are trying to decide what to do about all of this discrimination and crud going on around them. One is a rebel; one is somebody who is thinking wide; the third has a whole other approach behind blackness in this community. They were three brothers who had different ideas about gaining freedom.

With this play, we started doing things between the actors and the musicians. It was one of Cecil's first plays and he wanted to experiment with it. The actors had a lot of freedom to improvise, but he had like a chord progression for them to improvise off of. The most important thing was the expressions on the actors' faces, because they had very few lines. There was some dialogue, but it wasn't full of dialogue. Instead, there was a lot of space for thinking and choreography. And that is where the music came in. Each of the three actors' thought patterns were depicted through some musical instrument, played behind them as they walked and thought. The actors would never see the musicians, who were supposed to be invisible to the audience. One of the actors might have been thinking about bombing city hall or someplace. The flute player would be walking right behind him, fitting sounds to the actor's expressions. When the actors spoke, the musicians would be silent. When an actor was silent, deep in thought, the musician would start playing. Every performance was different and every performance was given in the community, because it was so out that we couldn't give it anywhere else.

Three Brothers was the first time that we had done that kind of thing. I was told it was similar to Japanese *Kabuki* theater, where they had a spirit who would always be following the actor around and never saying anything. They wore a hood and would be the mind of this character. The hardest part was the choreography, the steps between the actor and the musician. We couldn't have accidents. So the cats would be walking behind the actors with flutes and small instruments, so as not to get in the way. But each line had something to do with the next phrase, the next few bars of music. There might be a line, "I'm going to incinerate the establishment," that would be followed by an ominous musical phrase, as the actor crossed the stage. We spent a lot of time creating those kinds of things that we weren't used to seeing and hearing.

That was one of the activities we were doing with the Arkestra, and UGMA was bringing those kinds of talents together. Everyone was giving a little piece of their talent to make one thing happen, particularly on the last Sunday of the month. Every last Sunday, we had some program to give that had something to do with a message. It wasn't hard or hard-core but was easy to bring to kids, and it wouldn't make them feel strange.

The Ark's Musicians

We might play a gig in a schoolhouse or park, and by the time the concert was over, we'd have two or three new members. That's how we mostly recruited people over the years, by exposing youngsters to different things, sounds and motions that they hadn't been exposed to. Then they'd want to be a part of it. Sometimes they were very young and not even playing music, but they knew what their course was going to be. When they got to a certain age and wanted to play an instrument, or dance or do something else, they'd come to the UGMA house. Many parents would see the interest growing in their kids and they'd bring them by. And many of them would bring us other resources or put us in touch with other people. Once they believed in us, they would open up. That's how we did it mostly.

These people knew we were walking it. We didn't just talk and leave; we were there every day, doing the same things. All of a sudden it started to make sense to many people and they wanted their children involved with us. That's why it's so important to be seen in your community, if you're talking about being a part of it.

We had so many players come through the Ark, a lot of great players and a lot of potentially great players. Some went on and some are playing today in different settings. From the early 1960s through the mid-1970s, cats like Arthur Blythe, Azar Lawrence, Will Connell, David Murray, Lawrence "Butch" Morris, and his brother, Wilber Morris, were playing in the Ark. They were straight-ahead cats and could have made it anywhere they lived. They didn't have to go to New York but they had that drive and eventually did go.

Butch Morris learned his whole bit in the Ark. He and his brother both came right from high school, along with some of the other cats, like Azar Lawrence. Butch used to wear a porkpie hat and he always had nice, exotic ladies with him. I asked him once, "Butch, why you bring these exotic ladies around?"

"Ah, pops, you can look at 'em, man. It's cool. I just brought them around for the cats to look at them."

He started writing when he was a young man with us, and he was always quiet, serious, and wanting to learn, always absorbing things. Wilber, who played bass, was just the opposite, was flamboyant and talked a lot. And Azar also joined us young and played with us for years, before leaving for New York. He even wrote a piece, "Tapscott's Blues," that Woody Shaw recorded. He was avid, always there, asking questions and always rehearsing.

There are so many of those guys who are still playing and writing. A lot of them are still here and many are scattered everywhere, some even in Europe, but they stay in touch. Wherever I'm playing, they show up and we talk. They never forget where they came from. I've still got some of the first music that they wrote. I saw so many of these cats come up from the first note, but what I remember most is their dedication and that they were there, always there, and ready to give.

It was quite a period for musicians, and these people in turn brought in other people. Another one who made a name for himself was Rufus Olivier, who was the first bassoonist in the San Francisco Symphony and then with the San Francisco Opera. Me and Arthur got him off the streets one day, off Western Avenue, when he was about fourteen. He heard Arthur playing and came in to listen. Stanley Crouch came around in the early 1960s. He was teaching out in Claremont, east of Los Angeles, and whenever he was in town, he'd come over and play. Sometimes he'd do his oratorical thing. His album of spoken word, *Ain't No Ambulances for No Nigguhs Tonight,* was recorded during one of those gigs. Later on, he'd bring David Murray along with him.

Stanley almost got us killed one night on Vermont Avenue with the police. We were coming from Watts, and I was driving. The police pulled us over just because, and Stanley went off on them.

"Why'd you pull us over? Is it the car? Anything wrong with the car? You're doing it 'cause we're black. Look at you. You've already got your gun out to shoot us."

By this time, he had the cop saying, "No. No. Look, I don't . . ."

It worked out that night, but we never knew.

We met Everett Brown Jr. in the late 1960s. Arthur Blythe, myself, David Bryant, and Walter Savage were driving to the musicians' union, and we saw this cat walking down Vine Street with these colored bell bottoms on and with his own walk, a kind of sliding motion from side to side. We called out, "Hey, man, where you going?"

"I just left the musicians' union."

"Well, come on, get in, man."

He told us he was a drummer and had just got in from Kansas City. We took him with us, and he was in the Ark for years, until he got Parkinson's disease and moved back to Kansas City.

We got a few more drummers during this time — Bill Madison and Donald Dean. Bill Madison had come out of the neighborhood, a few years behind me at Jefferson High School. He used to hang with Frank Morgan, and during the 1950s and 1960s was in and out of town. When he settled back in, he hooked up with us. Donald was another cat from Kansas City who came to Los Angeles in the late 1960s thinking this was where the music was. We first started playing together on a gig with Curtis Amy at the Intermission Room on Adams and Crenshaw. He also played with Les McCann and Jimmy Smith.

We had some fine saxophonists, like Lattus McNeely, who had his own sound on alto saxophone. Then, a few years later, he just stopped. I think he got religion, maybe with the Muslims, but whoever he was with were down on the cats playing. Then we had another cat for a while—I can't remember his name—a brother so phenomenal, you knew something had to happen to him one way or the other. When he first came by, he couldn't play anything. He learned by coming around and listening, just standing in the corner by himself, listening to the cats and working on it. This went on for three or four years, and then one day he showed up to play. After watching him just standing there every day, we couldn't believe this. Somehow, he had really put his shit together. Then one day he left. Brother Percy said he'd just split, gone back to wherever, and we never saw him again.

Everyone in that group had their own distinct sound, because there was nobody to follow. These cats didn't follow the records so much. No one, except for Guido, was sounding like Charlie Parker, and that's what we really dug. They just started playing by hearing other cats who were alive around them and then developed their own sounds. Most didn't have any outside teachers. They worked on their own and then learned in the Arkestra. We used to teach each other how to read on the blackboard without any instruments. You'd just count. We had a clapping class, where you'd clap everything out. Then we'd have them connect that to their reading classes. They got an understanding of what time is about. Instead of just hanging, we'd teach. A lot of these people had time, all the time.

When we had a nucleus of people with a lot of time and a lot of interest, it was very easy to recruit. Musicians started coming by word of mouth into the Arkestra, some who were just beginning to play and others who had been playing for some time. We also had an age spread of a couple of generations. David Bryant was the oldest, and David Straughter, the youngest. We used to call it "the Pan Afrikan Peoples Arkestra from David to David." It was a mixture of ages, and we wanted it that way. It was necessary that the older cats be in the band. It was necessary in each section, so that the young cats could ask questions. We had about five bass players all the time and about four drummers. It was very nice. It was a good feeling to sit up and play a suite that you'd written about the ghetto, and everyone knew what it was.

The Fire This Time

8

By the mid 1960s, we turned most of our activity to Watts and developed a program at the Watts Happening Coffee House on 103rd Street. We were distributing food to the families in the area and giving concerts. The food we gave to people was donated by local markets. We'd go around to different stores and get what we could. People would bring food to our concerts to contribute. We found ways to make things happen without money. And people started helping out in many ways, with their skills or just contributing a little money here and there. All this was done for the children in Watts. Nobody was making any money then that we knew of, because everything we got from different folks, we passed out. There were no grants or anything like that in the early days.

There wasn't much activity in Watts in the early 1960s. The Watts Towers were there, but no one thought anything about them, except for the ones who grew up helping the old man, Simon Rodia, build the towers. There was no office or center there. There weren't many businesses left on 103rd Street. It had pretty much dried up. The Coffee House was the biggest spot there. It was an old furniture store, owned by a Jewish cat—always used to have a big cigar in his mouth—who was a furniture salesman around there. Evidently, he just gave the place up. After we'd been there a while, around 1964, 1965, we managed to get some of the government's War on Poverty money and turned the space into this big auditorium. Some of the guys who were into carpentry built a stage. That money didn't come right to UGMA. It went to local organizations first, and they passed some of it on to us.

Then the artists and writers started moving back into the area. They opened the Studio Watts, just around the corner from the Coffee House, where there'd be poetry readings with Jim Woods, Ojenke Saxon, Quincy Troupe, Jayne Cortez, and the Watts Prophets—Anthony Hamilton, Richard Dedeaux, Otis O'Solomon Smith—all these cats were coming around, and the singer Dee Dee McNeil. After the summer of 1965, the writer Budd Schulberg came down and watched, and then started the Watts Writers Workshop there, because he wanted to see these brothers write. He was one of the cats who had enough kick that he believed in what these guys out there were doing. Every time we'd play, they'd be on the set doing their thing. Kamau Daáood and Eric Priestley, who wrote a book, *Raw Dog,* about growing up in Watts, were contributing their poetry. We had a group of women, called Sapphire Streakin', who brought poetry and songs.

Up the street, across from the Coffee House, was the Mafundi Institute, which was built a little later with the government's War on Poverty money. It was a space for theater and actors that Roger Mosley and some other actors got together. William Marshall was there. The musicians and writers had a place, so then it was time for the theater people, who started performing plays there. We played for the ground breaking of the Mafundi Institute and helped put up all these things in the community.

All of a sudden we started getting educators and intellectuals, black ones, who wanted to come down here and talk to and feed the children. Everybody became part of the scene. No one was left out, and everyone felt like they were a part of it. There were people who had a lot to say and didn't have anyplace to say it. That's why they were constantly coming in. We even had some people in wheelchairs and some that were so-called mentally ill. They knew enough to know what was happening; they felt enough. All their lives they'd been treated differently and they weren't expecting to be treated as part of the community.

There were so many things happening. You'd walk down the

street and might see somebody dancing or singing or playing. All this was going on in the community, but no newspaper, no news, no writers. Nobody knew anything about it. Nothing like this had really existed since the Central Avenue days, but there was a hunger there. People knew something better could be done. So we said, "Why don't we pull this together and put on functions and show how we feel, where we've been, where we are, and where we want to go." And it was a multimedia kind of scene with the poets and dancers, writers and actors, as well as the musicians. Everybody was an artist out there, and we'd all work there, all the time.

We'd rehearse during the week like we were giving a paid concert. Every weekend there'd be performances, and everybody was really into it, was looking forward to it. The guys who had jobs, or the ones who were going to school, or ones who had a little work to do, were all looking forward to getting off or getting out, so they could come to rehearsal and play for four hours at night after a long day. The young folks going to grammar school would come right to the Coffee House after school. Their parents would pick them up from there.

No one was hip to the kinds of functions going on, but it was happening along 103rd Street from Central Avenue all the way to Long Beach Boulevard. People were quicker to recognize each other. Communication was back: "Hello, brother!" "Hello, sister!" "Hello, ma'am!"—real loud and clear and pleasant. People started coming to concerts with baked pies, baked cakes, baked cookies, just to give. They'd bring canned goods.

"What's the entrance fee?"

"Food."

People would come in with a can of beans. And somebody else would be happy because they'd have something to eat that day. And we'd take it to them personally after the concert. The community started functioning.

I enjoyed it so much because I got a piece of the action while I was there. I was able to smell the roses, while I was alive. The kids were always outside, listening to the Ark, going down the street and dancing to "The Dark Tree," just singing the rhythm and dancing. That really got me. It worked, because while they didn't know what they were doing, they were doing. They felt it and they responded to it.

You hear more about the horrible things in Watts, but a lot of good things happened out there as well. A lot of great people came out of there and are now doing things around the world. It proved a point to me: when you come together in your community, you can go anywhere in the world and do anything, and everybody will accept it, because they understand this. They understand togetherness and harmony.

The Summer of 1965

By the summer of 1965, we were very involved in the Watts community. Aside from the music, we had all sorts of classes there and a breakfast program, which was later supported by the Black Panthers. We had the youngsters in school and were teaching them about their history, as well as reading and writing. We had martial arts, poetry, and music classes outside of the regular schoolwork. There was a lot of poetry and dancing and singing in the streets, because we played out there all the time. Elaine Brown, the writer and ex–Black Panther leader, was part of it; she'd be singing. Stanley Crouch was part of it; he'd be getting up and talking, doing his oratorical thing on black history and black pride. All these people came and were involved in these kinds of activities that had to do with trying to help our own community. We were trying to do it the best way we could and see that the youngsters didn't starve.

The area was cut off; there wasn't much traffic coming through. I could park my car on the street, unlocked. We had gotten so fully out and into the community that I could drive my car to 103rd, leave the window down with my keys and all my stuff in the car, and walk away. The youngsters out there knew whose car it was, that it belonged to one of the band. "Uh-uh, that's one of the guys." That's when we knew we were correct, again.

We were doing the right thing, because now the youngsters started listening. They would see us all the time and they could talk to us whenever they wanted. We didn't just give them a big speech and then leave. They could ask us a question along the street or in a store. They knew we really cared for them and that they could come to us at any time. Just like when I was growing up, you'd see teachers in the grocery store and could ask them questions. You could go by their homes, because they all lived in the area. That's one real convincing way for a youngster to take note of someone, is if they see them all the time. That person might be known throughout the United States or all over the world, but in this neighborhood, they're one of the people, one of the community. And that's how kids, young folks, gain confidence. "If you want to teach me something, now I can listen to you, because I believe you. I believe you, because you're here." They won't say, "Oh, well, he's going to Beverly Hills. He ain't thinking about us now." So we were where it was important to be. If you're really thinking of trying to help the community, you can't just jump into it. You have to really figure it out and it's not easy.

So the Arkestra saw it coming that summer of 1965. We saw the anger. With all the poets and the music, it was climbing down. Some were screaming their poetry about black people and the police and dying. The tension was building, and it was just a matter of time before it exploded.

The police were shooting cats in the neighborhood. They were shooting black cats just for running away. Maybe they stole a car, had jumped out, and were running. They'd kill them. So many brothers were shot in the back. The police would come through the neighborhood and just tear it up. You'd have to get off the street. You couldn't be just walking, because the white policeman would call you "nigger" and shoot you. You'd try to ignore him, because if you said something to him, it would give him an excuse to shoot you. And you knew, and he knew, that he'd get away with it. It was really out.

About a year or two before the Watts insurrection, the police attacked the Muslim mosque at Fifty-sixth and Broadway. I was coming home from a job at two o'clock in the morning and I saw them. The cops were all over, telling everyone who passed by to move on or else. A brother, who lives down the street from me now, was shot in the back that night and he's been in a wheelchair ever since.

There was another incident around that time that really did it. The cops shot this brother who was taking his pregnant wife to the hospital on Avalon Boulevard, down the street from my house. Her water had burst. Because he was speeding, the police were chasing him. Then they shot and killed him, because he wouldn't stop. Later, they said the gun just went off. They shot the brother in the head, killed him instantly, and he was just trying to get to the hospital with his pregnant wife. That really got it out. It got so bad after that in the neighborhood that the police stopped coming into it. There weren't that many guns, mostly rifles, in the black neighborhood then but they were coming out of the houses now.

The first day of the insurrection, the shooting began in Will Rogers Park on 103rd Street and Central. We were farther down 103rd, playing as usual out in the street, and the kids were dancing to "The Dark Tree." The police came down the street and drove around the bandstand, holding their microphone out of the car for the cats downtown to hear. They said, "Listen. This is inciting the riot. This is why the riot is happening." Then we heard the sounds of ambulances and more police cars coming into the neighborhood. After a while, it seemed they had quelled it somewhat.

The next day, no one was on the streets; there weren't any dogs on the streets and it was in full bloom. It was happening. You could see the first smoke rising and hear the fire engines. When the National Guard came in, they blocked off my street, Fifty-sixth and Avalon. We had to be home by eight o'clock or else we couldn't get in. And I had gigs. There were cats right on the corner with guns. If you didn't live there, they wouldn't let you in or out after a certain hour. I said, "No way," and just broke through. I started to get very angry, because my kids couldn't go down the street and one of the kids on the block could get shot at any time, just because he or she was out in the street playing like they usually play. That made a lot of us fathers and mothers angry.

Cecilia and I went where we had to go, and wherever we went, there was the riot. I even took my family out to watch, to see what was happening. We drove down Slauson Boulevard to see it, to be a part of it. We were always in harm's way. We were supposed to be in by eight o'clock, but I'd get home at one or two. It even got to the point where this young, white National Guardsman, who didn't want to be there, would say, "Just go ahead, man."

Other times it didn't work out that way. Once, Cecilia and I were driving home, and they pulled us over, around the corner from our house. There were all these cops on our car. One pointed his gun at me. That pissed me off. He started talking to my wife, and she got scared.

I said, "You don't have to say a word to this motherfucker! You don't say nothing to him!"

He started getting pissed off, when an older guy came over, pushed him out of the way, and said, "Where do you live, sir?" When I told him around the corner, he told me to go ahead. It was really touchy, because they had killed a couple of people that day. The National Guard shot this one woman because she was speeding. They said she was trying to run them down and they killed her. So here we were, and this younger cat wanted to blow us away. They would have gotten away with it, because they could have said we broke a barrier and who would have known. If it wasn't for the older policeman, we'd have been shot, because they had orders to shoot to kill and they could just fire on civilians. Was that out?

It put me in a very hard place, thinking-wise. I had to get myself together again, because I was angry. Especially when they held the gun against my wife, and she hadn't done anything, hadn't said anything. We were ready to get shot. I was ready, because I had to have some respect in my family. You're just going to come over here and put a gun in my car, and I live around the corner—no!

A few days later, we were playing inside the Watts Happening Coffee House. Butch Morris was in the band then. The police broke in with their shotguns and told me to stop the music. I wouldn't stop. The guy in charge pulled back the hammer of his gun and yelled, "I said stop the goddamn music!" Meanwhile, they were lining up these pregnant women, who were there for a class, by one of the walls. I put my hand up in the air to stop the band. The cop put his gun back on the safety and headed out. As he walked past all the kids who were listening to the music, David Bryant, or one of the other bass players, looking right at the police, started the line from "The Dark Tree," and we all started playing again.

The scene on 103rd Street in Watts lasted until the late sixties and then it tapered off. After the insurrection, there was some money coming in from the government and other sources, as well as job offers for a lot of the cats. Some of them started becoming actors. All of a sudden there were jobs, and a lot of people split from the set.

The Music

After the insurrection, every chance I had, I was writing that music. When I later did the Elaine Brown album, *Seize the Time,* I put my heart into it, man. I put all that into it. It had really gotten to me. And all around me, there were a lot of wild brothers who just wanted to die, to go downtown and kill everyone and die. People were pissed off and were gathering together to throw firebombs. It was really out. So we said that we'd best do it the best way we know, and that was through the Ark. And the Ark got stronger and stronger. The people got strong behind it. We settled down a lot of people into thinking again, instead of destroying, by playing, talking, by just being there.

I first met Elaine through Stanley Crouch. He brought her around and said, "Horace! I want you to hear this singer, man. She's written some great tunes, and you'll love it."

"Yeah. Okay."

I wasn't expecting much. But she came on the set and started singing her songs about freedom, and she was accepted right away. She wasn't a Panther then, had come out of a bourgeois family, and was a very beautiful and shy woman. The shyness held her back, but she could sing, and she was different because of her writings, the quality of her words and songs. She was off into it heavy and had done a lot of homework. That's what drew me. She wrote songs of freedom, and I loved it. I thought, "Ah, this is it." So we started pushing and rehearsing and pushing, rehearsing, pushing, until she was past the shyness and got to the point where she wanted to sing.

By then, she had joined these different groups and she was writing all these wonderful compositions, beautiful words and lines about the community, and I loved her for it.

We were building things around her songs, because her ideas were going straight the way we were going. She put it into sound and words, and her expressions and the way she sang, it would send chills through us just to listen to her. We became very tight because of that. It had nothing to do with her being a Panther, or who she knew and all that. But she was becoming an intricate part of the music coming out of the community.

All the songs on *Seize the Time* were Elaine's. I arranged them, played piano, and led the band. It was so simple to me at the time, because I was so deep into it. Everything she brought to me was just right on the mark. The songs were about what had been happening in the communities, especially in Los Angeles and Oakland. The music was very political and was intended to enlighten people in the community about what was happening. She had all the cats on the session: Lester Robertson, Ike Williams, Everett Brown Jr. All the guys loved it, and I enjoyed doing it, because I had a chance to express some things musically with someone who felt the same way. *Seize the Time* was quite an album, but they took it off the market. They seized it, and you could only hear it underground.

A few years later, Elaine did another album, *Elaine Brown,* for a Motown subsidiary label. She got me to arrange the music again, and I put the band together. We had Buddy Collette on this session and a large string section. It was a wonderful record, but there was no way it would ever get played on the radio. It was just as political as the first album. One of the songs was about Jonathan Jackson, George Jackson's younger brother, who was killed trying to free him during a court hearing in northern California.

Some years before, I had thought about this sleeping black giant, somewhere, finally waking up and taking care of business and freeing his people. When John Coltrane wrote "Giant Steps," the giant was awakened and started taking those steps from Trane's music. Then my sister had an old, old book of black folklore. When I opened it, it fell right to High John the Conqueror, who was a giant, a sleeping giant come to save his people. That was how "The

Giant Is Awakened" came about. It was just something I felt I'd caught hold of, while at the same time realizing that I wasn't the only one to catch hold of this. Many of us get ideas, feelings, maybe at different times, different places, but the same ideas and feelings come to each person, sometimes simultaneously, without our realizing it.

When I was thinking about that awakened giant in this part of the world, so were some other people. Every time we'd play "The Giant Is Awakened," the audience would all stand up, salute; some would be crying. If you could have seen how those audiences reacted when we'd play that. And we always played what used to be called the Negro National Anthem, "Lift Every Voice," at the end of every concert. We were seriously into it, to the point where it didn't have anything to do with any one person or star; it had to do with everybody putting in a little sharing.

In 1969, I didn't want to make the album that became *The Giant Is Awakened.* When producer Bob Thiele approached me about recording, I asked, "What are you going to do with this?" I just wasn't interested in doing it. I didn't know what he was going to do with my music; I had the kind of attitude that wasn't very trusting. Here was another cat who was going to exploit this black music. Stanley Crouch, John Carter, and some others were pushing Thiele to record us. So I talked to the cats in the band—Arthur Blythe, David Bryant, Walter Savage Jr., and Everett Brown Jr.—about it and said, "We have to take a vote on this, man. If you cats want to do it, and you outvote me, okay." They outvoted me.

I knew that we could do what we wanted, because Bob Thiele came looking for me. What impressed me about him was that he came into the ghetto. He came into my neighborhood, when I was near Fifty-sixth Street and Avalon, where you didn't come by yourself if you were a white cat from New York with a pipe. This cat came to the ghetto looking for my ass, just drove right up and said, "Look, all I want to do is put you on wax. I think you deserve to be on record." I told him we'd do it. It wasn't any big thing to me. Thiele had gotten off into this Flying Dutchman record label and he wanted to record everything that no one else wanted, that made statements. He also recorded John Carter and Bobby Bradford, and later Stanley Crouch's *Ain't No Ambulances for No Nigguhs Tonight*. John had told me it was cool to record with this cat.

We recorded *The Giant Is Awakened* and part of another album that I never finished. Thiele and I had some arguments. While I agreed to do the recording, I still didn't want them controlling everything. So I said, "Okay, I'll do the album, but I want to do the finish work, here or in New York, if necessary." He gave me some wild story in a letter that they couldn't do it here and "We're going to hold your ideas in abeyance." I'll never forget that word; that was the first time I'd seen it. They just went ahead, produced the album, and put it out without letting me put anything into the final record. He just did it on his own. I would have voiced it differently. I had other ideas of how I wanted it to be heard, especially the piano. The way I was playing, I just wanted it like a seam, floating through the whole thing, instead of being dominant over everything else. It should have been more a part of everything that was going. I felt that with the technology of the time, it wouldn't be that hard to do. So it was just a matter of him not allowing me to be a part of that process, and that really ticked me off.

When the album came out, the so-called out people listened to it and it got some play overseas, especially in the Eastern bloc countries. They wanted all the stuff we were doing. I don't know today how they found out about us. I figured it just had to be word of mouth. That's where all my money came from, the Communist countries, like Poland and Russia.

I had another bad recording experience the previous year doing Sonny Criss's album, *Sonny's Dream (Birth of the New Cool)*. Sonny and I were working for a woman named Mary Henry, who had an organization that was quietly working in the community to help people. She liked me and Sonny, and hired us to work in her community center. We'd give regular concerts there and got paid every week. Sonny had just come back from Europe and was pretty angry because he couldn't get any gigs here. So I was trying to set him up performing, and we were also talking about preserving the music.

One day, Sonny told me he'd like to do an album of my music. He picked some of my compositions that he wanted to record, and I wrote a new piece for him called "Sonny's Dream." We put a band together—all cats from the Ark—and started playing the tunes at our gigs. We figured that by the time we got to the studio for the recording sessions, we wouldn't even need the music, because the band would have it.

The first day we went to the studio to record, we found another band there. All these other cats were around, like Dick Nash, Conte Condoli, and Pete Christlieb. I didn't even know who Pete was then; he was just out of school. We came walking in with our guys and, man, we went off. I went off on Sonny first and then the producer from the record company. Don Schlitten from Prestige Records had brought in all these other cats. Sonny went crazy. He got drunk and got to hollering and screaming. So we had to get out of there and cool it. I walked out of the studio.

Cecilia came after me and said, "Baby, you spent the money already. You can get sued for this." We had paid bills and got out of some problems. So I had to go back and do it. We did get Everett Brown on drums, and their cats read the music well, but our cats had it down. They didn't need the music in front of them and we were getting a sound after playing the tunes at all the gigs. We had rehearsed every day, all day, because we had nothing but time. There wasn't much else going on for us during the day. And when we went to the clubs at night, we'd be just poppin'. I told the cats who did the recording that I wasn't angry with them, that this had nothing to do with them. It was between me and this guy, Schlitten.

That was a rough day, a real rough day.

After the experiences with Prestige and Flying Dutchman, my reputation was like, "He's really gone crazy now. No telling what he might do in the studio."

In the Middle of It

9

As we grew and spent a lot of time out in the streets performing, we ran into more problems with the police. We got busted by the FBI one time. The second UGMA house at Fifty-sixth and Figueroa was two stories and housed a lot of musicians. We'd rehearse there; thirty cats would be downstairs playing. And during the 1960s, all the revolutionaries, people like H. Rap Brown and Stokely Carmichael, would come to the UGMA house, and they had all kinds of weapons. They'd be upstairs talking, making their plans, while we were downstairs rehearsing.

One day, we'd taken a break from the rehearsing and were outside in the parking lot, smoking marijuana. Two or three carloads of police passed by, but didn't stop. All these black cats out there standing around, some smoking, and the police just drove by. I said, "Wait a minute, man. What is this? How come they haven't driven over here and asked what we are doing?" That stayed on my mind.

About two days later, after another rehearsal, we took a break and I drove home, about two or three blocks away. When I came back, all the cats were in jail. The FBI had busted the whole house. Those carloads of cops had just been watching the place for the feds, who were looking for firearms, not dope. There was some marijuana there, but they went right past it and headed upstairs looking for ammunition and guns. Those cats they didn't take away ran from the pad. It was empty when I got back.

That same evening, we rehearsed like nothing ever happened.

The police came again, just rolling through. We said, "Okay, go ahead," and went back to playing. It was like they were invisible. We didn't recognize them. We had nothing to hide. We knew where we were. "Go and tear the place up if you like." They didn't find anything at all.

We were targeted now, and stayed that way for a long time. They would follow me and a lot of the cats. I had a tail everywhere I went. When I'd have a gig at the Troubadour, they'd follow me to work and then they'd follow me home. Whenever I left the house, I'd look in the rearview mirror and there would be that car. This went on for about a year. I'd be coming home and there would be two guys at my doorstep in Hawaiian shirts and dark sunglasses. One day, I came home from a rehearsal and Cecilia was at the door talking to these cats. They had their backs to the street, and she was into it. When she saw me coming down the street, she made radical eye movements to warn me. I kept driving and stayed away from the pad for two days. They were after me, because of my so-called affiliation with all these groups, and wanted to bust me. So I just stayed off the set; I didn't come home and didn't call, and no one told them where I was. For a long time, I didn't sign my name on anything and tried to stay out of it, make it harder for them to track me.

We also got the police on us for bringing some of these groups together, which we would do musically. We'd talk about what was happening in the community, and the poets would say something about racism and protest in their poetry. The lyrics to our music were all written about our situation. So cats started forming together, trying to do things in the community, and all of a sudden, became political activists.

All kinds of political people came to us, including white ones, all the cats, cats who the FBI were after. They'd come to watch; they could sit there and everything would be cool, because all the cats would know who this person was. We had a kind of unity with these cats. Budd Schulberg had been around the Communist Party at one time, so now we were called "Commie supporters." So naturally, the FBI was going to be there.

The J. Edgar Hoover thing was really heavy. I was in their files, like the rest of the cats, as if I was carrying a gun. But I was more dangerous, so to speak, because I could get on the microphone, say or play something, and people would get up and understand, dance to it or stop doing what they were doing, because we said something. And not just me but the cats in the Arkestra and other cats, like the Watts Prophets. The young people would look up to you, listen to you, and believe you.

Even though all this pressure was on us, it seemed to inspire the people in the Arkestra. They wanted to write more and they wrote about it. They wrote about several killings on different streets. Their song titles would be "Fifty So-and-So and So-and-So Street." We were inspired more than before, because the Watts rebellion showed that people were listening, and people were tired of racism and of just about any kind of bigotry.

"What can we do?" was now the question. "How can we do it?"

All kinds of activities, all kinds of classes, started happening right after that. Things started blossoming in the community. Even the common, everyday person—black folks in the neighborhood—started asking questions. People who used to go along with every-thing were now asking, "Well, why?" Remember, during the years 1964–1967, there were major rebellions in cities all over the country. This was when Muhammad Ali said no, too, to the Vietnam War and the draft. We rallied for that. We were down on Fifty-sixth Street and Broadway when he was there, and we were playing behind him.

By this time, everything had come all the way up to the ceiling. Everything was happening: Angela Davis speaking, the Panthers on the rise, Huey Newton up in Oakland, Stanley Crouch speaking hard-core, and all the things we were trying to do down here. So we were in danger.

Struggles in the Community

It seemed that in some kind of way, we—the Ark, myself—were always in the middle of it. By 1968, after Martin Luther King was iced, it got to the point where some cats in the band wanted to burn the musicians' union down. One Sunday afternoon, Linda, Arthur, David Bryant, Leroy Brooks, and myself were driving down Vine Street in Hollywood. Leroy, who had a Molotov cocktail with him, said, "Let's go by the union."

He was really going off.

"If you don't take me there, I'm going to go by myself."

So we took him there. Monday morning, he wanted all the people to see it burned to the ground. We managed to talk him out of it, but he just had to throw it anyway.

"Well, I won't throw it against a window but I got to throw it."

He threw it against a wall and scorched the building a bit. He just had to get that anger out. Terrible anger.

We were always hassling with the union. Around this time, I went to one board meeting to try and get some money, again, for the Ark members playing down in South Park. They had been supporting bands in other communities. We'd been playing there for some time and hadn't been getting paid for it. What the union did was send a mixed band down to play in South Park and just ignored us. Pissed me off.

One Sunday, their band was playing and the union president was there. Me and David Bryant went by to check it out, and then went on to our gig with the Ark at the Malcolm X Center, which was a space run by some of our supporters. After we left, two Black Panthers got on the stage with their guns and demanded to know, "Where's the Ark?!" They shot some rounds in the air, and the band broke up.

Monday morning, the president of the union called my house: "Horace, your Arkestra has the job at South Park next week."

"But none of my Arkestra is in the union."

"It doesn't make any difference."

So we started getting paid by the union. They claimed that I sent the Panthers to blow them away. Today, he still thinks I sent those cats. But I don't know who those cats were, just two Panthers who went to the park expecting to hear us. After that, they started calling me for gigs, all kinds of gigs over here, because they thought I was going to raid their things or cause disturbances.

After these kinds of things and all the events of the 1960s, all our thoughts and activities were focused in one area. Our music, literature, films, and tapes were focused on the struggles in the community.

"So why don't you stop all this business, man, and go to New York and make a record?"

I had forgotten all about that; it had left my mind. I had no idea what was happening in that world. Records and all that, I didn't even think about it.

We started going to the college campuses. I got a job at the University of California, Riverside, because of the black students there. They had a little insurrection at Riverside, and they wanted me and another person to teach them. It was just an example of what they were really after. The class was called "Black Experience in the Fine Arts."

We went to prisons all the time. After being sent to prison, guys would write to try and arrange us playing there. Sometimes the officials would approve it; sometimes not. One of the cats once tried to get the band up to Soledad. He and some of the other convicts had arranged everything. At the last minute the warden said, "No, we're not sending the bus down to get that band. You're in prison." But others did send buses for us, and we played mostly at the California Institution for Men in Chino and the women's prison.

One time when we arrived to play, they wouldn't let one of the band members in because he'd been in jail there. We refused to go in until he was allowed inside. They also wanted to tone down our poet, Kamau Daáood, because he was upsetting the prisoners with his poems about what was going on at the time. The warden came down and stopped us, because the cats were listening to all that music and the words this cat was screaming out to them, and they were crying and yelling. They closed the concert down before they had a riot.

Many times we'd be at prisons and were locked down, because the cats would be having a riot in some other part of the yard. The cats in the concert hall wanted to hear the music, and these other cats would be having a race riot. It was out there—the Hispanics and the blacks. Later on, we'd have Roberto Miguel Miranda with us, and they just loved it. When we'd play, they'd get emotional. You'd see cats, hard-core criminals, crying.

Sometimes, brothers would hook up with us when they got out of the joint. Some were hooked up before they went in. Two in the Ark went to jail for murder. One, a tenor player, murdered his old lady's boyfriend—a crime of passion. He later told me that he found her with another cat, had a flash, and just lost it. He eventually served his time, got out, and just disappeared. I tried to bring him around to certain things, but it didn't happen.

We had a lot of opportunities to go to different places, places we hadn't been before. We were invited into different neighborhoods. Many of these gigs were for Communist and other left-wing organizations, the groups that were against the government. That's when we made a little money, when we played for those groups at rallies or whatever. Every now and then we'd get invited out of the area, and then we started getting invitations to play festivals in various places.

We played at Angela Davis events, when people were fighting for her freedom. For a long time, we were doing things for Geronimo Pratt, an L.A. Black Panther leader who was wrongly convicted of murder in the early 1970s. He was only released from prison in 1997—twenty-seven years in prison for a murder he didn't commit. All these kinds of functions that had to do with political prisoners, we did. If we knew they were in jail because they were political prisoners, we would play for them. It didn't matter what group they came from. They were black, and we had to get them out. We knew what the deal was: J. Edgar Hoover and the FBI had targeted the black community. It was an all-out attack. They even had spies in the community, black spies. Some tried to get into the Ark and UGMA. We busted a couple of them. Cats just noticed a lot of small things, put the picture together, and passed the word around. We wouldn't do anything to them; somebody else would, but we wouldn't. We just ignored them.

Talk about freedom, respect, and those kinds of things was spreading by the late 1960s. Cats started cutting off their hair and wearing naturals; women were wearing naturals, and now they've got something to talk about. There were cats in the Ark going different ways politically. We had some of the Black Panthers in our group. One who got killed at UCLA, John Huggins, was in our choir. I loved John. He had a great personality. We also had some of the guys in the US Organization, Maulana Ron Karenga's group, and some Black Muslims. Every time they had a function, our Arkestra was called. And throughout this period, I was in and out of all their offices. The Ark knew people in just about every organization.

If these cats had disagreements, and the Arkestra was playing, no more disagreement. These cats were actually shooting at each other, but they did stop when the music began and they did listen. We were trying to get them to stop shooting each other and we saved a lot of lives, because the music itself cooled the cats out. They were all in the music. It settled them down to the point where they had enough time to remember that they used to go to grammar school together. They used to live across the street from each other. But the music has always been known to do that, and that's why we were so important in our community for a while. The Arkestra became a beacon for the rest of the community, for the other organizations that grew up out of the community, none musical, but they saw the togetherness, all the camaraderie with this Arkestra and what it was about. There was one goal.

Both the Black Panthers and the US Organization people respected us and loved us. Both sides knew what we were about, and we knew what they were about. A lot of the publicity about their hostility was off. It wasn't happening like they said it was. We knew there were outside forces stirring up a lot of this antagonism, and that's why it was important for us to bring these groups together. A lot of the shootings weren't done by these people but by the hired hands of our government. A lot of it didn't happen between these groups but it was put on them. It was a dangerous time and J. Edgar Hoover was a dangerous man.

Later, they started the Black Caucus within the neighborhood, where all the black groups started meeting: the US Organization, the Panthers, the Muslims, and the New African Army group. And the Ark cats would be right there, while they're going through their things, and they'd recognize us for who we were in the community. And in each one of these groups, we had somebody from our group. But we were one group. We were the Ark. One reason we were successful this way was because we got started early in the community when no one else was doing it, and people remembered and respected us for that. They remembered what we had said then and what we did, and they knew we were right.

It was another kind of time, because a lot of people started waking up to a lot of things that didn't occur to them before. And they always wanted to know why I was like I was, because I had gotten out of the real hate bag. I was only thinking about me and my people. I wasn't thinking about fighting anybody anymore. I was thinking about getting my people educated enough and to respect each other again.

People were always asking us what we were.

"Are you guys Muslims?"

"No, we're not Muslims."

"Are you Black Panthers?"

"No, we're not."

"Are you US Organization people?"

"No."

"Well, what are you?"

"We're black Americans, and want to live in the American way."
You dig?

10

When I first started doing these things, and we weren't very well known, I was able to find work. It wasn't until the late 1960s, early 1970s, when I was associated with a lot of the activity that was going on, that I got shut out of most gigs.

After I left Lionel Hampton's band and had just started setting up the Ark, I got my gig back at the Troubadour club, which had moved to Santa Monica Boulevard, playing with my trio six nights a week for sixty dollars. The guy who owned the club, Doug Weston, was a radical, a beatnik, and if you didn't play what he called "jazz" in his club, don't even come in there. I stayed at the Troubadour for two years. It was a good gig and covered a lot of the bills. Meanwhile, I'm organizing all these cats into the Ark.

All the people that J. Edgar Hoover was against in those days, white and black, would all come through that club. All the so-called discards from society would always be there, the creative people, like Ava Gardner and Lenny Bruce. That's why I enjoyed that gig, because it attracted creative people and I got to play exactly what I wanted to play. I had control of the music, and we fed them the new music. And all kinds of people came down and played with us, including Bill Pickens, Bobby Hutcherson, Albert Stinson, Roy Ayers, Walter Benton, Rafmad Jamal, Elmo Hope, Guido Sinclair, Charles Lloyd, Jimmy Woods, and King Pleasure.

It wasn't long before law enforcement started hassling us, because of the mixing that was going on, all the white women coming and listening to all these black cats playing. The cops would be waiting for you when you left the club. You'd drive away with some lady, and they'd pull you over, anything to hassle you. They once tried it at the club, but everyone jumped on them. It was out. Everyone in the club came out saying, "Why are you bothering those guys? Because they're black?" All these whites started telling them how prejudiced the police were, making a stand. It got to be a big thing, and it became dangerous for me to come home sometimes, because the cops would be following me.

But economically it was pretty fruitful, and Cecilia and I had a lot of support from our parents and the whole family. They supported us because we were really serious, and after a while we needed it.

The Studio Scene

When some cats became aware of what we were really doing in the community, they helped, and I was able to get by doing a little ghostwriting. As early as 1959, when I started thinking that I should get off the road and also about what I wanted to do musically, I had to think about what I'd do for employment. "If I go into this phase of music, can I make any money? What can I do?" I figured that if I became a ghostwriter in Los Angeles, I could get enough money to take care of the family, and have plenty of time to deal with the Arkestra and the community.

Different professional black musicians gave me a hand. They found out what I was into and said, "Oh, man, I can't believe this. Come on. Since you're doing that, I've got this here. Maybe you can make some money doing this." Then it started working from both sides. Cats started accepting me as a person. They liked my work first and then my attitude. They started getting me gigs, but silently. I didn't want it any other way but silently. Too much attention and soon people would be calling me for all sorts of things that could get in the way of the Ark and UGMA. Kirk Stuart, the late pianist, used to give me a lot of work, quietly, for Sarah Vaughan and other people he was writing for. It was enough.

Gerald Wilson was ghostwriting in the studios. He wrote a lot of music that came out under Dmitri Tiomkin's name. The fact is, for the generations coming in the year 2000 and beyond, Gerald wrote the music. He did a lot of ghostwriting for many of those Hollywood writers. They would write four bars, and Gerald would take the rest. That's the way I got the bulk of my writing experience, from being around Gerald and cats like Gil Fuller.

I became Gil Fuller's protégé during the 1960s. He wrote for Dizzy Gillespie and those cats in the early days, pieces like "Manteca." He also composed "The Shadow of Your Smile" and the music for *The Sandpiper* during the late 1960s. His name wasn't on it at all. They used to tell me all that, and I'd seen the music; they'd show me the scores. It wasn't a lie. Gil was a driving force and he'd take me everywhere he went. He'd come to my door every morning, waking my ass up, and lay stuff on me, musically and socially. Somehow he found me. He'd heard I was rehearsing my band and he just came to get me. I loved this cat, and we got pretty tight for a long time.

I started working in the studios because of cats like Gerald, Gil, and Buddy Collette. They would hire me, hire their guys, so to speak, to come in. They made sure we acted correctly. We could take care of the music, but how was our attitude? That was the biggest part and that was where the biggest problem was. I'd go in two or three times a week to make tracks for vocalists or whomever. It was money. At that time, seventy-five dollars was the top price for the lowest-paid musician for about three hours of studio work. It was pretty nice and it was steady. There were also occasional Hollywood parties. So the union amalgamation benefited me during these years.

But I had my run-ins with a lot of the white musicians in the studios. Once, I was in the studio, sitting, waiting, and one of the white guys said, "Hey, Tapscott, what's the problem with you? Why are you sitting there sulking? You're making seventy-five dollars for doing nothing." That pissed me off, so I jumped him. We weren't going to hit each other in the mouth, so I shoved him. He happened to be one of the top-notch trumpet players. I also found out later that his father was a head studio cat. After that, I stopped getting called for a lot of dates, because of my so-called attitude. And not just me; others weren't called back, because of the way they would talk music and were used to doing things. There were a lot of problems, of course, when integration in the studios had just begun. The cultures started clashing, and when you stopped playing the music, everyone went their different ways.

When I did the second Elaine Brown album in the early 1970s, I had a run-in with a studio string section. The strings always have an attitude, especially when it comes to the other musicians — "You're important, but . . ." These cats are used to coming to the studio all the time. There's a group of them and they know each other. They have a little money and boats out at the marina.

So here I come to do the violin track for Elaine's album, and I'm facing a studio string section and a bassoonist. They'd never seen me before, gave me a quick look, and kept talking about their boats. As I passed out the music, I could hear them talking about how much it cost to maintain those boats. When I stood up on the podium to conduct them, they just kept on talking. Finally, the head violinist turned to me and asked, "Are we ready now?"

"Yeah, I'm ready."

And they settled in with the attitude — "Let's get this over with now."

We started the playback of the music that had already been laid down, and I took it from the top. We got to the part where the bassoon was supposed to run with the bass guitar that had already been recorded, and he couldn't get the part. It ran by him too quickly. We stopped, and the violin players with their cocky attitude worked on it. We tried it again, and this time the cellist took the part and missed it. They were reading the music, but just couldn't get the rhythm of it.

"Okay, we'll just leave those two bars out and leave the recorded tape as it is."

When I said that, the head violinist jumped up, "Can we have a minute, please, sir?"

"Sure."

I walked out, and they went back to my music to see if it was written correctly. They realized it was, that the mathematics were correct, and when I came back they were ready to try it again. They still couldn't get it, and I told them to just forget it.

"Oh, no!"

They just couldn't accept it and were pretty shaken up. The bassoon player cried.

"Sir, for fourteen years I've been sitting in studio chairs, and this is the first time I've come across something that I couldn't play."

Of course, he could play the notes, but not the way I wanted them played.

They kept calling me "sir" after those two bars. By this time, they had come out of their act and they were respecting me. When we moved on, they were ready. I had challenged them, and their attitude changed. It was a struggle, but I really enjoyed that session. After that, they treated me like I was Henry Mancini.

Motown and the Supremes

When Motown was trying to get themselves together on the West Coast in the late 1960s, I did a lot of those gigs. They had formed a West Coast band, and Bobby Gross, my friend from Los Angeles City College, had hooked up with them and brought me in.

You'd think things would have been different for black artists with Motown, but they weren't. Those cats who used to write for Motown and groups like the Supremes were black writers. Gil Askey was the main cat who made Motown. Those sounds you hear behind the Supremes, Marvin Gaye, the Four Tops, all those people, were Gil's. He was the writer who made all those kids sound good and he showed me how to write for a vocalist. Gil also made new dances and new beats that he never got credit for. The music was just flowing out of this cat. He was *the cat* and my man never got the notice for it. He made the Motown sound, and he never got the money and the notoriety he should have. Now he lives in Australia.

I was their pianist when Motown came out to the West Coast. Gil and Preston Love had the California Motown band. We'd travel on the bus with the Supremes and play each place. Diana Ross would never call my name correctly. I hated that. The rest of the chicks, Florence Ballard and Mary Wilson, would come in and say hello to the band. When you're a singer who needs accompanying, you want to get to know your accompanist. If not, they can do you in. Diana could have taken time to learn a name or come in to say hello to the cats. One time at a festival, we were the only ones on stage. The band had to be down on the floor, so there wasn't anybody on stage but me and the singers. She looked at me and said, "Tapshoot" or "Boopdabip" or whatever. I just looked the other way, ignored her.

Many great cats just didn't get the respect and the recognition from the studios and the recording companies. Gil Askey created all this music and went unnoticed. He was treated like a worker and then one day he was gone. People never liked to talk about it. You'd just hear, "Them jive motherfuckers." Gerald Wilson used to come by pissed off. He'd drive down here and scream and holler about everything, because this was the only place he could do that and not be called crazy. Then one time he just gave it up. All these guys were in there recording, and something must have hit Gerald the wrong way. He went out into the studio, took up all his music, said something like "Y'all can go jump in a lake," and walked out. And you have to remember that this cat is a master writer. I remember Duke Ellington coming down here to get Gerald to do some writing for him. That's why I got out of the so-called studio music scene after seeing all these guys and what happened to them. And by the late 1960s, most places didn't want me.

Family Matters: My Father's Son

By that time it was getting tight, because I had ten kids—six boys and four girls. The first five were by Cecilia, and then one by Joyce Butler. Her family came from Kansas City in the early 1950s and, at first, didn't have anyplace to stay. So my mother put up two of the girls. That's how Joyce and I met, and we were teenagers together. We were close and so were our families. Joyce's daddy loved me. There weren't too many people surprised when she had my daughter Nyja in 1963, and our families are still close. Mama loved both Cecilia and Joyce, and used to tell me, "Now, don't you mess up with these girls." But I didn't listen. I was young and crazy and full of life.

There were some other ladies, and we had some kids who I care for very much, but they weren't planned. Some agreed to not have the child, but then changed their minds at the last moment. And about this time, everyone seemed to be upset with me. Man, I was the ball that was bouncing around in the middle of all this. But the bottom line was that each of these mothers, except one, allowed me to see the children. I had a son, Michael Tapscott, with Vicky Hamilton, a vocalist, and she'd bring him around to play with the other children. He plays guitar now, plays his ass off. He's got a group called East/West and gigs at places like the Whiskey. He's got the talent. Then there's the twins, Rashied and Kenya, whose mother is Carrie Wagner, another vocalist. There was also a daughter, Emanon—again by a vocalist, Alexandria—who was put up for adoption and whom I've never met. All I've been told is that she went to school in Long Beach, and so we've never hooked up. It's up to her, if we ever do. But I've been thinking about her ever since, and for a long time I drove down the streets staring at people, looking for a resemblance.

No one will ever believe this, but none of this did I initiate. And, man, the babies after just one time! I'd be sitting there, and . . . "Here."

One time? Just one time! Poof!

What is this?

In my mind, I talked to my father quite a bit in those days. I started to realize what had happened to him and started seeing things from his point of view. Regardless of all the ladies he'd knocked up, and all the kids he had, he stayed there in Houston and did care for as many of the kids as he could.

But I'm glad it went down the way it did. If I had to do it over, I'd probably do it the same way, but I'd be a little more aware of what I was getting into. Then, I was a young cat and consequences didn't exist. I was enjoying the lilies of the field, even though I had my own rose garden.

It was really rough for Cecilia, and she had to go through some changes during those years. Being in music, there were chicks all around and they were always on you, no matter what you'd tell them. Sometimes I'd get trapped in it; sometimes I wouldn't. Cecilia went through a lot of trials and tribulations with friends telling her that she shouldn't go through all this with this guy. She went through a lot of hell for it, but got to a point where she believed she could handle it. She also figured that I wasn't as bad as I seemed. I was always at the pad and taking care of business.

The first few years of marriage are just learning about each other. It was after ten or twelve years of marriage that I realized what it was about as far as I was concerned—not only what society expects but what I wanted to give over to my wife and to these lives that I was bringing into the world. It was a slow change with me, and I'm still learning and growing. After years of marriage, you fall in love. You know what's important, what the difference is between lust and love. You can say "I love you" for real. There's nothing like loyalty and belief in somebody. That's always been a part of my life, since my earliest training. I've never believed in breaking strings, if you've helped make them. You build something with someone and you keep it. You find a way. Loyalty . . . especially loyalty. That's what Cecilia had and has now. After forty years with a person you don't take it for granted, but you don't have to speak a lot. I could sit here right now and think of something, and this woman could come in and tell me what I was thinking. It's become a spiritual blending.

So I didn't have to leave and I wasn't threatened. They knew I was in the music and that was a different scene. They knew what I was involved in and what I was about, so there was a different atmosphere. The mothers were all very independent and only asked for things when they really needed it. We all respected each other. We certainly had our problems, but I'm glad they're all here. I used to take all the kids, at one time or another, to rehearsals with me. That was the one time they'd all be together. I think I've been pretty lucky and I love all my kids. I married the right woman in the first place and then I was lucky enough with the other women to work things out. With different people, I could have ended up in jail. But they were cool and never pressured me. They knew what I was doing in the community and what kind of community we were working to create for our kids to grow up in. The kids always came first and they were all exposed to what I was doing, except the one I've never met.

Without this kind of support, I couldn't have made it. Even when they didn't believe, my family has staunchly supported me, because I believed. That's how I lasted through the hard years and up to now. There's nothing like family, and I'm the living proof of that. Nothing could ever happen that would make me lose respect for family and that to the nth degree. With a family you can take chances, because you have a backup. And as we got into the middle of it, I needed that.

Shut Out

As UGMA and the Ark became known, there were long stretches when I couldn't work anywhere. Especially after the second album with Elaine Brown, I was shut out, and we depended on Cecilia working. I wasn't able to get any kind of job. I wasn't able to work in the studios. I couldn't get certain gigs, because of my persona. Whenever my name would come up in the studios, they'd ask for another arranger. They said I was hard to deal with, hard to get along with, or I had an attitude. "He might stop the band and fight." It wasn't true at all but they stopped me from working. I didn't get any more calls. Some of the white cats who wanted to hire me told me what was going down.

It was tough for a while, because I played in everything that J. Edgar Hoover didn't dig—the Communist thing, the Muslim thing. I played for everything that was "against the American society." But the people I was affiliated with were just talking about respect. "Have respect for me and mine, and I'll have respect for you and yours. Then we can have respect for each other." That's all it was about. It had nothing to do with hate and killing.

But there were also a lot of patrons around, people who would just send me money, anonymously, out of the blue. Sometimes, I'd look in my mailbox and there'd be some money from someone.

"For you and your family, Horace."

"To help you along."

All anonymous, no one would tell me who they were. At first, I couldn't imagine what was going on. I even thought it might be a trick. "What is this, a setup?" As time went on, I started putting things together and realized the support we had. Yeah, that was out, wasn't it?

I did all kinds of hustles to get by and keep my babies fed. I never committed crimes, but at one point in the late 1960s through the early 1970s, I got in with this pimp and went to play at his pad in the Hollywood Hills for the whores and their customers. He had six chicks, and they all drove Mustangs. They were called the Mustang gang. Al Hines and Arnold Palmer, the drummer, were with me. We'd be sitting up in the living room playing. Some business cat might like the music and drop some money on us. Meanwhile, Zeke would give us $1,000 for the gig. I'd bring that money home, and we'd be eating, the light bills would be paid, and nobody would ask any questions.

Every now and then I'd get an out-of-town gig that paid some money. I accompanied a few singers, like Mickey Lynn and Lorez Alexandria, in Vegas for a few weeks at a time. When the Ark would get a college gig, usually through the Black Students Union, they'd raise so much money for us. That was important when these Black Students Unions started helping me work. But I hardly ever left town, though; it was so busy here with community activities. After a while, my affiliation with the Ark, and the music I was writing, led to pretty steady work. People would come by and ask me to do this or that for them. And that enabled me to get by monetarily. I never did make big money, but it got to a level that at least every week I knew I had a gig.

Once, in the early 1970s, I got an offer out of the blue from a white college in one of those northeastern cities to join their faculty and lead a seventy-five-piece orchestra and one-hundred-voice choir. I have no idea how they found out about me. They just sent me a letter offering me this gig, telling me how much money I'd be making, and what kind of situation I'd be in. I refused it, naturally, because it would have taken me so far out of the community and put me in an all-white setting. At the time, I was trying to educate my own and I couldn't understand, "Why me? Why not some educated white professor?" I even thought it might have been a trick to get me out of town. But it was a great feeling, just the fact that they hit on me and that I could say, "No, thank you."

So I was home a lot. My kids saw me every day of their lives. I changed every one of their diapers and I sat with them. We never went hungry; the kids had clothes and their supplies for school. They'd know their homework, because their father would be there doing it with them. I could spell and add, and I was proud of that, and I wanted them to be able to do that. I could comprehend what I read to them. I tried to expose the family to different kinds of cultures. I did pretty well up to a point and I had a lot of help.

I don't have any regrets about how it went down. That's how we did it through those years. I was able to do it my way, by being who I was. I was able to have a family and a band.

11

About five or six years after the inception of UGMA, we changed
our name to the Union of God's Musicians and Artists Ascension
(UGMAA). This was after a few years of building our own clientele,
our own listeners, by being constantly there for them and taking
the music all over the community, especially where there were
children. We forced it on people; they just had to accept us, even
if they didn't know what was going on. We wanted to reach families and parents, and after a while it got to the point where they
weren't afraid to bring their children to us.

But as the underground, we were always a target for the "lawful"
faction of the community. They called us "that radical group of
musicians," "that underground group of radicals who are producing those 'hate songs.'" They weren't used to hearing what they
were hearing; they weren't used to the way the music was being
presented; they weren't used to the way the people were dressing
for these events. The Ark would only wear African clothing, and
in the days of the early 1960s, that was intimidating to white and
black people.

We had to get out of that, if we wanted to affect more of the
community. We wanted our community, the black community at
least, to accept us, and we didn't want them against us any more
than some of them already were in a sense. We wanted to be able
to approach people and to let them know that we understood what
they were talking about, that we were part of what they were,

and that we were just messengers. We were more like the vanguard showing what's really going on behind the African American, what our tradition was. And even that name, African American, was intimidating. People didn't like to be called "African," just like years before nobody wanted to be called "black." So we had to learn how to get over to them our message about themselves, about what society was doing to a race of people, without making it seem like we were sticking pins into them, and doing all of that through the arts.

We began with just some small words, with understanding people's names, for instance. We had people writing poems and things who were using all of these names about themselves and changing the names of who they were. A lot of these people came to the conclusion that the names they had here in America were slave names and they wanted to change them to free names. I questioned it, because the names they changed to were slave names in Africa from the Arabs. They took on Arabic names and their religion, Islam. It seemed they were just giving up one slave name for another, Robert for Hassan or William for Muhammad. You don't know what your ancestral name is. So if you don't know what your name is, and the only way you're hooked up with your parents is through this American name, it doesn't make sense to give it up, because then you'd be cut off from your whole family.

Those seemingly tiny, minute things that people hardly think about were what we were working on—those subtleties behind race, those subtleties behind being proud of yourself by showing that pride in creating something, by giving something to the society regardless of whether you agree with it or not, but are still a part of it. This led us into a whole discussion of identity and who we are as a people.

After a while, as we became more aboveground, we started realizing what our real role was. In the beginning, it was more like breaking the old mold, the old routines; just take a bulldozer and run it down. Then, we had to think about how to build it up to what we were talking about. That's when we became the Union of God's Musicians and Artists Ascension. When someone asked, "What does UGMAA stand for?" we could answer that this band is about depicting the lives of black people in their communities all over this country, where it has been turned around and people have been made to feel unworthy. We were trying to kill that kind of attitude about black folks through the arts.

We chose the name because the black cats in my age bracket were all brought up in segregated America, which meant we spent a lot of time going to church. "You will be at church and you will do this, and you will learn these things." We spent all day in churches and we still had a respect for that type of feeling that the religion's supposed to have been fostering. I tried hard not to disrespect my elders and I wanted to tear down the things they'd had to face. But I also had to have some sensitivity to what they went through in my actions. By using the "Union of God's Musicians," they understood the word *God*. They'd been hearing it all their lives. Okay, so we utilized it. "Musicians and Artists Ascension" I picked because that was the idea we had in mind: that we were going to ascend through the arts to bring about recognition and understanding of each other. We thought we had to do this as a people before we could reach out to someone else.

By unifying all the different aspects of the arts in this one area, we were heading in a direction that was going to bring us, bring our people, out of the descending mode they'd been in for years, and allow us, as a people, to start feeling proud of ourselves. There were a lot of black people who didn't realize how much they had contributed to this society. They were never told, and we tried to show them that in our actions, as well as the importance of our African heritage.

Africa had a big impact on us. I was aware of the anticolonial struggles going on and I wanted to know how come we never had any kind of hookup to Africa. When I was growing up, if you were a black in the United States, you didn't want to be thought of as African. They were a whole different people. That's how much we'd been turned. They had cut the string, and we didn't have anything to hang onto.

So we stayed underground until those times when many different people started coming to our concerts with their children and their grandparents. People would leave the regular Baptist Church on Sunday and come down to listen to us wherever we'd be playing. We increasingly became a rallying group for the community and would sometimes have speakers, as well as the music. Someone like Malcolm X or some professor from the South might come and speak. We brought these people, educated black men and women, into the community so that our community could be informed about what was going on. Then, they could start making up their own minds about what they wanted and what they didn't want. Too many ideas had been accepted, because the black community was told to accept them. Soon, groups started sprouting up all over the place to pursue information about our history.

This way of approaching people was so necessary, because at that time anyone who would go against the man—the white man—was dangerous. If you said something about Jesus Christ being black, many would react, "Whoa! Are you crazy? You'd better get out of here. Don't come on this block no more. Don't even walk near this church." We had to deal with that kind of attitude without getting crazy and mad, and we would get mad. But then we had to realize why they were acting like that and try something else. Let them see what was happening and why, and then let them decide. They'd start asking you questions, which you could then answer. All of a sudden, they might remember things and start putting them together.

Consequently, UGMA became UGMAA, because we wanted to re-educate, to show people that we had a heritage and were part of a race to be proud of. We wanted to show how much of a contribution black people have made to this whole society, and how much of that we hadn't been given credit for. And we demanded that this happen. We wanted our grandchildren to grow up realizing that they were not just here, that they had something to do with this country. People who were trapped in this society, mind wise, would always come to the Ark to relax, to listen, to be able to function outside, to get some more strength, so they could leave and go back into the war zone.

It was very important that we made that motion, that sound, that moan, that started more people looking and saying, "Well, maybe they're not teaching hate. Let me see." And anyone who had any kind of campaign that had to do with uplifting black people, UGMAA was right behind them in any way we could assist them. That's the gig we took on. "We're just informing you of what's going on. We're not telling you what to do or how to do it, and we're not putting this person up against that person, because he or she speaks about black people better. All we're doing is trying to show you the whole picture of what's happening, because of our lack of knowing and realizing, educating and enlightening our children. We have to show you what it is that will gain you respect in this country."

We became an organization that was going to inform, somewhat entice, and help bring a community to the point of recognizing who and what they were. Before we could make a dent or a mark in this society, we had to learn who we were and what our function was, and why. "How come I want to go to college? How come I can't go to college? How come the curriculum at my high school is at a lower level?" Once you start investigating these questions, getting past those things that were snuck through after the end of segregation, then you can think about becoming a ruling part of this society, about making laws and governing it.

We felt that you had to better yourself first, before the country could be better. You had to educate yourself, before the country could become a better place for education. You had to do all these things yourself, just as you had to take care of your family. That didn't only mean putting bread and food in there; you had to put some knowledge and information on the table. That was very important to us—always had been since the beginning of the Ark— but now we were focused on that and that's what we tried to do.

In the early 1970s, we did an independent film, *Passing Through,* that attempted to do that. One day we were rehearsing in my garage and Arthur Blythe said something to Lester Robertson. Ted Lange, the actor, was standing outside, heard it, and said, "What?

What did he say, man? Damn! That said it all! Let me write this down." From there he started writing a script with Larry Clark, the photographer and filmmaker, who was a student at UCLA then, about the Ark. Their main character, Warmack, was based on me and our approach. A lot of the cats from the Ark are in the film, like Adele Sebastian and Jesse Sharps, and Ernie Roberts plays Warmack's saxophone.

After a while, we were asked to come to schools, junior colleges, and colleges all over the state because of our activities. We went to the University of California at Riverside, at Davis, at Berkeley, and to Laney and Merritt Colleges in Oakland. This was the entire Ark, traveling in three cars. I was even asked to teach classes at Riverside City College and then at the University of California there, where I had about ninety students in that course called "Black Experience in the Fine Arts." An important part of that class was sending students out to listen to live music, to talk to the musicians, and then to write about their experiences. The class had its ups and downs. The up part was the interest the students had in the subject. The down part of that class was dealing with the girls. They'd all sit in the front with their big naturals or perms and their short skirts, showing all their thighs. Finally, I just stopped the class one day and said, "Ladies and Gentleman, this is a wonderful, beautiful morning class and this row up front here is excellent. However, if I'm to get this subject over to you, you ladies are going to have to lighten up on me." They all cracked up. Right away they knew I was human, and we became good friends.

We also set up a UGMAA Fine Arts Institute in Riverside—another UGMAA house—and had a lot of support at those colleges from the students and some of the faculty, who helped us get some financial backing for our work out there. We staged regular performances and exhibits of all kinds by local artists, and even put together a TV show for the local public television channel. It was called *The Store Front,* was produced by Sue Booker, and ran a few times. William Marshall was on, and it featured me performing solo and answering questions. We were pretty active in Riverside for about one year.

We were even being sought after by guys running for political

office in the community. They'd call me up and ask, "Horace, could I get you and the Arkestra to play at a rally I'm having at the park? I'm trying to run for council," or whatever. We played for a lot of different people, because they were black politicians, period. We just felt like, hey, they should have a chance to mess up as well, just like the white cats. When former Mayor Tom Bradley was first running for city council, we'd play at any of his functions. People like that and Robert Farrell, Nate Holden. Whatever it took to get that respect was where we were coming from, to get an African American seat at the particular table that runs this country. We wanted to make sure that somebody was available, someone who was a wordsmith, to be up front taking care of the technicalities of black people.

We started getting calls from more and more of these cats, who started coming to our rehearsals, and we began playing at many of these gatherings. We'd have parties in the street and we'd have speakers representing different ideas and groups, so people could hear all that. The Arkestra would be there to play, regardless of whether we agreed or not with all the people speaking. The point was that they were supposed to be listened to by the people in the community, and we were behind that.

After we had some politicians elected who were black and started getting some experience of black political leadership, then we only hooked up with black people who we thought were going to represent us. These kinds of situations would lead to a lot of questions and discussions in the Ark. We didn't do anything haphazardly and then not just because someone was black. We wanted to know what they were going to do. If they were musicians, would they be in the Arkestra? What were they going to do about the street cleaning in the black community? How many times was this cat going to come down the street? We wanted those things answered. What would they do about having the police stay out of different areas and just protect the community? Somebody might object, "Well, man, I don't want to play there, because these people did such and such, and I don't think we should play for them."

Yeah, we had those kinds of discussions. It didn't have anything to do with a person's way of thinking, their politics; it had to do with what that person was supposed to have been doing for you community wise. That was really important to us. If the Ark hadn't seen a person doing anything, if they hadn't seen that person contributing toward what we were talking about, then we wouldn't play for that person, wouldn't rally for him or her, because we didn't believe in that person. It wouldn't have mattered if there were two black people running for the same office. We played for both, if we believed in what they were talking about and doing, and neither of them if we didn't. And after a cat had been in office, if we didn't see they were doing anything for the black community they claimed to represent, then it was over.

That's how we got hooked up in politics. It came from our demands for respect. We had started musically, because we could grab people's attention right away. Now we were trying to support politics that contributed to this, politics that were about us coming up, nothing about going down.

Sun Ra and Rahsaan Roland Kirk

We did a lot of things in the community that we didn't advertise, because it was done just for the community. Whenever some of the cats were in town, they'd call me and come down to talk to the children. We'd get the children ready for them; they'd be looking out. Some cats who would be passing through, like Rahsaan Roland Kirk, would eat this up. He'd run down here to be a part of it. When Rahsaan would come to the neighborhood, he'd take the time to just sit and talk. And he could talk to the kids. They could ask him anything, and he'd answer them, right out front with them. They loved him, and he did it, man. He used to come by and play with two horns in his mouth. The children would be in total glee, mesmerized. One day he told me, "Before I leave here, every black kid in the neighborhood is going to be playing two horns at once. I'm gonna see to that. That's my role, Horace."

At that time, I had my class at the University of California at Riverside, and he'd want to go out there with me every morning. One time I had to leave without him, because he was late and it's a long drive from Los Angeles. He got a ride with somebody else and finally showed up after I had started the class. With everyone sitting there, he came in and started walking down the aisle: "God-damnit, Horace, you left me! Why you leave me, man?" He called me all kinds of things.

I yelled, "Shut up, you black ass, blind motherfucker!" and he fell out. "Young folks, this is Rahsaan Roland Kirk."

When he finished with that class, all the young cats just had their mouths open. "What did he just do?" He was something and he loved doing that class. It was one of his happiest moments, and they found him very interesting.

I enjoyed his music, because his music was his personality, and he was a regular street cat. He didn't hold back. I'll never forget that one day when he tore up Shelly's Manne Hole in Hollywood. What I liked about Shelly Manne was that he was so cool. He'd just sit there and let Rahsaan go off. They had a local disc jockey, Rick Holmes, I think, as MC one night. When Rahsaan came walking in with his group, Rick said, "Ah, Rahsaan Roland Kirk."

"Who's that? That Rick Holmes? Rick Holmes, motherfucker! How come I don't hear Horace Tapscott and these other cats on the radio? Play the cats, man!"

Then Rahsaan started throwing things, breaking the place up. When I walked in later, Shelly was sitting there, looking at me and just shaking his head.

Cecilia would be crying, whenever he played. Close to the end, we went to his last concert, and he had to be helped on stage. He couldn't use his left side by then. When he got on stage, he said, "Well, folks, tonight I'm going to be playing with only one hand, one arm, but I'm going to play it like I've never played it before." And he did. People were crying.

Not only Rahsaan but a lot of the professional cats got the word about what we were doing in the community and they'd come here.

"I want to do something, man. What can I do?"

"What's my part?"

That kind of attitude. Everyone would accept them as one of the cats, and they'd love that. And the musicians who came to play in the community were mostly the people who were considered outside, like Rahsaan and Sun Ra.

During the 1960s, we played on the last Sunday of every month at Foshay Junior High School, along with the Bobby Bradford-John Carter Quintet, for people in the neighborhood. Then we moved on to the Widney High School for the Handicapped. Every now and then Sun Ra and his Arkestra would be there. One day, Sun Ra just called and told me he was coming to town. He had heard about me, and I knew what he was doing. Whenever some of our guys were back east, they'd play in his Ark, and whenever some of his came out here, they'd sit in with us. The same kind of interchange also happened with Muhal Richard Abrams's Association for the Advancement of Creative Musicians in Chicago.

When Sun Ra came out with his Ark, we had access to an auditorium at the Widney High School, and so our Arkestras played together in a few concerts. The only problem we had was one night when Sun Ra, after a while, got to talking and time was just passing on. I kept saying to him, "Ra, my man, got to close up."

Finally, the janitor, who helped us and really dug the show, looked at me and said, "Horace, I got to do this," and started blinking the lights.

"Why they blink the lights on me, man?!" Ra started yelling and then he put a curse on Los Angeles.

I said, "Ra, don't do that, man. We have to play here next week."

The custodian was just doing us a favor. He dug our music and came in on his day off to open the auditorium for us without anybody's permission. It was getting late, he had to split, and Ra just kept on talking.

"Ra, you're gonna get this guy in trouble."

I explained to him what the situation was and that he was being selfish. The janitor had to be respected, too.

"Okay. Okay. Okay. Okay."

Then they played "Jupiter"; the people danced, and the concert was over.

Sun Ra knew why I had put our Arkestra together and he knew I was one of his admirers. The old man would come by and preach to me for a long time after we played together. After I had the cerebral aneurysm in 1978, the whole band came by my place. They were passing through on their way up north and had heard about my stroke. Around 2:00 A.M., Sun Ra's Arkestra pulled up outside my house and started banging on the front door. Half his band was asleep in the car. The women, the dancers, were coming in and using the bathroom. John Gilmore and the other cats were in the front room. Ra was blabbing away, and I was sitting there in a state of oblivion, while my wife slept through it all. She didn't wake up. By sunrise Sun Ra was still talking. Finally, John and some of the cats said, "We've got to go. We've got to go," and they finally left.

Whenever Sun Ra was in town, we got together. I enjoyed the brother. I liked the way he did things, musically and socially, especially the way he dealt with people. Whenever anyone would ask him a question, he'd really get into it and get to rappin' about space or whatever with whomever it was.

"Why do you do so-and-so?"

You wouldn't ask that, unless you were ready for a serious answer. He'd take time. Sun Ra proved himself by being in it for forty years. I always appreciated that and I appreciated his attitude. He stuck with his vision.

Settling into the Community

12

In the early 1970s, after we left Brother Percy's house in South Central Los Angeles, UGMAA had a small office in a house off Western Avenue called the Great House. Since that wasn't much room, we also rented a three-room space in an office building near the Crenshaw/Baldwin Hills shopping center. We were in that office space for nine months, eight months of it for free because the building was in escrow, and then we met Reverend Wolfe.

We always seemed to have help from the community, even to the extent of offering us facilities. During the 1970s, Reverend Wolfe, an old Jamaican brother, gave us an entire print shop—a three-story building, and all the machinery and equipment—because he saw we were very serious. This brother saw us in the community and he wanted to be a part of it. He was in his early seventies, was about to retire, and offered us his business.

"I'm going to close this place down, but you guys need some space to do your function. You need your own printing press. You need your own publicity."

He gave us a price, and then kept lowering it when we hesitated. Finally, we told him we couldn't buy it; we didn't have any money. So he grabbed his chest and said, "Something tells me I should give this to you." He let us have the place for one dollar, and we only saw him occasionally after that. Isn't that something?

We moved into this big, three-story building on Vermont Avenue near Eighty-fourth Street. Now, we weren't moving from house to house. We had a big place and started settling down in the community. Different people with expertise in repairing and paperhanging and roofing came along to fix the place up. People, who were in a position to, gave all these office-type things to us. One guy said, "I have an old truck that hasn't run, and if you guys can fix it, you can have it." This kept happening. We had a guy, Barry Cisco, who was an accountant and was so inspired by our activities, that he volunteered his services and started taking care of the books for us. And he started touching other people who we never would have reached. He started the paperwork for us becoming a foundation, so that we could apply for grants and things of that sort. With his help, we became the UGMAA Foundation, a nonprofit organization. Marla Gibbs set up the Sisters of Music to support the band and arrange concerts for the Ark. It was nice.

We weren't just an orchestra rehearsing for a gig and then leaving. We were something that was going to be there all the time. People in this area could count on it. As had happened in Watts and elsewhere, we started getting food for people who were hungry. No matter what part of the community we were in, we always did that, and people would always bring food to our gigs and events. Cats would donate food, and we'd pass it out. Again, people started donating their time teaching kids different things. They'd come down to our shop and teach classes. We were accepted in the community.

We had a large rehearsal space and we reopened the print shop, calling it "the Shop." My future son-in-law, Michael Dett Wilcots, was very experienced in printing and graphic arts, and he took over running the business end of it. The equipment was old, but we were able to make it work and raise a little cash through printing. We weren't trying to make a lot of money. It was more or less just survival money and being independent. We utilized it to spread the word of our existence, to get us more publicity and exposure. After a couple of months, we started doing print jobs for the neighborhood. People started coming in to get their work copied, or they'd bring in flyers and things of that nature. That's about as far as we got in the printing business, because the equipment was so old.

Upstairs we had office space, and we moved in our files and

Pan Afrikan Peoples Arkestra, South Park, Los Angeles, May 1970. Horace (piano, left), Arthur Blythe (alto saxophone, center), and "Voices of UGMAA" (right). (Photo by Michael Dett Wilcots.)

Pan Afrikan Peoples Arkestra, South Park, Los Angeles, May 1970. Foreground: Jimmy Hoskins (drums). To his right: Everett Brown (drums), Cerion Middleton III (tenor saxophone), and Will Connell (alto saxophone). (Photo by Michael Dett Wilcots.)

Linda Hill ("Lino") at the Great House, 1970s. (Photo by Michael Dett Wilcots.)

Horace, South Park, Los Angeles, Winter 1971. (Pencil/charcoal and photograph by Michael Dett Wilcots.)

Pan Afrikan Peoples Arkestra, South Park, Los Angeles, spring 1971. Left to right: Horace (piano), David Bryant (bass), "Voices of UGMAA," Ernest Straughter, Linda Hill, Robert Roy, Ray Straughter (tenor saxophone), Will Connell (alto saxophone), Willie Samprite, Walter (unknown), and Butch Morris. (Photo by Michael Dett Wilcots.)

Pan Afrikan Peoples Arkestra, South Park, spring 1971.
(Photo by Michael Dett Wilcots and Kamau Daáood.)

Pan Afrikan Peoples Arkestra, Widney High School, August 1971. Left to right: Ernest Cojoe (congas), Horace (piano), and Everett Brown (drums). (Photo by Michael Dett Wilcots.)

Everett Brown.

Pan Afrikan Peoples Arkestra, Los Angeles, March 1974. Left to right: Steven Meeks (baritone saxophone), Pamela Jackson (flute), Adele Sebastian (flute), Jesse Sharps (tenor saxophone), Gary Bias (alto saxophone), unknown (trombone), Lester Robertson (trombone). (Photo by Michael Dett Wilcots.)

Pan Afrikan Peoples Arkestra, Los Angeles, March 1974. Horace (piano) and Greg Tell (drums). (Photo by Michael Dett Wilcots.)

Pan Afrikan Peoples Arkestra, Los Angeles, March 1974. Left to right: Linda Hill, Horace (flute), Jahid Abdullah (horn), and Steven Meeks (baritone saxophone). (Photo by Michael Dett Wilcots.)

Lester Robertson, Ladera Park, Los Angeles, spring 1971. (Photo by Michael Dett Wilcots.)

Samuel R. Browne, at his home in Los Angeles, fall 1972. (Photo by Michael Dett Wilcots.)

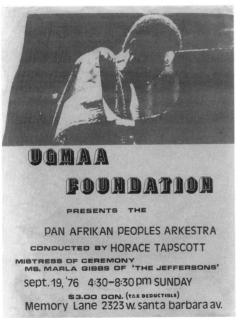

PAPA flyer. Photo is from the Los Angeles Music Center performance of *Ancestral Echoes* with the Watts Symphony Orchestra in the mid-1970s. (Photo by Michael Dett Wilcots.)

UGMAA FOUNDATION

PRESENTS THE

PAN AFRIKAN PEOPLES ARKESTRA

CONDUCTED BY HORACE TAPSCOTT

MISTRESS OF CEREMONY
MS. MARLA GIBBS OF 'THE JEFFERSONS'

sept. 19, '76   4:30–8:30 pm SUNDAY

$3.00 DON. (TAX DEDUCTIBLE)
Memory Lane 2323 w. santa barbara av.

UGMAA actors workshop, Los Angeles, December 1976. Linda Hill (left) and Dorian Gibbs, Marla's son, upstairs at the Shop. (Photo by Michael Dett Wilcots.)

Kwanzaa celebration, 1976.

Horace conducting the Ark at the Immanuel United Church of Christ, late 1970s. Left to right: Walter Savage (bass), Michael Dett Wilcots (recording with headphones), Kamonta Polk (bass), Adele Sebastian (flute), Jesse Sharps (soprano saxophone), Ismael Balaka (drums), Dadisi Wells (Komolafe) (flute), Michael Session (alto saxophone), Wendell Williams (french horn), Bill Madison (drums), Amos Delone (baritone saxophone), Charles Chandler (tenor saxophone), James Andrews (tenor saxophone), Steve Smith (trumpet), Lester Robertson (trombone), and Michael Daniels (congas). (Photo by Craig Anthony.)

Outside the Immanuel United Church of Christ, 1978. (Photo by Michael Dett Wilcots.)

Recording the album *In New York* with Cecilia looking on. New York City, 1979.

(Below) Pan Afrikan Peoples Arkestra, UCLA, summer 1981. Left to right: Linda Hill (piano), Alan Hines (bass), David Bryant (bass), Henry Franklin (bass), Fritz Wise (drums), Dadisi Komolafe, and Herbert Callies.

records from our previous office setup. Thanks to some support from Mary Henry's CETA Program at the Avalon/Carver Community Center, we were able to hire some staff. We also utilized those offices for children's classes on the weekends.

This was what we had been doing since the early 1960s, but now we had our own place. We had classes in music, storytelling, and even some "lightweight" music classes for very young people, where we would try out different methods of teaching music. We would try to identify those children who might not be good readers first off but could really hear music. Then, we'd hone them to the point where they would be playing without knowing what they were doing. After that, we'd put them in a course on reading music. We didn't want to lock them up from the top, starting them off with the paper and notes. They weren't ready for censorship, and we wanted them to be as open as possible to sounds. We'd have them playing with each other, putting things together, humming out a phrase, all long before they reason.

Then, we'd start them on a real simple class procedure, using a blackboard to teach them how to read. They didn't have any instruments; they just learned to read using their hands to clap out rhythms, to know the value of each note and rest and all of those musical notations. It was like it was separate from their playing, almost as if they were in another class just taking mathematics. So I used that kind of system. Then, after all that preparation without the paper and notes, the movement into reading seemed more a natural thing.

The biggest problem was to have a gathering where the children would feel relaxed. We had several instructors who had their way of getting to the children, getting them to like you and to relax around you. These kids were young and that's why it was so delicate. We'd have their parents bring them to our concerts. We wanted them to be a part of everything we did. It got to the point where they were very relaxed around all these grown-ups and all the different lifestyles, African lifestyles, and they got used to all these different things. It was a whole process and it was daily. It got so that the kids always wanted to come to the UGMAA house. And during this time, we continued visiting the schools, playing for the children and talking with them about Louis Armstrong and Duke Ellington. We never received any money for doing it, but we were there.

We utilized this space to the point that the whole area started opening up. On Saturdays, it would be really colorful around the Shop. People would come out on the streets, come by the building, just to be there, because something was happening. It was a very fruitful period for us in a lot of ways, because we reached a lot of other people who we ordinarily didn't reach on regular occasions, such as the concerts. We had people who would then start coming to the concerts, who had never been before, had never heard the kind of music we were playing. These were all the people in the neighborhood, the African Americans living there. When they came to believe in us, they started supporting us in all kinds of ways, hooking us up with resources that we needed, just passing the word on from mouth to mouth, which enabled us to stretch out.

By this time, the personnel of the Ark was changing quite a bit. Between 1973 and 1976, a lot of the guys migrated to New York, some went to other places, and some just stopped playing. Many of the guys who went to New York got hooked into the avant-garde scene there, the loft scene that was happening in the 1970s, and they're still there doing it. Stanley Crouch, Arthur Blythe, Butch Morris, Wilber Morris, David Murray, Azar Lawrence, Will Connell—just a lot of the cats split for New York. They'd be asked by the cats back there, "What's happening? How come so many guys come from there?"

"Well, it's the Arkestra. We come out of the Ark," they'd say.

McCoy Tyner used to come out here and say, "Every time some cat plays, he's talking about Horace Tapscott and the Arkestra. Every time I've got somebody playing with me, he came out of your Ark."

When I go to New York, I'm accepted like I live there. One night a few years ago, I was back there and went to see the cats playing at Sweet Basil. Butch Morris was conducting David Murray's band, and they had Will and Wilber, also from the Ark, with them. I walked into the club and there was Butch leading the band, just like he did with us in the churches. The whole band saw me, stopped playing, stood, and clapped. People looked around and said, "What's happening?" Then Butch and the cats came over, and were hugging me and shit. It was something, man. It was out. I'd never experienced that. That's the first time I'd had a lump in my throat. I said, "I'll be damned." That was really beautiful.

These cats are steady, so we know it wasn't in vain, because they stayed on it. And they always come back to play. If we give a concert and they're in town, they come and play. They don't want their names advertised; they just want to sit in with the cats. One time we were playing at the Immanuel United Church of Christ and Azar Lawrence was visiting from New York. He had been gone a long time. He came in with his lady and sat down to listen. The next thing you know, he took his horn out and started walking down the aisle playing the tune. It stayed in his head and he still knew all the tunes. Those moments are nice, bright, and precious moments. The cats come out of nowhere and start playing. They're beautiful.

During another visit to New York, I saw my bass player, Marcus McLaurine, who used to be in the Ark. He came after these other cats. Marcus grew up in Omaha and came out of a group around Preston Love, who mentioned my name to him. When he came to Los Angeles, he was in his early twenties and hooked up with the Ark. He played with us for a while and then headed for New York in the later 1980s. He's made a name for himself there and is on a lot of new records that are coming out.

Meanwhile, other cats were starting to come around. Drummers Sonship Theus and Fritz Wise, bassist Roberto Miguel Miranda, pianist Nate Morgan, saxophonists Michael Session and Dadisi Komolafe, trumpeter Steve Smith, and some of the other cats were just teenagers and would be at rehearsals listening. It seemed that each time two or three of them left, four or five would come in their place, and they were all ready for it. Some of the cats were practicing to get in the Ark, because they were inspired by all these cats playing. There was always somebody stepping up with their instrument. It kept changing, but there was still a nucleus of seven or eight players who stayed for years, some up to the present.

Roberto was around twenty when I first met him. He hadn't been playing that long but he wanted to be part of the music. He had stopped running around with gangs and was working in the kitchen washing dishes at Shelly's Manne Hole, just to be around the music. His style was different then, but the cat was really starting to play and he was ready for an open scene like we had.

All the cats had a chance to do different things. That's what was so beautiful.

"I'd like to try this, Horace."

"Well, write it out, man."

"What do you think would happen if I do this?"

"Well, show me." You dig? "All the cats are here. Let's play it."

That's how our classes went. A cat would write something one night and the next day he'd hear it in our classes with the Ark. It might all be wrong, but the cat heard it and would say, "All I have to do now is this and that." Instead of me showing them on the blackboard, they had a chance to hear it and then work with it. We spent a lot of time playing and listening to each other's music, talking about it and adding to it, trying to find different ways to put it over. One time, we had a project where I had everybody in the band write one bar of music without seeing any of the others. The result was interesting. The cats really learned to play free, to explore.

Michael Session used to come around when he was young, around twelve or thirteen. When we played over at Nickerson Gardens in the projects, Michael would show up to admire Lester Robertson's old lady, Esther, who used to teach dance for us. He and his brother would be peeking in the window, watching Esther dance. He didn't make any moves toward the band until he was in his twenties. And he hadn't studied music at all until then. He and another guy started coming around, not saying anything, just hanging out. Then, a few years later, he came by and said he wanted to play in the band. We put him in a section. He was quiet and wouldn't take any solos for the first few months. He had to face the draft and went into the service for a few years. When he came back, he was ready. Since then, he's been a fireball in the Ark with a real distinct sound.

Dadisi Komolafe started coming around in the 1970s, but he was a very young kid then. He was a small cat who was hanging around the action, but wasn't playing anything. The next thing we knew, he'd picked up an instrument. He was just a real talented person. He picked it up, started playing, would come around the Ark all the time, just listening and then asking questions. He built up a sound on alto sax and flute. He later got in trouble with drugs and then jail, but he's coming back now and has a lot of support. He's a good cat, looking well and playing again.

Another high schooler who started coming around was Fritz Wise and he's been here ever since. I saw those hands of his grow fast and then become the fastest as time went on—strong, fast hands. Another drummer and high schooler, Sonship Theus, came around. His name then was Woody, until one day, he said, "I'm Sonship."

"Okay."

He was always an outstanding player, a special kind of player with a real gift for rhythm and sound. And Ndugu Chancler, another fine drummer, was around, though he didn't come by as much.

Saxophonist Gary Bias, Ray Brown, a trumpet player, and Reggie Lewis, a trombonist, all came out of the Ark, and played in the Earth, Wind, and Fire band. Vibraphonist Rickey Kelly also started coming around the Ark then.

People were always coming by the rehearsals. Sometimes the cats would bring them, and sometimes they'd just show up on their own to listen and check it out. A lot of cats were trying to get in the Arkestra, and many thought, at first, that because they couldn't read, they'd be turned down.

"I can't read."

I'd say, "Well, you're the first one we want."

That's how we did it, that and a cadre of people who stuck together, time after time after time. Even when we weren't playing, just being together, talking, and then playing, that strong binding brought others into us. Some might have needed guidance, and some maybe needed another avenue for their art. Whatever it was, the Ark was there, in the community, and the people knew us and appreciated it. We considered ourselves as carriers of the culture.

The Ark personnel had all experienced a personal calling of the creative soul to come together. "The Call" was felt by everyone, including the audience, some of whom later became members.

We never turned people away. But once I did have to fire two cats off the bandstand. It didn't have anything to do with the music; it was only because of serious disrespectfulness. One cat complained that he didn't get paid a certain amount of money and accused us of tricking him out of it. Well, that was all he had to say. I told him, "Man, if you ever get on a bandstand with me again, I'm going upside your head." I don't play that. "Get off! And don't come back anymore!" The first thing we were against was tricking each other. We never played together again. The other cat just didn't care enough about the music. He wouldn't show up for rehearsals; didn't think it was important enough. Then one day, after people started coming to hear the band, he wanted to get on stage. We didn't want him. I was on stage, and he grabbed my ankles.

"I could pull you down from there, if I wanted."

I said, "And I could step in your face, right now."

He cut me loose, and I never saw him again.

The musicians I like to play with are the ones who I still like being around when they don't have their instruments. There are a lot of cats who play good, but who you don't want to be around, who don't take care of business, who don't have any respect for the music, even if they're playing it. I don't need that. All my life I've been in music, so I don't treat it that way. It's something that's very necessary for me, and anybody who I deal with has to have that belief. The ego stuff is never a part of my agenda. I don't deal with egos. These are the kind of people who I avoid if possible. I won't let them hang me up and I'll avoid a gig rather than get in that kind of situation.

After a while, we started getting offers to do things in other neighborhoods. Can you believe that? But we stayed in that neighborhood, at Vermont and Eighty-fourth, until we couldn't hang there anymore. It got rough, economy wise, keeping up the overhead on the Shop and things like that. We did it as long as we could and had that place for four years before we had to move on.

Not long after we had moved into the print building, we also started rehearsing and performing at the Immanuel United Church of Christ on Eighty-fifth Street and Holmes Avenue. Reverend Edgar Edwards was the pastor and he allowed us to play in his church. I had seen this place in a vision before we got there. When I first saw it, I said, "This is it." I didn't get excited or anything. I knew. I just walked in and said, "Yeah. This is it." I saw it all, and the next thing I knew, we were in there.

We didn't have any plans to play in a church but the pastor was so cool and he was ready for it. I fell in love with this pastor, because he was different, a real deal preacher. He was what I used to look for in a churchman: a preacher in the community, one who was a part of the community and helped the community. They had a lot of brown people over there, poor, going to school, and he would feed these people every morning for free. He'd look for jobs for people. He took care of the community; even went to people's houses. That's what he'd use the church money for. He believed in it. That knocked me out. We wanted to be involved with that. So he invited us, and we became a part of it.

When we hooked up, the church was having problems. He didn't really have a congregation; there wasn't anyone coming to his church, and the New York organization that provided funding was thinking about stopping his money. So we played there on the second and last Sundays of the month for free, and started attracting an audience. Of course, we'd play elsewhere on the other Sundays, and the last few years at the church, we were just playing on the last Sunday. But this allowed the church to continue getting that money from New York, and it was fine with me. It made us feel good, because we were helping the church and the reverend continue.

Reverend Edwards was the first cat to have a sanctuary for "illegal aliens." There were all these cots set up in the gym part of the church, and all these Mexican cats, who couldn't speak English, from south of Guadalajara would sneak down into the church to listen to our rehearsals. We'd make sure there was an opening between the church and their sanctuary, so they could come through, listen, and go back without being seen from the outside by the sheriff. Once, the reverend took us up there to look around. I couldn't believe it. He had about twenty to twenty-five people who he was feeding and housing.

I loved that old man. He believed in what he was doing. And when he allowed us to have our music there, I knew it was the correct thing to do, and we kept on doing it.

When we first started playing, the concerts were called "The Seed," and we played upstairs in conjunction with another cultural organization. Then, we performed a sunrise Easter service concert downstairs in the sanctuary and soon moved down there for all our performances. For those Easter services, we'd have half a dozen trumpets and trombones standing outside the church, blowing as the sun came up. Then they'd march into the church, and we'd continue playing until about seven-thirty in the morning.

About our fourth year at the church, white families started coming to Eighty-fifth and Holmes, coming down into a section of the city where it was said white people were scared to go. We're talking about white families from Van Nuys in the San Fernando Valley bringing their babies to Eighty-fifth Street. Whatever it was they were coming for was stronger than what they were supposed to have feared. These cats would bring their families, kids jumping out of the cars and running around playing, and we never had any hassles. This was a changeover from one or two people in the audience to all kinds of people, coming from all over the city, and bringing their kids. Every time we'd have a packed crowd.

The reverend did have some problems with the other preachers down the street from the church. They complained, "What kind of music is going on in that church? This is blasphemy!" Those are the kinds of problems you had among your own kind. But the reverend was ready for them.

"Well, I read out of the same Bible that you read: 'And I heard the trumpets sound. Let the trumpet sound, let the sound of the music roar.'"

That was his backup, you dig?

The sheriff would come around to check it out all the time, but the music had gotten to the point where it just drew people from all over every time we played. It was nice to sit in that church with the cats playing and look around, at first to see an all-black crowd, then all of a sudden a mixed black and white crowd.

We also attracted all kinds of political groups. It wasn't anything for the Communist Party and other left-wing groups to be around at all our concerts. We accepted that right away; we knew who those people were. But then there were some others who started coming. It was very strange, and I knew some of these people had to be spies. We'd been through it before.

We even started having the white critics come into the neighborhood, because they'd heard about the Ark, and they started writing about us without anyone asking them. I didn't buy nobody no coffee. I didn't ask to get any special table for anyone. I didn't even speak to them; I'd walk past. But they'd write about the music and that's when they first started writing about me. But the first writers covering us were some black writers.

During this time, we were also being invited to places outside the community. We might be invited to play at a function in the Pasadena black community. Each cat might get fifteen dollars or so, but it was enough to buy some food and things for their families. And the gigs became pretty regular.

It seemed that we were reaching all areas of society. I even had doctors show up and then come to my home to give us free examinations. They said they wanted me to stay alive. Wasn't that nice? Those kinds of things you didn't expect. "Let me check out your children." And through all this, in a neighborhood supposedly known for thievery, you'd leave your car out, windows down, and all your shit in there. No problem. Now, that was worth more than making any money.

We left the church when Reverend Edwards died, nine years after our first rehearsal there. He was a hip old man. He was on it.

The Cerebral Aneurysm

One day during the summer of 1978, I was on my way somewhere. I got out of the car, and friends later told me that I started speaking randomly and going back into the past. I was getting pretty out. I even started pissing on myself. But I wasn't feeling any pain and I had no idea what was happening. They took me to the hospital. My son-in-law started calling all the smoke men that I'd dealt with. He thought I might have gotten some bad stuff, maybe been tricked with something. But all of them said they hadn't seen me in a while.

They took me to this small, west side hospital, and those people passed me onto Kaiser. I was in emergency for a while; a lot of people passed me by, and a few checked me out, then moved on. Finally, this one doctor came up, took a look at me, and started yelling, "Stat! This man's got ten minutes to live!" They got me stabilized, did a spinal tap, and ran all sorts of tests. When they got me awake enough with drugs, I was told by this doctor that I was having a cerebral aneurysm. I might live and I might not. I had confidence in this doctor, because we talked and he told me that he was in the Nazi concentration camps when he was a kid. He was a Jewish doctor and a straight-ahead kind of cat.

"Mr. Tapscott, all I can tell you is that you might not make it. Even if the operation is successful, you might not make it. But we have to operate, because if we don't, you will die for sure."

"Hey, go for it."

Just before the operation, I was in this room with these six other guys, four black males and two white. All these guys had aneurysms, and the doctors and nurses were talking to us. At one point, I went back into the past. It was 1953, and I was in the service. This nurse was standing next to me, and I looked up at her: "Bitch! Why you standing next to me?! I'll kill you! Get away from me!"

She said, "Okay, Mr. Tapscott," and patted me on the back.

Then I thought, "What am I doing?" It was like there were two of me, and one was saying to the other, "Why you doing that? Why you talking to her like that?"

"Damn, I got to get out of here and go over to the barracks."

"No, you don't."

"Yes, I do."

It was out.

While I was lying on the table during the surgery, I died—flat lined—for a few moments. Some other being was with me, and we were sitting off to the side. I looked over and saw myself, the nurses and doctors running. Someone came running up to the door and asked, "Is he going to make it?"

The nurse said, "I'm not sure."

Then I remember going down a dark area toward a light and coming to the end of this trail. There was my best friend, when I was seventeen years old. He was a trombone player, Arthone Elster, who had died when he was eighteen from leukemia. Arthone was there to greet me and called me by my nickname from the old days, "Hey, Ace, how you doin', man?" Behind him, people were dancing and waving at me. There was one girl, Lottie Mae, who was my next-door neighbor in Houston and who had died very young. She smiled at me. And there were some of my old relatives, just dancing. Arthone reached his hand out to me. All I had to do was step inside and continue this good feeling I had. Then a voice said, "You can stay here, Horace, if you like, but I know that you want to be at the Ark rehearsal." It was feeling so good that I damned near stayed. All I had to do was walk in through this gate. That's the last thing I remember, until I came to after the operation.

When I woke up, the first thing I did was try to move my fingers and then yelled, "I can move my fingers, Doc! I can move my fingers!"

They said they'd had a lot of problems with me. I started pulling the bandages off of my head, walking through the hospital buck naked, running through the halls trying to get out. Afterward, I couldn't remember doing any of this. It was something. I was in a coma for a while. Cecilia lost twenty-five pounds just coming to my bedside. It looked so bad for me that a radio station even started playing my music. They'd never played it much before. Yeah, I tricked them. But before I left the hospital, my doctor told me, "If you have another one, Horace, forget it. Just say 'bye.'"

I always had a lot of support, the whole time I was dealing with this. I'd wake up in the hospital and the room would be full of people. William Marshall would be the tallest one, standing in the back. They were all there waiting for me to wake up. One time I woke up and started yelling, "What you-all doing here?!" I was jumping on everybody. "Get out of here!"

"Okay, man, we're gone."

I put them all out.

Another next-door neighbor from the early days in Houston would visit me every day. Her name was Ernestine Davis, and we used to call her "Chicken." When we were kids, we used to walk together all the time. She was the only chick I had as a close friend. We were tight. She had become a nurse. I didn't know it at the time but she had been diagnosed with cancer. I couldn't talk but she was at my bedside every morning; just rallied me up, giving me inspiration. And all the time, she was dying of cancer. By the time I got out of the hospital a few months later, she had died.

As I came back, could reason, and was starting to feel like myself again, I walked out of my room to go see these six other cats who had the aneurysms. Every one of them had died. I'll never forget that. I was the only one who survived it. I spent a year recovering in our back room at home, staring out the window at the trees, trying to get my thought pattern together, and thinking of those other guys dying and my surviving it.

Being laid up as long as I was, I traveled inward a lot. Cats told me after that my playing had changed. The music was the same, but the approach seemed different to them. An experience like this has to affect you, even in ways you might not be aware of, but I couldn't see anything in me changing. I didn't feel different and I still thought the same as before. I knew what my interests were and I just continued straight ahead. I don't think my music has changed much or evolved, although it has deepened.

When I finally got out of the hospital at the end of 1978, some friends had a party for me at a club near Redondo and Pico Boulevards. Charles Owens was playing when I walked through the door. He looked over and said, "Damn! Ghosts! Ghosts in the house!" I almost looked like one. I was moving pretty slow and my head was still bald. My son Darion delayed his wedding until I got out. But he had to dress me and hold me up for the ceremony.

It took me about a year or so to get most of my memory back. I went to New York in early 1979, and all I could remember was the piano and the tunes I played. I met Art Davis and Roy Haynes, and we cut an album there called *In New York*. But everything else was blank, a few bits and pieces, but really nothing. I talked to Melba Liston, who had a stroke a few years later, and she said the same thing. The music was still there, but she couldn't remember most of the other things.

During those days the greatest thing happened to me. I got something I needed when I was on the radio at either KPFK or KCRW. While I was being interviewed, the telephone rang. It was a woman calling from almost her deathbed in the hospital to tell me that my music had helped to heal her, someone with a real soft voice, sobbing as she spoke, like she had been under some kind of dark cloth, saying that finally some light came in because of the sounds.

"Thank you so very much for playing and please don't stop."

I never knew her name, never met her. I don't know if she's still alive or not. But what she said to me justified everything that I believed in. There wasn't anything happening money-wise and sometimes you're down in the dumps, but you have to pull your head up. When things like that happen, those little small things, well, that was the idea of the sounds in the first place.

There were still times ahead when I needed that kind of support. A few years later, in 1990, I had to deal with another aneurysm when it happened to my second son. Vincent was a silent cat, real black and beautiful. He was always aware of what was going on around him and had a great personality, a charisma that brought people to him. He married Paula out of high school, and they had five kids, plus one from Vincent's earlier girlfriend. Not long after graduating from Crenshaw High School, he had to go into the army and was sent overseas. After his experience in Vietnam, something happened to him mentally. He came out of the service very sick. Then, some years later, Paula was murdered and it became very hard for him, trying to raise those kids and all. But he never complained.

About a year after Paula's death, he started having these head-aches. He called me one day and said he couldn't stop the head-aches. I went over to the pad and held him in my arms, waiting for the paramedics. He said, "Dad, it hurts." Finally the paramed-ics came, and I told them my son was probably having a stroke. They took him to the hospital in Marina del Rey and put him on life support. But I told them to pull the plug, that he was dead. He had died in my arms at the pad from the same thing I had—a cerebral aneurysm. He was a good cat. It was too bad he couldn't last longer.

Movements to the Present

13

After we closed the Shop, we fell back on the Western Avenue house near Twenty-fourth Street. We still had the office there, but now we took over the whole place. It was a big, two-story, twelve- or thirteen-room building, which was later torn down to make way for a whole apartment complex. There were a few places like this that were usually run by various organizations. They weren't really homes; no one lived there, although one of the band members had been living in this house for a while. One of the caretakers, a landlord-type cat, dug us and let us have this house for a minimal amount of rent.

A lot of cats started living there, and sometimes it got pretty crazy with all the activity—some cats sleeping, some playing, and others drifting in and out. Michael Session called it Quagmire Manor and later wrote a tune about it, "Quagmire Manor at 5 A.M." Steve Turre passed through on his way to New York and stayed with us for a year or two. All kinds of cats used to come by, including a lot of the older musicians and some of the Central Avenue cats, like Roy Porter and Buddy Harper, and they'd listen. Here was a band that was rehearsing all the time, and a lot of them would bring their music. Here was a chance to get it played. When Buddy Harper died, Jesse Sharps was passing by his place and he found all of Buddy's music piled up on the front curb for the garbage truck. He picked up every bit of it, and we saved it.

We moved into the Western Avenue house before I had the aneurysm, and it lasted into the early 1980s, about 1980 or 1981. That was the last UGMAA house. Cats started leaving, again some going to New York and other places as well. By then, a lot of our activities had been cut back and, for the size we had, we didn't really need the house. We could always find someplace to rehearse. Sometimes, we'd be at my house near Crenshaw High School. Cecilia and I had moved the family here in 1966. We also had a couple of places nearby in the village, before it became famous as Leimert Park. The artists were already there, and by the mid-1980s, we were set up in a studio. It's funny how we'd just set up in places and then they'd become something. Now, Leimert Park and Degnan Boulevard have become a cultural center.

In the late 1970s, early 1980s, Degnan Boulevard had all these little stores, small businesses like cosmetics and such, that closed down. There were a lot of vacant places, and the artists started moving in. The first thing that appeared was this art gallery run by these two brothers. A drummer, Carl Burnett, opened a performance space around the corner on Forty-third Street, and cats would come and play on the weekends. It got pretty popular. Kamau Daáood then found a space on Degnan Boulevard, and told me and Billy Higgins about it. The three of us opened it as a performance center and called it the World Stage. That was in the late 1980s, after the Olympics in Los Angeles. Carl's place had closed up and we took over, musically, in the area.

By the early 1990s, the World Stage had taken off, and more clubs and enterprises were opening—a dance studio, art galleries, clothing stores, a book and record shop, 5th Street Dick's for food and music, and Babe's and Ricky's Inn for blues. Ben Caldwell opened KAOS, a place for the youngsters to go, and that's a godsend to the community, because it keeps the youngsters together. It's an important spot for the hip-hop generation, a place where there are regular performances of their music. But the main function is to teach youngsters about TV and movie production, learning all the technical things that go into producing shows and films. Ben was another of those persons who had an idea and wanted to contribute something. He went to film school at UCLA and used to teach at

Howard University in Washington, D.C.—used to teach about me—and then decided to come back out here and get KAOS going.

Now, all generations are in this village, the music of all generations, and there's no crime on the boulevard. The area can still use a lot of help, but it has maintained itself and is growing.

The UGMAA Foundation is still going. There's David Bryant, Marla Gibbs, William Marshall, and some of the other people who have worked with us still around. We use the foundation to support specific events and things of that sort. If we can get the Ark settled into playing in one spot, once a week, then it might become even more of a force again.

Recording the Music

By the late 1970s, I hadn't recorded any of my music since *The Giant Is Awakened* session with Bob Thiele in 1969. We talked about forming our own record company, but we didn't have the resources to follow through on it. In 1978, though, two people who had followed the Ark for many years got involved with us to change that: Toshiya Taenaka and Tom Albach.

Tosh was a student at Polytechnic High School in Los Angeles and had been following our music. He enjoyed it so much, he told us that one day he was going to come back and record us when he made some money. That's eventually what he did. A few years later, Tosh wrote me a letter and said that he was finally in a position to do it. If I would agree, he'd start recording. That's how I started with Interplay Records, a label he put together.

I did *Songs of the Unsung* with him, which was my first solo album, in February 1978. The following January, after I'd recovered enough from the aneurysm, we went to New York and did the *In New York* date for Interplay with Art Davis and Roy Haynes. Nica, the Baroness de Koenigswarter, was there for two days. She wanted me to spend some time with Thelonious Monk, but we never hooked up.

People have talked about my music as post-Monk or whatever, and I don't mind. It's just that the only encounter me and Monk ever had was over a blond at the Five Spot in New York, when I was back there with Hamp's band. Clark Terry and I went to the club with these two Danish ladies. Lester was supposed to have one of them, but was somewhere else. So Clark Terry walked up and said to the one, "Hey baby, don't you know who I am?"

"Who?"

"I'm Clark Terry, baby!"

"Who?"

"That's all right, baby, you'll know who I am sooner or later."

So we went to the Five Spot, and this blond was sitting next to me, up front, close to the piano. Monk was playing and just staring at the blond. He started gesturing to me, and I shook my head no. That was my one encounter with Monk, and we didn't say one word.

By the early 1980s, Tosh was spending most of his time in Tokyo, working with his dad in the import/export business. He did record me a few more times until around 1983, but as far as I know, those sessions haven't been released. I've heard stories about some of them being released in Japan. A ten-minute version of "Sketches of Drunken Mary" that I did with Roberto and Everett in 1983 appeared on a Japanese CD in 1990, called *Modern Jazz Piano Forum*. I didn't know anything about it. When I saw the CD seven years later, that was the first time I became aware of it. This was done without my permission, and I haven't seen any money. I hope there aren't any more CDs like that. I don't want Tosh to become a dishonorable person in this country.

Aside from Tosh, the only person who wanted to record us was this six-foot, blond, blue-eyed, German American cat, Tom Albach, my man, who used to come down to the neighborhood. I noticed him years before we hooked up. Wherever I was, he'd always be there and he never said anything to me. He came to our concerts for four or five years without saying anything, just listening. He never bugged us, and after each performance, he'd say good-bye and leave.

Then one day, he suggested doing some recordings at the church, the Immanuel United Church of Christ, and founded Nimbus Records to do it. Tom had never had anything to do with the music business. He was a gambler, a successful one, and put out all his own money, rented the best equipment for us, and brought in some new pianos. He loved the music and he loved the way we were doing it. It was raw, and he wanted it in that form, not messed up in a studio.

Tom was always real strong in his beliefs and that would get him into trouble sometimes. But I liked that he was always up front about everything. It got to the point where the cats began to trust him and looked forward to his being there. He said what he had to say and got the respect of everybody; came and told his story, and took care of a lot of the cats, helped the ones who needed it to get back on their feet. If someone in the band was in trouble, he was there. He'd help cats with jail trouble or help them keep their pad, their car. Tom became a household word, and all those guys never forgot that.

The first recordings, beginning in early 1978 and going through mid-1979, were of the Ark. Those first three albums — *Flight 17, The Call,* and *Live at the I.U.C.C.* — were raw. Some of our best recordings were done in the Immanuel United Church of Christ. And I liked the way they were recorded, because it was just the way we performed there and in various places. I knew they could have been better in terms of recording technique, but it was the kind of sound I wanted.

Most of the music on those three albums was written by members of the Ark. "Flight 17" was written by Herbert Baker, while he was a student at Dorsey High School. He died before he graduated, at the age of seventeen in a car wreck one night. I'd known him since he was a babe in arms, and he was just a natural musician. He was always coming around when he was very young and he was at *The Giant Is Awakened* recording session when he was about fifteen or sixteen. We dedicated that first Ark album to his memory.

We then did some small-group recordings — duos, trios, sextets — and between 1982 and 1984, recorded the solo piano sessions at the Lobero Theater in Santa Barbara. It was a great time, an artistic time, and Tom just loved the art. When I was putting my albums together, I decided what was going on the albums. Just me. That's why I agreed to record with Tom, and he kept his word. He was the only one. Tom Albach was an important part of what we did. He's got a niche in the Arkestra that no white has ever had.

Not long after the Ark sessions, we started talking about who else in the band to record. There were a lot of little groups that had formed within the Ark, and they were writing and rehearsing all the time. By the mid-1980s, Nimbus had albums of groups led by Linda Hill, Dadisi Komolafe, Nate Morgan, Roberto Miguel Miranda, Gary Bias, Adele Sebastian, Curtis Clark, Jesse Sharps, and Rickey Kelly. Most of the music on these albums was their own, and most of the sidemen on those were Ark members, as well as other musicians who supported what we were doing, like Billy Higgins.

I was continuing to compose as well during this time. Through the years, I've noticed that just before I write a tune, there comes this loud ringing in my ear. The next thing I know, I'm writing a tune. I've never tried to figure out why. It just happens that way. Sometimes the whole tune is in my head. They come to me at all times, in all kinds of situations, and it's always the music first. A piece like "Mothership"—I don't know where it came from. I just sat down one day and wrote it. Afterward, I find the titles or themes that seem to fit the music. The mothership was the ark, the vessel that saves the music after the forty-day flood of commercialism.

Even if I begin with a musical idea, a line, or even a complete composition, I'll associate it with other ideas or people when picking a title. "The Dark Tree," for example, has to do with the tree of life of a race of people that was dark, and everybody went past it and all its history. The whole tree of a civilization was just passed over and left in the dark, but there it still stood. Musically, though, "The Dark Tree" began as a dance. I took the rhythm from Desi Arnaz doing "Babalú." Yeah, I loved Desi Arnaz and the rhythms he had going, reaching back to the Afro-Cuban roots. By the time I finished that tune, it scared me because of that rhythm. I could hear all these drums, down low, playing that rhythm and telling me something was coming. Since I was a kid, I've had that feeling— expectant, ominous—about drums, and I've built a lot of tunes off that drumbeat. We used to play a piece called "Warriors All" that had that same feeling. One time, Kamau Daáood came up to us and said, "Please don't play that anymore, Horace." It got him depressed, sad, crying, because it called up so much from the past.

I use a lot of different rhythms, meters, in my compositions, but it's something that just comes from the rhythms of everyday life. When I'm walking down the street, I might do something in five, or I might do something in six that could run into five. I might see somebody walking and think what time is that. Every day, you see different patterns and rhythms going on, and it's just paying attention to what's around you.

I've recorded mostly my music, but I also play and have recorded some standards, like "Oleo," " 'Round Midnight," "Now's the Time," "Alone Together," "Lush Life," ones that I really enjoy. I like a lot of standards, and if I have the chance in the future, I'll record more. Cecilia wants me to record with piano and strings. But first, I want to get down all my stuff, originals by myself and some other cats.

An International Audience

We once had an offer to play at the first Pan-African Festival in West Africa. Earlier, many of the Africans who were visiting or going to school here and living in Brentwood, far from the neighborhood, would come to our concerts. They didn't really have any hookup with the rest of the African Americans. But they dug our music, and arranged, through this African American organization in Washington, D.C., to send us thirty passports, so the Ark could play at this festival. About one week before our departure, the people in Washington "lost" our passports. Only ours were lost. They had musicians from the East Coast and elsewhere going, but ours they couldn't find. We worked hard to get thirty passports for all these people, including Ark families, to go overseas, waiting to go to mother Africa, and these cats lost them.

My son-in-law and I spent money out of our own pockets to take a trip to Washington, D.C., to meet with one of these cats who said he was going to help us. This was a guy who used to be here, used to be in the community, and was a community leader with his group of actors and actresses, just like UGMAA. He had told us, "Oh, Horace, it's going to be great when I get to Washington and I'm sitting in the chair of the National Endowment for the Arts. I'm going to take care of my people back there, because you all deserve it."

We were there an hour early for a nine o'clock Monday morning appointment. We waited and waited. Well, the cat never showed up. We called around, and he couldn't be found. And I'd known this guy a long time. That night, we had to catch a plane and come all the way back with nothing. I haven't talked to him since.

This had nothing to do with race; this had to do with class. Because it was the black cats in Washington who did it to us. After that first festival, they found our passports and sent them back. That was cold-blooded. I've had a lot of things happen to me, but that was so cold. For whatever reasons, some black people didn't want to deal with us. So we just stayed here, in our community. That was a great disappointment. The cats were ready, the families were all excited, and some of the Ark members were even planning on staying over there.

In the 1970s, I started getting more attention throughout Europe. It happened because a lot of the guys going back and forth mentioned my name, or people would read that they had played with me. The attitude seemed to be, "Well, I want to see this guy who we hear so much about." That's how it began. When a lot of our guys left Los Angeles to go back East, or whenever they traveled abroad, they'd talk about Los Angeles. Horace Silver said, "Man, I'd been hearing about you twenty years before I met you."

And McCoy Tyner told me, "There ain't no music coming from out there, unless your name is on it."

Europe has always been great. I've been over there solo, with small groups, and with the Ark. And the people over there know the history; they ask me about all the musicians in the Ark, even about some who haven't played with us in years. But they know and they ask me why Americans don't recognize their own classical music. Sometimes, they talk about America so bad that *I've* got to take up for America!

I love the theaters over there, especially the amphitheaters. I'll never forget a concert we played in Verona, Italy. Andrew Hill and I were on stage for a sound check. While Andrew played without a microphone, he could be heard everywhere throughout the theater. I couldn't get over it. They also had the greatest equipment. Andrew and I went backstage, and the cat asked us which piano we'd like to use. We saw all these pianos back there, covered up, and had our choice of a couple of Boesendorfers and Steinways. They were all locked up and covered with red velvet cloth. Nobody messes with the piano but the pianist. They don't allow anybody to touch it, except the cat who's going to play it. There's nothing like playing over there. They recognize the art. They love it and respect it like a dog.

During the 1980s, I had opportunities to play with a lot of great cats, pianists who are good friends, cats who I've been listening to for years and admire—Andrew Hill, Cecil Taylor, Mal Waldron, and Randy Weston. These cats are like brothers to me. Mal is the older brother, Randy's next, then Cecil, me, and Andrew. Whenever they're in town, they're over here eating. One night Andrew, Mal, and Randy were over here, and you talk about cats eating. They hadn't had any home cooking in a long time!

Mal is direct, consistent, and has never changed. He's always had a sound he believed in. We played together in Santa Barbara once, two pianos, and it worked. A few years later, I did a two-piano thing with Cecil Taylor. In 1984, Randy, Andrew, and I had a piano summit in Los Angeles at the Wilshire Ebell Theatre. It was fun, each of us playing two sections of the concert. We've been talking about doing it again. Randy has tried to get all of us over to Morocco for a gig, along with Mal and maybe Abdullah Ibrahim, but it hasn't worked out yet.

Cecil will let you know that there are so many sounds left unheard and untouched on the piano. The way he hits the keys is just different from everybody else, but all these cats are like that, individual approaches, and probably more with Cecil than anybody. He has just broadened our music so much. He plays piano like it's a full orchestra. Randy, on the other hand, gets off into exotic rhythm lines and adds all these other colors coming out of those lines. Andrew approaches things more like Cecil. When I hear his music, I hear all natural instruments being played. Each of these guys have in common the way they set a theme that seems to roll through the whole composition and keeps everything intact and on course. When I listen to music and buy CDs, it's the music of these cats. I love to listen to it, and we're all hooked up.

In 1988, I joined with John Carter, Bobby Bradford, Arthur Blythe, James Newton, Roberto Miguel Miranda, and Donald Dean as the Together Again band for a few gigs. It was nice playing with these cats, and Cecil, Mal, Andrew, and Randy, because I admire their consistency. They're still here, doing what they started doing back then, adding to it, but still doing it their way. I knew they were real men when I met them.

About twenty years ago, I was working these concerts in Oakland with Andrew Hill and groups like Bebop and Beyond. I noticed that every time I played, there'd be this young Chinese kid sitting up front and bowing to me. Finally, he came up and introduced himself as a high school student and a pianist who really enjoyed my music. He said his name was Jon Jang. Year after year I'd come up there, and year after year Jon would be there. We started growing, and he started asking questions. He wanted to know about the Pan Afrikan Peoples Arkestra. That interested him, because he was tired of what was happening to the Chinese people in this country and he wanted to get something across musically. So he figured he'd do it the way we did it down here and created the Pan Asian Arkestra. Through the years, he's grown to the point where he's going to China, to Beijing. Jon's now established himself as a cat to be dealt with.

After a while, we got to the point where we were pretty tight. He started writing me and sending me things, inviting me to different places, to his wedding. Jon recently arranged for me to do the music for the seventeenth Asian American Jazz Festival in San Francisco in May 1998. They commissioned me to compose for it, and I wrote a piece called *Two Shades of Soul*. It was a good experience for me and I got a chance to explore, working with Jon and the other musicians. Chinese music has never been foreign to me, because I can hear a lot of things within it. And when I was growing up in Houston, there was a Chinese guy who used to run the local food store across the street from us and who would let us have food when we needed it just by signing a piece of paper. He was the first Asian I'd seen in my life. I've never forgotten that and have always felt a kind of kinship with the Chinese people. The San Francisco festival gave me the chance to put images like that together in my mind. In *Two Shades of Soul,* I was able to write my version of how I see Chinese living under the stresses and strains.

Piano Player in the Hood

I've done some rap recordings with my other son-in-law, Darryll, who's JMD of the Underground Railway, Nedra Wheeler, and the Freestyle Fellowship—four real-talented young brothers. They were doing some pieces talking about the community and they got me in on it. We did a piece called "Hot" together. I'm on two or three parts of the rap, just jamming, no rapping. I left that to those guys. They also did one piece called "O.G.—Piano Player in the Hood." (That's what they call the older guys in the neighborhood, O.G.s.) Now that was nice. I wasn't on that one but the cats were reaching back and respecting.

Not long ago, I was playing at the World Stage on Degnan Boulevard in Leimert Park and I walked around the corner to Ben Caldwell's place, KAOS, where some of the young brothers were playing. One of the cats saw me come in and started into a rap with "There's a legend in the house." They kept on playing and they were poppin'.

I've also done a session with some rappers in Atlanta. Amil Gibbs ("Game") asked me to do a demo—"Rewind Time"—with them. And these kids pay you good!

"Here you go, pops."

I've had chances to stretch out with these cats, playing and talking with them. I started telling these young rappers that their music has been happening for years. They got real interested, and I told them to check out people like Louis Jordan. *Know* that nothing in the music is just beginning. It's all come out of the black community and has been for years. All you have to do is ask. They have to realize that they're taking up and adding to what had come before, and talking about the same kinds of things. The only difference now is the profanity, but the subjects are the same.

One thing I like about the hip-hop generation now is that their minds are opening up. They're intelligent in the first place, but now they're opening up to the hows and whys of rap, and where did it come from, and how does it hook up to the past and the present. The hip-hop generation has found out about the Watts Prophets—Brother Amde, Brother Richard Dedeaux, and Brother Otis O'Solomon. They've found out about them and they love them. They've started realizing that they are part of a long cultural tradition. And by this, they're starting to understand what their position is and then taking it to another level. They're realizing they don't have to use all the profanity, only when it's necessary. They're starting to understand what it's all about.

The Ark into the 1990s

In the 1980s and 1990s, we've had new people coming around the band. Billy Hinton, James Andrews, Mike Daniels, Vergilio Figueroa, Kafi Roberts, Sabir Mateen, and Kamonta Polk came in the 1980s. Bill Madison came back then, and his son, Archie Johnson, a trombone player, joined us. The Ark started changing and has been really Pan Afrikan. Some of the guys have come from different countries, from West Africa, East Africa, the Caribbean, Brazil. I featured them in September 1993 at the Los Angeles Festival. On the last day, Degnan Boulevard was closed off and a bandstand set up by the park. The Ark closed the festival that day. We were thirty-pieces strong and did my composition, *Ancestral Echoes,* just one piece for the whole concert. I wrote it about 1968, and it had only been performed once before, never recorded. The Watts Symphony performed it at the Los Angeles Music Center in October 1976. The piece is scored for something much bigger than the Ark. But for the Los Angeles Festival, we had all these cats there and these dancers. It was really something else. These cats are bringing in their renditions of the music to the Ark and enhancing it, just expanding it. Same blood, but different cultures, and they're coming together. The music of the Ark hasn't changed much but expanded or grown from our foundation.

Over the years, we've had a few white musicians playing in the Ark. Vinny Golia has been around us since the early 1970s, and he calls me all the time: "Hey, I want to play." Joshua, this Jewish cat, plays saxophone with us. We saw him playing outside the Music Center in downtown Los Angeles one night, doing his Coltrane shit, and hooked up with him. He's never given us his last name. When cats asked him, he just said, "Joshua."

"All right. Joshua."

There's also Alex Cline, drummer, percussionist. Because of his playing, he fit right in. Cecilia loves his playing, along the lines of Sonship.

But the Pan Afrikan Peoples Arkestra was, and is, a lot more than an Arkestra. Many families that had been broken up because of the cats doing their music, came together again when they got involved in the Arkestra. A lot of things happened because of the Arkestra; things outside of music happened because of the Arkestra and its calling different groups together. We were the reason a lot of other groups—nonmusical, nonartistic groups—came together to better their community, to do little things that they hadn't thought about doing before but was brought to their attention by the Ark. You know how music can.

Many people began and developed their artistic lives because of the Ark. People in our audiences would be inspired to do so many things. Some, who became writers, started by sitting in one of our audiences. People have come up and told me, "The Ark allowed me to be introduced to my wife."

"The Ark allowed me to do something with my kids."

Some of them might not have remembered the music but they do remember being there and being a part of it, and raising their children around it. So we've had a function: the only group, outside the church, that came together all the time. People saw it and people had a part in it.

That made more sense to me than just making the records—being able to put your hands on somebody. When people in our band would get pregnant, we made sure to be around for the baby's birth and have a party. When the child would come out, we'd be there playing for him or her. Some cat might write a tune about the newborn right then and there. We certainly had our hassles, but it was a lot of fun.

People now come up to us, saying, "I remember when I was a kid this group was together. Wow, you all are still playing." They're grown up and here are these same guys, their hair a little grayer, they move a littler slower, but they're still playing great. And that in itself is a real reward. The real struggle has been to prove the point that it can be done. "I believe this and I'm staying here, and this will work. Believe me, believe me, believe me. Watch me, watch me, watch me. I'm here, I'm here, I'm here."

Now, I get asked questions on gigs at colleges about all of this and I look forward to telling this story to an audience of American kids of all races. I look forward to the young people changing this whole thing up and to there being a multiracial society. But you have to have a background for all this, and we are the background. We were on the front line for a purpose. We don't know what's going to happen next, only that we have done our job, and we want to see that this next group, that wants to take us to that place, doesn't have to cross this pit.

14

I'm pretty much satisfied with my life up to this point, musically. I have no regrets. None. I'm cool with the way I've done it. I'm still here and healthy enough, and I've got a large family that's still supporting me regardless. They think their old man's a crazy nut; they treat me like I'm out, but they still support me. I've got one grandson, Cabell, who collects all my stuff, plaques and notices about where I play, and puts them on his wall. Isn't that nice? He'll see me and just grin, because his parents, Barbara and Darion, will have told him another story about me.

Cabell and Martin, another grandson, are both learning to play the drums. Cabell's daddy, Darion, is a natural for the drums, but he never played. We bought him a set of drums, but he never wanted to be a professional musician. My oldest son, Laurence, is a hell of a pianist and also writes, but he only plays in his back room; he never plays in public. Sometimes, he'll be back there and he might let me hear something that he wrote. He's damn near seven feet tall and he's sounding like Randy Weston. He *plays*.

Renée's daughter, Raisha, my six-foot-one granddaughter, plays the flute with me every now and then, when she gets serious. She's been through Crenshaw High School and the army, and is now back. I told her that when she's ready, she can come here in the back room again, because she's got the chops and the ability to learn real quick.

My kids, and now the grandkids, grew up as I did in creative surroundings. It's been quite an experience for me as an individual and as a father, even though it was strange.

"The Tapscott's house, that's a strange house."

Strange in the sense that it's cool; they all liked it. I'd take my kids to the most wanted and unwanted places, so they would have all of it. They'd get a sense of the whole and where they might fit in; they'd know what was going on, and that they must have a part in it and contribute, as they saw it. Every one of them had different ideas about one thing or another. The basics were the same, but they had different ways of approaching the world, because they were shot out there, exposed to it. They got to know all kinds of personalities and weren't afraid of anybody. The kids could walk up to a person and say, "Hello, how are you doing?" and talk to him, regardless of whether he was acting crazy. My daughter, Renée, would walk up and say, "Hi," and he'd come out of his act, because here's somebody who really meant it.

Those are the things I thought about passing on to my children and for them to pass on to their children, to reach an area where you can be respected for being who you are and what you contribute, and that you're part of this society, as much as anybody else. And to appreciate differences, because that's what nature is all about: differences. All of it together makes one beautiful landscape. All these different colors can be put together to make the picture we're after. But people have to be treated equally, before you can get the best out of everyone.

That's the way I see it, and everything we see is like that. Everything that we feel seems to be like that. And that's the way I walk. That's why I love traveling, going someplace and listening, and looking, and understanding about the human race. What's happening with the human race, regardless of what all of us have been taught. What is happening with the human race as a whole and what is your part in this.

That kind of thinking gets confusing sometimes, because it's like running through a maze. But it's a way of life that I guess I've chosen to live, though it is flexible. It has to be flexible, but it has to have a base on which to be flexible. It's not one of those rays that just shoots through and brilliantly clarifies for a moment, before disappearing. It still has a foundation to it. It's like the Ark itself—a saving, preserving kind of attitude, like the trees. The roots are still there, but it's flexible. It might grow this way. I always had to keep that in mind.

Sometimes I get to the point where I want to communicate so badly, because I want to reach people as a way toward reaching "Peace, and to all people, goodwill." If people can do it for one week at Christmas, you know it can happen. It's like Negro history. When it began, it was Negro History Week. You had a week to realize that Negroes existed. Then a few decades later, it became Negro History Month, although it seemed strange to be set in the shortest month of the year. But today, the African American can be appreciated all year long for his and her contributions. We're just part of society now. If you're going to have a holiday, let's have a holiday for the human race.

All those are small things, but all my life those little old things are like ticks on me, chinches in the bed. You're trying to sleep on a good mattress, and the chinches are biting you, but the bed seems comfortable. That's what it's been, those little old small things.

Keeping the Motion

I'm still at it. I don't have a regular practice or warm-up routine, because I'm playing all the time. But there are certain things I practice, like compositions of other writers that I might want to play or record. I've been practicing one piece, a suite by R. Nathaniel Dett called *In the Bottoms.* This is in keeping with my goal of exposing black composers, known and unknown. But that's as far as it goes. Sometimes, I might sit at the piano for fifteen minutes or so and just go back and forth with two fingers, getting inside those fingers. Mostly, my warm-up and practice is long walks and stretching my arms and fingers, just loosening up. Before a concert, I'll go in the dressing room, shut the door and be quiet, talk to the spirits for a moment, and then split.

I still enjoy performing before an audience. There's nothing like working with a bunch of people, playing the music, everybody

giving their share, and the audience involved with it and respond-
ing. I love it. And, fortunately, I'm at the point where I can travel
around the world and feel good about traveling. I just take my
old lady with me and we just enjoy it, making that contribution
toward what Duke always called good music. His music wasn't jazz
or swing music; it was just good music. And that's the way I wanted
to do it. I wanted to be able to play good music every time I performed. You can call it this and you can call it that, but to me it's
all blues. And what I play are African American classics.

I travel some each year and have been to Europe quite a bit. One
of my favorite musicians, Benny Carter, came with an entourage
to see me one night a few years ago at Catalina's Bar and Grill
in Hollywood. Benny had been traveling all over the world, and
people were always asking him about Horace Tapscott. He said,
"I wanted to find out who they were talking about." Afterward,
Benny told me, "I don't play it but I enjoy it. I know where you're
coming from." Not long after that, I went overseas, and we were
on the same gig together in Italy for his eighty-second birthday.
That was a great feeling, moments like that with a great artist, one
of the greatest of all time.

Because of all this traveling recently, I've had to spend time on
airplanes. I still remember looking up at them with my mother,
when I was a kid. I didn't think anything special, except for what
my mother would say, "Ain't nothing supposed to fly but a bird."
She never got on an airplane. "The only way I'll get on an airplane
is if you're shipping my body back." Now, of course, I have to fly
and I'm used to traveling on airplanes. But when I board and I'm
settling into my seat, waiting for the rest of the people, listening
to that chatter all the way down the plane, this voice comes above
all the rest and says, "Ain't nothing supposed to fly but a bird." And
there I am, shook up like clabbered milk. Then the motors start,
and I know I've got to go to Europe. I always go through that,
each time, and the cats in the band mess with me.

It seems that there are more people interested in recording us
these days. We've done some CDs for hat ART and Arabesque, and
there are some tapes circulating with other companies. We'll see.
Most of these are with small groups, but I'd like to have another

(Above) Pan Afrikan Peoples Arkestra at Foshay Junior High School, early 1980s. Left to right: Sabir Mateen, Lawrence Kafi Roberts, Kamonta Polk, Jesse Sharps, Adele Sebastian, Horace, Herbert Callies, Linda Hill, and Bill Madison.

(Right) In performance, early 1980s.

With Cecilia, May 1982.

Jazz Center of New York concert, early 1980s.

(Above) Los Angeles Mayor Tom Bradley presenting Horace with an award from the city of Verona, Italy. (©BonGiovanni.)

(Right) World Piano Summit, 1984.

An Evening of Improvisational Solo Piano

WORLD PIANO SUMMIT

featuring

Randy Weston, Andrew Hill and Horace Tapscott

Friday, February 17, 1984 8 p.m.
Wilshire Ebell Theatre
4401 West 8th Street
(near Wilshire & Crenshaw)
Los Angeles, CA 90005

For ticket information please call the theatre at (213) 939-1128

Produced by David Keller and Nimbus Records

With mom, Mary Lou
Malone.

(Below, left) Monk solo
series, 1984.

(Below, right) Reverend
Edwards, minister of
the Immanuel United
Church of Christ and
co-coordinator of the
Pan Afrikan Peoples
Arkestra "Last Sunday
of the Month
Concerts."

The Smithsonian Resident Associate Program
and District Curators Inc. present

THE THELONIOUS MONK
SOLO PIANO SERIES
Vol. 1

featuring
HORACE TAPSCOTT
and RANDY WESTON

Friday, June 8, 1984
8 p.m.

BAIRD AUDITORIUM
National Museum of Natural History

Presented with support from the
National Endowment for the Arts

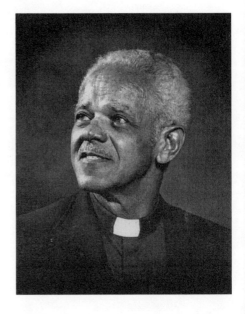

With Cecilia in New York, 1992. (Photo by Craig Anthony.)

(Below) Outside the Village Vanguard, New York City, 1992. Left to right: Roberto Miguel Miranda, Horace, and Fritz Wise.

For Lester Robertson, April 1993.

(Below, left) Australia, 1994.

MISSING FROM MIFA
Contemporary Jazz ignored in this year's Melbourne International Arts Festival

Is Horace Tapscott the greatest pianist you've never heard of?

Based in Los Angeles since the mid-1940s, Horace began his career working with such names as Dexter Gordon, Lionel Hampton, Eric Dolphy, Don Cherry, Gerald Wilson and Sonny Criss. He made a great album with Arthur Blythe in 1969. More recently, he has recorded albums with sidemen like Roy Haynes, Andrew Cyrille and John Carter. So why haven't you heard of him until now?

Instead of trying to make a name for himself in New York, Horace has spent his career in Los Angeles, playing creative music, recording for small independent labels and working to forge a bond between his Pan-Afrikan Peoples Arkestra and the local black community. It hasn't made him rich or famous, but his peers regard him as a giant of American music. Here's your chance to hear why.

"Horace Tapscott is an unsung genius of creative black music, and he deserves your attention."
The Wire (UK)

"Tapscott has developed a personal style out of Monk. He can spank the keys percussively or caress them tenderly, splash extravagant chords or slice them lean and razor-sharp." Down Beat

"He is a tremendously powerful and original pianist, on a par with such established giants of the modern era as McCoy Tyner and Don Pullen."
Adrian Jackson, 'Rhythms'

THE HORACE TAPSCOTT TRIO
with Roberto Miranda (Bass) & Darryl Moore (Drums) can be heard at:

MIETTA'S
Alfred Place Melbourne on Thursday 2 November. *Bookings:* 9654 2366

WANGARATTA FESTIVAL OF JAZZ
Saturday 4 November: Solo concert • Sunday 5 November: Trio concert
Monday 6 November: Orchestra concert, with members of Australian Art Orchestra
Book on 1 800 803 944 or at Bass outlets or on 11500

Presented by Mietta's and the Wangaratta Festival of Jazz in association with the Sydney Improvised Music Association

WEST COAST HOT

HORACE TAPSCOTT & ROBERTO MIRANDA

Samstag, 21. März 1998, 20.00h
Altes Rathaus (Konzertsaal)
Weil am Rhein, Hinterdorfstr.39

Karten: Städt. Kulturamt, Humboldtstr.2, Tel.07621/704 411
und Ohrwurm, Lörrach:Sounds, Basel: BaZ am Barfi, Musik
Hug, Musik Wyler

Veranstalter: Städtisches Kulturamt Weil am Rhein

Flyer for appearance by Horace and bassist Roberto Miguel Miranda in Europe, March 1998.

(Below) Horace signing a copy of *Central Avenue Sounds: Jazz in Los Angeles* (University of California Press, 1998), which he coedited and contributed a chapter to, at Vroman's Bookstore in Pasadena, California, 4 April 1998. (Photo by Elaine Pastras.)

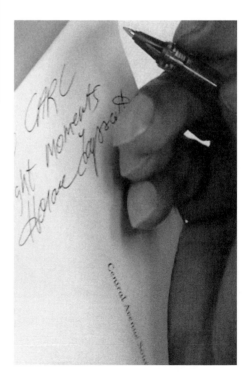

Horace and Steve Isoardi at the World Stage in Leimert Park.
(Photo by Tamar Lando.)

Horace Tapscott,
April 6, 1934–February 27, 1999.

(Below) Flyer for the Horace
Tapscott tribute, which took
place the day after his passing,
late in the evening of
27 February 1999.

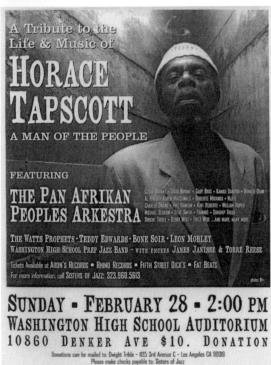

Ark session. I've been trying to record more, trying to get everything down that's been done through the years, and that I thought was nice and hasn't been recorded. That's almost done, maybe another record date will finish it, then I'll go to the next stage: new projects, some that I've been thinking about for a while.

I'm still doing a musical that I've been writing for years about the community, *Impressions of the Ghetto*. It's based on people I've known and things like that. I don't know if I'll ever hear it. I've also been writing a musical play in my mind for years that tells the story of the music and the times from the late 1940s on, from the time I became conscious of it and a part of it. The play deals with how and the reasons why the music and society changed. I'm telling some of it in this book, but not like I could through music, where I could portray it better. I have it all together in my head.

Marching band music is still being written. I've got a marching band and I've scored "Lino's Pad" for the Kwanzaa and Martin Luther King Jr. parades. I see movement, movements in my music. I've got a tune, "Nyja's Theme," with five different patterns going in it. And then Billy Higgins and those cats have started a drum thing for the parades. So there's a lot of music coming out of the community.

Most of the schools around here no longer have school bands, and the youngsters ought to be able to see a seventy-five-piece band marching down Crenshaw Boulevard. I'd like to be a part of a parade with a large band, and everyone there looking with their kids. That's nice to be able to do that. It might be just the thing to ignite the other youngsters. "Hey, I want to be in that band! Mama! Daddy!" Then they might go buy them a trombone or a tuba. They get exposed to it and that's important. It was shoved in my face from the womb.

My music has stayed the same from the time I started writing until now. It still talks about the same kinds of issues; it still has the same kind of fire that it had before. There are no basic changes in my way of approaching it. My music is mostly written out of the same vein, because it still has something to do with everyday life. Every time I write something, it's about what I've been a part of or seen. If the community changes, then so goes the music. That's just the way it is. I can write about red roses on a bush like every-one else, because we have them here. But it's where those red roses are growing that is really what my music is about. It's always been based on that, and in that sense I don't think it has changed.

I have a critic, a lifetime critic who I grew up with, and every time he hears my music, he'll let me know. He's not a musician at all and doesn't have anything to do with music. He just knows me, and we're best friends. He'll say, "Horace, your music is sound-ing different." And I'll ask him to tell me how. He's the only cat I really listen to, because he's actually been there, and he always has something to say about it. He always comes to where I'm playing and the next day he's always over here. Sometimes, he'll recognize a sound that will remind him of the past, like my mother's whistle signal. When he heard that, he said, "Oh, yeah." So that cat's my major critic. Wendell Black is his name.

The respect of my peers is what's really important to me, too. Guys like Mal Waldron, Randy Weston, Andrew Hill, Cecil Tay-lor, McCoy Tyner, Steve Lacy—these cats know what's happening. They've been there. Every time we see each other, we get along, because we know each other and it doesn't have anything to do with ego. That's the best part. We've all got something to offer. And that's the way I've always thought about it. I've never thought about competing to the point of destruction, or cats not trusting each other, because he might have practiced a little more or had an opportunity for this. All of a sudden the music wouldn't be music anymore, as far as I'm concerned. I remember busting up a band a couple of times, because the attitude was wrong. I didn't want to play with them and I let them know that. As it says on some of our albums, "Our music is contributive, rather than competitive."

To gain the respect of your peers, and knowing that you're real and genuine, already puts you ahead of the game, as far as your confidence and status is concerned. And your performance is rated by your actions and reactions to the things that are around you. I was never a person who talked a lot of rules and regulations. You act first. You walk it, then you talk it. That's the idea to have.

When the cats come to town, they come over here and eat and hang out, talk about their kids and grandkids. Those are simple things, and I'm a simple person. I can deal with that. Because the simpler you are, the more you allow yourself to cop much more in appreciating what's around you that is exciting. That's the way I raised my family. Just do it simple, because we're going to run into a whole lot of crud out there. And if we don't have a simple stabilization going for us, we'll be lost in this crowd. We've tried to stay with the simplest of things, just love and respect and recognition in its righteous ways, and we've built on that.

The Lost Generation

Looking back now, what we had in the communities of the Third Ward in Houston and along Central Avenue in Los Angeles was during a time when segregation was the art of the day. We were brought together by force. Today, the community scene is much smaller and more voluntary, but we have it happening in Leimert Park, down on Degnan Boulevard, down here on Fifty-fourth Street. Artistically and musically speaking, we have that kind of atmosphere and that kind of environment.

Nothing is ever going to be like it was before. But this new generation has to have something of their own, rather than what they have to speak of so far. Individuals and a people can become invisible again. Not long ago, it looked like the Afro-American Museum at Exposition Park in Los Angeles was going to close, because of budget cuts. How can you close an archival place, a library and arts place that has records of a people who live in this country, especially of a people who hadn't been in the regular books and libraries? What does that mean? Kids need a place where they can walk in and say, "I can find something out about myself in this museum." If it ever closes, what do I say to my grandson, Martin, when he asks, "Why did they close this one and not another one?"

People did start fighting for that museum. One day a youngster, a real solid young black kid, appeared out in front with a sign: "No library, no justice, no peace." Soon many people joined him. There are issues that are important and must be dealt with, and the library is definitely important in the community, a library in everybody's community. So cut liquor stores; cut all those other things that won't be missed as much as knowledge, something as powerful as knowledge.

These are things that have to be dealt with now, above ground, by all people. You've got to maintain some kind of standard for the next generation. That's just it, man, because your time is almost up. So what are you going to do in your time? Have all your years here been just a waste?

The generations that came before us got the hard core of this country's racism. Then they had these children, and these cats got a little better, because they didn't want to have a slave frame of mind, like their fathers and grandfathers. They wanted to go to these great schools, the integrated schools, to learn. My generation came along, still in the heart of it, with a different attitude, because when we were growing up, we saw so many things happen to our parents and we saw how we were treated as black people, and how black males were the ones who had the roughest part in the whole society. The teachers we had, like Samuel Browne at Jefferson High School and several others, were telling us what we had to have to make it in this kind of society, in this racist society, as he called it. You have to gain respect. You don't have to get anybody to like you. Your biggest thing is to get the respect. Once you get that, the other things will come to you. That generation I grew up in, came up for respect. That's all we had, and the only outlet was music and sports, because we weren't allowed to be doctors, architects, or people of that nature.

With the generation after us, it seems that a hitch started to break, that it was starting to decline. The goals were different, which was cool, but then they got caught up in the drug scene, which was a hard scene, and the war scene. They got messed up in between both of those things. Most of the drugs started in the Vietnam War. That's where most of the drug addicts came from, and the black ones who came out had the police on their cases, just as it happened during the Korean War. The black soldiers were always on the front line, so on your belt you had morphine. If you got hurt or shot, you're going to shoot up. This guy has given his body and soul for this particular country; he gets an addiction doing that and is then thrown out on society. I knew a lot of guys, including a bunch of my personal friends, who died out on the streets or in jail with no family anymore. These were straitlaced people! When they got out, the armed forces called the local law enforcement and told them who was coming into the community again—dope addicts.

Now when I see my children—I call all the black teenagers and all those young adults, my children—and how they're acting, there's a reason for it. Sometimes I'm very pissed off at it. "Hey, man, they know better than that. They're much more intelligent. They don't have to do this." Then sometimes I feel very bad, because it was handed down to them and I was one of the ones who handed it to them. But I also know there are other things that are much more powerful that we're up against.

One of the problems we face is that most people see the world, our world, only through the media and not from the core of it. In the rebellion of 1992 in Los Angeles, all you saw was a helicopter view of what was happening. So naturally, people thought, "Shit, everything is worse over there." But they never showed us walking the streets, the kids in the neighborhoods playing. They just showed where the fire was burning, and where gangs of people were running and carrying goods. Not everything going on was as bad as they were saying. But by just focusing on those aspects of the community, it made the problem worse than it was, actually encouraged people to join in the worst part. Unless you're a part of it, you don't really know. If you have that responsibility to report the happenings, then you have to become a part of it and know what you're speaking about. Otherwise, the reporting is just keeping people away from each other. It's polarizing society to a level that doesn't have to be, to a level that makes people put up their guard on both sides.

Another problem is in things like the attacks on affirmative action. I know for a fact that you're supposed to do things on your own. What I really hate most today is all the unemployed black cats hanging around the corners and stores. These cats piss me off. They're supposed to be working, to be taking care of their families. No matter how you got there, you've got to take some of the blame yourself. You can't be talking about white folks. You got to clean up your shit, then you've got something to say.

But I also come from that age where I know why things have got like they are. If you're not paying back the money that you owe these people that you made slaves—300 to 400 years of taunting and knocking a people down—you've got to do something, because the racism lingers. It may be more subtle, but it's there. There won't be any lawyers or doctors of color in the century 2000 if it keeps up. What do you expect to come from that kind of activity? How long is this supposed to go on? I know the subtle racism is much worse than it was, when you could see it out front in the 1940s and the 1950s. And it's destroying anything that could help.

All of us are putting our little old poison in this society. It's shaken up. Everything is shaken up. Families aren't recognized as families anymore. Neighbors aren't neighbors. People don't look at each other anymore. All those kinds of things that make a community happen, people are afraid to do. It doesn't have anything to do with one race or one person; it has to do with all of us.

I live across the street from Crenshaw High School. It was a first-rate school when they built it. Starting a few years ago, they didn't have enough books for the kids. How did that happen? I couldn't believe it. My granddaughter, Raisha, came up to me after her first day and said, "They don't have any books, papa." All they've got over there is a championship basketball team, and that's beginning to be a joke. "Well, they've got a good basketball . . ." Maybe one of these guys is going to make a lot of money, but all of them can't be athletes, and that one can't read.

We realized that by the early 1960s, black men were an endangered species. The more society killed, the less it had to worry about this world becoming multicolored. Narcotics had already been in the neighborhood, but it seemed that by this time they started coming in rough, real bad. Then all of a sudden, in the mid-1970s, firearms started getting into this community from out of nowhere. Guns started showing up in young cats' hands. You'd see guns and ammunition being sold on the street out of panel trucks.

They had gangs for a long time, but it would be fists or knives, not guns. And as long as the black teenagers were killing each other, it was cool. I have never known kids getting guns as easy as they were. I didn't make them. We didn't make them. So where were they coming from? Those kinds of heavy-duty things have been in my head for the last two decades.

Years ago, I did a composition called *The Lost Generation of the Nile,* and it happened. Two decades of lost black boys never got to the age of sixteen. That's terrible. I cannot sleep well. How can you just walk the streets and think everything is all right, knowing that's happening and knowing that the ones who are still here are dead anyway, because society has made sure that they won't go any further than here. That's sickening to me!

And you can't speak to the youngsters; they act like you're invisible. I see my young people just ignore you totally. It hurts to walk down the street and they don't even see you; they don't make eye contact. It's like you're not there. That hurts, because even though they're younger and you're older, you've got something in common. You can speak and teach one another, and not be intimidated by the other.

Sometimes, you'll be driving down the street and cats will be stopping in the middle of it, talking, holding up traffic, like you're nothing. That bugs me to death. It's like, "You'd better not say nothing to me about this. I'll take my gun out and shoot you." That's worse than anything you can think of. It's dirty; it's contaminated all the way to the sperm, because this cat's going to make a baby and feed that to him or her.

When you lose respect for your elders, don't look for respect anywhere else, from anybody else. That's the biggest problem today. And to me it seems like it's worse than it was, because then the young people had some respect for their elders, and that's not here now. I walk the streets every day. It's not all of them but the ones who you do see are enough.

In the 1960s, when George Jackson wrote his prison letters, black kids didn't expect to live to be eighteen. It's even lower now—fifteen—and worse than it's ever been. It went haywire; all the things that we had started to build in the 1950s, that new freedom era, learn and get a better education, all that has gone down the drain. After all that has happened since the 1960s, now youngsters are shooting at each other, because "You're on my turf," and they don't own nothing. That's the sick part of it. You don't have a building you can call your own, you don't have any land you can call your own, and you're going to shoot this other person. That's ignorance, and I can't believe it's happening and can't help thinking, "Mothers and fathers have died through the generations for it to come to this? To shoot at each other for what?" They don't have any idea at all, and that's what makes them much more dangerous. They just don't care. I want to ask them, "Why are you looking forward to dying?"

What happened? Where is the pride? Where is the learning? The poison that seeped through whole generations is still here and it's just tearing them to pieces. It's killing them like they don't mean anything at all, and everything that I believe in and thought about doesn't mean anything anymore. It's like there were no grandparents; there were no parents. They're invisible.

It's terrible to think that these youngsters are running this whole society by their actions. They drive people off the street. People don't want to go anywhere. It's horrible and it's been put upon. It's not something that just happened; it's been put upon—the dope first, now the guns—by the establishment, by those in power, by those lawmakers who are running things. And it began by not giving the youngsters anyplace to go and taking away what little there was.

Today, protest is writing on the walls—graffiti. These young cats now are tagging, writing in their particular language. If it meant something, if it had something to do with coming together, it would be all right. But it doesn't have any meaning; they're not saying anything except, "Well, if you don't want me to do this, then I'll do it."

There's no longer any direction from the top, and a large part of the reason is that many of the people, who were in those earlier groups, sold out. If they were going to be in it, they're supposed to be in it now, today, even if they're in a wheelchair. And if they're not doing it, they're supposed to be telling someone else what to do about it, or showing them which way to do it, because it's never over. How come what we were talking about or practiced then isn't functioning as an everyday thing for us now? It doesn't stop. The young people who have come up didn't have it, because these same people, who might have made a bigger difference, went maybe in the direction of the White House. Of course, some were sent to another house, like Geronimo Pratt and all those cats who were wiped out by J. Edgar Hoover's FBI.

It was my fault, my generation's fault, that this got so far. It's my son's fault now, and it's going to be their son's fault, if nothing is done about it. I believe it happened mostly because things were left undone. During the early days of the 1960s, when the guys were fighting for freedom, they got it to a point where they made everyone pay attention. Then they started working it for themselves. These black leaders became the kind of American that they were used to seeing and hearing, someone who takes from the people for themselves. They started filling their own pockets, rather than doing it for the whole. And it is still facing us, because too many people haven't come to the notion that we're all trying to become human.

You have to be here and you have to stay on it. You can't just do your little business and then split. You've got to be here, even though it's rough and nasty. Every family here has been hurt by something going on that had to do with their children; every one of us. For me, the answer isn't to move away, to run away, because wherever I go, I take it with me. If I'm right here in it, at least I can say, "I don't like this but now maybe I can go and help this guy scratch a tag off his wall."

Do something!

The only thing these cats are going to recognize is stamina. If you're going to be here, and they keep seeing you, sooner or later they're going to approach you. I don't care how long it takes; they'll notice, and come and say, "O.G., let me help."

It's not like I have the answers to it. All I have for myself is what I think is the best way for me to deal with it, until they throw the dirt on me. Otherwise, there's no point in being here.

"What did you do in the world, daddy?"

You were born and you died, so what happened in-between?

I gave a lot; I've added a lot. I've put a lot of kids and seeds out there, and I just can't abandon that. William Marshall used to have fun quoting some lines from a play: "Get away from me, boy! I did it. Make it on your own!" They can't make it on their own, if the community isn't there to be a part of their own, you dig? I'm more content if I know our young kids are getting a better shot at living, not just at education but a better shot at living and having a mind open to the fact that there are other things going on in the world, other than in their own little old block.

"So what's next? What do you do about this?"

At least try something. If you can't do anything, then throw a bomb and let's start all over. If people don't start asking, "What can I do now?" then it's the bomb. Just get rid of the whole thing. Start from scratch. Blow it all up; explode it, because the tentacles just reach out everywhere. It has always been my thought that this whole thing has to come down and go back up again, because it's been built on lies and stealing, on exploitation, and it can't be fixed. It's just got to whoosh! And then rebuild, really rebuild. If you've got that much poison in it, it has to come down, because it's been passed on from generation to generation. That's the only way I can see it.

It seems that it's only when the shit hits the fan and spreads that we begin again. This country has to have a real big jolt to understand what it's really about. That's the only way everybody will take notice that they are just one country here. If you're the home of the brave, the land of the free, then act like it. If you want to be the strongest thing in the hemisphere, then act like it, feed all the people that's necessary. That doesn't happen.

I still see the racism. No matter how much education there is, I can't see any progress happening. None. I don't see any after all this time, despite all the little black people in little offices. It's just much bigger than individuals.

"So what are you after? What are you trying to prove in this society?"

I just want some respect. I want real respect, because I give real respect. And you can't get that without giving it. That's all I'm looking for in this world, from man to man and woman to woman, man or woman, respect. That's all it comes down to. I'd like to be able, before they throw the dirt on me, to walk again through a neighborhood and everybody's speaking; bars are off the doors and windows. That's really dreaming, but I'd love to see that one more time, to live in that kind of community. If my grandkids are walking down the street, I'd like to see this lady on the other side say, "What are you doing over here? You belong down there. Do your parents know you're here?" That kind of attitude, because you're caring about each other. I grew up in that kind of setting, which made me like I am today, always ready to accept a person for who they are and they accept me for who I am. Respect for one another. I'd like to have some respect as a person, as a race, as a country.

You can't get that without giving it. So my way of giving it and getting it is in the little functions I'm into every day and have to be done every day: contact, information, actions, and passing it on. Like Mr. Browne told me, if I promised that I'd pass it on, he'd give me the magic. That's what I wanted to do and I've been doing that.

I have been consistent in this way of thinking, of demanding respect, demanding recognition, and demanding that the children, mine and yours, benefit from all the things that we've contributed. That's why I came out of the womb—I found out before I go to the tomb—that they had to have that respect and understanding for a race of people and their contribution to this country. America might not be known as America for everybody while you and I are still here; things are still happening. But the contribution that's being made is constantly working that way, which means that it wasn't all in vain.

Nothing feels better to me than being able to walk through the village and see functions happening. I like that, to get to the core, and I like being a part of that scene. If I can do anything about helping to maintain it, that's what I'll do. You'd have to really have something to get me out of where I am now, and that wouldn't have anything to do with money at all. I'm really proud of that. I know how I feel about things. I'm not guessing and I'm not bitter anymore. I worked my way out of that, because I knew I had to work my way out of that if I was going to try to do anything else.

So I feel pretty good about myself in the scheme of things and I'm not expecting anything special at all. On my tombstone it'll say, "He loved what he did and he'd do it again." I found my part to play and I fit in, just my part and not as so-and-so fit in, or as Coltrane did it. At the end, I want to be able to say, to show, that I lived in the community and I appreciated it, that I wanted to keep it up and I wanted to be a part of it, because I loved people and I learned to love life.

Postscript:

From the Funeral Service

For Cecilia

Father Amde, I want you to speak, but I don't want you to say anything about me. . . . Talk about the most wonderful, loving person in my life, my wife Cecilia.

I want the world to know what a queenly, grand lady she has always been with me, my soul mate. . . . Tell the world how she made me strong when I was weak. Sometimes I did not know if I should go on. She always understood, even when I did a little of this or a little of that.

She was forever forgiving and so very protective of me. Always there for me. Being the wife of an artist was not easy but until the end she loved me and I her.

Most of my life I spent with Celia and I do not regret one moment of it. Without Celia, there would not have been balance in my life or a complete Horace Tapscott. Thank you, Celia, my wife.

—Horace Tapscott

PAPA,
The Lean Griot

for Horace Tapscott, pianist, arranger, composer, community leader

I am Horace Tapscott
my fingers are dancing grassroots
I do not fit into form, I create form
my ears are radar charting the whispers of my ancestors
I seek the divinity in outcasts, the richness of rebels
I will pray for you on this snaggle-toothed piano
songs for the unsung
whose lineage was fed to sharks in the Atlantic
I will concertize you into trance, here in this garage
conjure spirits that will sing you into remembrance
on this piano so far out of tune it opens doors to other worlds
I will climb inside this piano searching for our history
I will assemble a choir of unborn voices
to teach you what the future sounds like
I will love you with the warmth of the African sun
I walk these sacred streets remembering kola nuts and cowrie shells
and how well our uncles wore their trousers
I am Horace Tapscott
and I am not for sale

the eyes look inward as the story is told
voices painted in the dignity of old photographs
we have seen blood on the piano keys
cobalt blue chains, slurred notes
as truth wells up in the corner of eyes

our richness like honey stuck to the tips of singing fingers
with palms held up in gestures of prayer
smoke thick as frankincense dance on pilgrimage
fade like golden echoes at the porch of our ears
to have seen life moving smooth as a red dress
on a purple spirit on a slow yellow day

cracked open the moment like children laughing
with their mouths held wide trying to catch the sun

remembering when our ways were straight and rooted
when we did what we had to do with what we had to do it with

under the sheltering wings of family
walking lines to our selves with spirit guides
elders correcting children
the way folks held their heads
the gathering of smiles
family, a circle of love

oh singing fingers, oh swell fire in the chest
we should know such joy

a thousand eyes watching children grow next to flowers
as old ones pray over food
where men with shiny shoes, swap scars and work songs
men knotted at the gut level in a common pool of sweat
remove their hats to pray, remember . . .

and women form bands of healing
quilting rhythms and tucking them into an ark of stars
sail through a storm of hardships
deep changes bring out the beauty of a song
where babies hide their fingers in gray beards

weaving teardrops and laughter
into a bright cloth of collected wisdom
etched in multicolored ink on memories' wall
love would hover in a room
like the scent of good cooking
and fall down like warm hands on the backs of travelers

a family was a circle of love
a community was a family
we did what we had to do with what we had to do it with

oh singing road of destiny, blanket of night whispers
rose essence and spirit hum
talking wood and flame dancer
street theater and heart sport

music oozing from each breath
kissing our ears like angels
the sacredness of strife
take time and give it to others
take time and give it to others

the eyes look inward as the story is told
voice painted in the dignity of old photographs
we have seen blood on the piano keys
cobalt blue chains, slurred notes

I am Horace Tapscott
my fingers are dancing grassroots
I do not fit in form, I create form
my ears are radar charting the whispers of my ancestors
I seek the divinity in outcasts, the richness of rebels
I walk these sacred streets remembering
kola nuts and cowrie shells
and how well our uncles wore their trousers
I am Horace Tapscott
and I am not for sale

—Kamau Daáood

Appendix

A Partial List of UGMAA Artists, 1961–1998

Note: This list has been compiled from various sources and makes no claim to completeness. It is as accurate as various records and memories have allowed. Undoubtedly, some brothers and sisters have been overlooked, and to them our sincere apologies.

Abdullah, Jahid (congas, horns)
Alaah'deen (vocalist)
Amatullah, Afifa (vocalist)
Amatullah, Amina (vocalist)
Andrews, James (tenor saxophone, bass clarinet)
Baker, Herbert (piano)
Balaka, Ismael (drums)
Baxter, Steve (trombone)
Bias, Gary (soprano saxophone, alto saxophone, flute)
Billingslea, Nikia (vocalist)
Blackburn, Lou (trombone)
Blue, John (drums)
Blythe, Arthur (alto saxophone)
Bohanon, George (trombone)
Bolden, Willie (trombone)
Boone, Omega (vocalist)
Bradford, Bobby (trumpet, cornet)

Brashear, Oscar (trumpet)
Brewster, Roy (trumpet)
Brooks, Leroy (drums)
Brown, Elaine (vocalist)
Brown, Everett Jr., (drums)
Brown, Joe (baritone saxophone)
Brown, Ray (trumpet)
Brown, Troy (trumpet)
Bryant, David (bass)
Bullen, Reggie (trumpet)
Burbage, Andre (drums)
Butler, Charles (vocalist)
Calhoun, Rastine (tenor saxophone)
Callender, Red (bass, tuba)
Callies, Herbert (clarinet)
Carey, Norma (vocalist)
Carter, John (alto saxophone, clarinet)
Chambers, Dante (vocalist)

Chancler, Ndugu (drums)
Chandler, Charles (tenor saxophone)
Chanima, Sister (vocalist)
Chapman, Tracy (flute)
Clark, Curtis (piano)
Cline, Alex (drums)
Cojoe, Ernest (congas)
Conly, Al (saxes)
Connell, Will (alto saxophone)
Cooper, Zeke (alto saxophone)
Cortez, Danny (trumpet)
Criss, Sonny (alto saxophone)
Crouch, Stanley (drums)
Daáood, Kamau (word musician)
Daniels, Mike (percussion)
Davis, Richard (trumpet)
Dean, Donald (drums)
Delone, Amos (baritone saxophone)
Draper, Ray (tuba)
Dresser, Mark (bass)
Duffy, Patricia (vocalist)
Ector, Joel (bass)
Fatisha, Sister (vocalist)
Figueroa, Virgilio (percussion)
Fisher, Rene (vocalist)
Fowlkes, Charles (alto saxophone)
Franklin, Henry (bass)
Gibbs, Marla (actress)
Goldsmith, George (drums)
Golia, Vinny (reeds)
Golson, Reggie (drums)
Green, Thurman (trombone)
Groce, Denise (vocalist)
Hall, Albert (trombone)
Harris, Billie (reeds)
Hart, Aubrey (flute)
Hasan, Brother (tenor saxophone)
Heard, John (bass)

Hearn, Brenda (vocalist)
Herrera, Richard (bass)
Hill, Linda (piano, vocalist)
Hines, Alan Kopkee (bass)
Hinton, Billy (drums)
Hoskins, Jimmy (drums)
Huggins, John (vocalist)
Hunt, Cynthia (vocalist)
Isis, Sister (vocalist)
Jackson, Pamela (flute)
Jíhad, Ali (vocalist)
Johnson, Archie (trombone)
Jordan, Waberi (vocalist)
Joshua [natural sound] (reeds, flute)
Kambul, Somayah "Peaches" Moore (vocalist, Autoharp)
Kelly, Rickey (vibes)
Komolafe, Dadisi (alto saxophone, flute)
Kopano, Chini (vocalist)
Kylo, Kylo (trumpet)
Lanetta, Sister (vocalist)
Lark, Aminifu Francis (vocalist)
Lawrence, Azar (saxes)
Lee, James (trumpet)
Legohn, Fundi (french horn)
Lenita, Sister (vocalist)
Lewis, Reggie (trombone)
Littleton, Don (drums)
Littleton, Jeff (bass)
Lloyd, Charles (alto saxophone)
Lott, Mark (trumpet)
Madison, Bill (drums)
Marshall, William (actor)
Martin, Greg (oboe)
Mathias, Eddie (bass)
Mateen, Sabir (tenor saxophone)
McKinney, Sherman (banjo)
McLaurine, Marcus (bass)

McNeely, Lattus (alto saxophone)

Meeks, Steven (baritone saxophone)

Middleton, Cerion III (tenor saxophone)

Minor, Rickey (electric bass)

Miranda, Roberto Miguel (bass)

Morgan, Nate (piano)

Morris, Lawrence "Butch" (cornet)

Morris, Wilber (bass)

Murray, David (tenor saxophone)

Nakia (vocalist)

Ndugu (vocalist)

Newton, James (flute)

Ngite (percussion)

Northington, Larry (alto saxophone)

Ojenke (poet)

Olivier, Rufus (bassoon)

Owens, Charles (reeds)

Palmer, Arnold (drums)

Pleasants, Edwin (flute)

Polk, Kamonta Lawrence (bass)

Porter, Rudolph (saxes, bassoon)

Priestley, Eric (poet)

Ranelin, Phil (trombone)

Reese, Torre (vocalist)

Riley, Herman (tenor saxophone)

Roberson, Chico (flute, alto saxophone)

Roberts, Ernest Fuasi (tenor saxophone)

Roberts, Lawrence Kafi (soprano saxophone, flute)

Robertson, Lester (trombone)

Rodriguez, Freddie (tenor saxophone)

Romero, Danyel (trumpet)

Roper, William (tuba)

Rose, Maria (vocalist)

Roy, Robert (flute)

Ruffin, Eugene (bass clarinet, bass)

Samprite, Willie L. (trumpet)

Sanyika, Dadisi (flute)

Saracho, En Medio (vibes, piano)

Saracho, Gary (vibes)

Savage Jr., Walter (bass)

Sebastian, Adele (flute)

Session, Elesia (vocalist)

Session, Michael (saxes)

Shabaka, Jamil (saxes)

Sharps, Jesse (reeds)

Sinclair, Guido (alto saxophone)

Smith, Christy (bass)

Smith, Glenda (vocalist)

Smith, Steve (trumpet)

Solder, Steve (drums)

Spears, Louis (bass, cello)

Spears, Maurice (trombone)

Stanton, Michael (piano)

Straughter, David (drums)

Straughter, Ernest (piano, flute)

Straughter, Ray (reeds)

Subita, Sister (vocalist)

Sutton, Ike (trumpet)

Taumbu (percussion)

Taylor, Bernice (vocalist)

Tell, Greg (drums)

Theus, Sonship (drums)

Thomas, Leon (vocalist)

Tilman, David "Eric" (piano)

Trible, Denise (vocalist)

Trible, Dwight (vocalist)

Turre, Steve (trombone)

Vernetta, Sister (vocalist)

Wainwright, E. W. (drums)

Walker, Desta (tenor saxophone)

Ware, Trevor (strings)

Watt, Robert (french horn)

Weber, Mark (photographer)
West, Bobby (piano)
Whitaker-Ward, Carolyn (vocalist)
Wilcots, Michael Dett (archivist)
Wilcots, Raisha (flute)
Williams, Ike (trumpet)
Williams, John (baritone saxophone)
Williams, Wendall (french horn)
Williamson, Tom (bass)
Wise, Fritz (drums)
Woods, Daa'oud (percussion)
Woods, Jimmy (alto saxophone)
Winn, Walter (drums)
Wynn/Jones, Alphonso (bass)
Zulu I (body musician)
Zulu II (body musician)

Discography 1:

Horace Tapscott

Note: An asterisk (*) indicates an original composition by Horace Tapscott.

SOLO

Songs of the Unsung. Interplay IP–7714. Hollywood, 18 February 1978. Horace Tapscott (piano).

"Songs of the Unsung"*
"Blue Essence"
"Bakai"
"In Times like These"
"Mary on Sunday"*
"Lush Life"
"The Goat and Ram Jam"
"Something for Kenny"

Billie Harris. *I Want Some Water.* Nimbus West NS–510 C. 1999. Horace Tapscott solo piano on one selection recorded in Los Angeles, 1979.

"Why Don't You Listen?"*

The Tapscott Sessions, Vol. 1. Nimbus NS–1581. Santa Barbara, June 1982. Horace Tapscott (piano).

"Jenny's Spirit's Waltz"*

"Speedy Mike"
"Mother Ship"*
"This Is for Benny"*
"Alone Together"
"Haunted"

The Tapscott Sessions, Vol. 4. Nimbus NS–1814. Santa Barbara, September 1982. Horace Tapscott (piano).

"A Dress for Renée"*
"The Hero's Last Dance"*
"Shades of Soweto"*
"Whit"
"First Call of the Humming Bird"*
"Toward the Sunset"*
"As of Yet"
"Forgiving"*

The Tapscott Sessions, Vol. 2. Nimbus NS–1692. Santa Barbara, November 1982. Horace Tapscott (piano).

"Struggle X: An Afro-American Dream"*
"Many Nights Ago"

The Tapscott Sessions, Vol. 7. Nimbus NS–2147. Santa Barbara, February 1983. Horace Tapscott (piano).

"Riding the San Andreas"*
"Amanda's Tone Poem"*
"Southwestern Avenue Shuffle"*
"Yesterday's Dream"*
" 'Round Midnight"
"On the Nile"
"Sonnet of Butterfly McQueen"*

The Tapscott Sessions, Vol. 3. Nimbus NS–1703. Santa Barbara, April 1983. Horace Tapscott (piano).

"The Tuus"*
"Lately's Light-Green Blues"*
"Reflections of Self"*
"Kopkee's Blues"*
"After the Storm"*

The Tapscott Sessions, Vol. 6. Nimbus NS–2036. Santa Barbara, October 1983. Horace Tapscott (piano).

"Ancestral Echoes"*
"Jessica"
"Restless Nights"
"Chartreuse Blues"*
"The Golden Pearl"*
"New Horizon"

The Tapscott Sessions, Vol. 5. Nimbus NS–1925. Santa Barbara, January 1984. Horace Tapscott (piano).

"Stringeurisms"*
"I'll Have One When It's Over"*
"Blues in Pirouette"*
"Perfumes in the Night"
"Hy-Pockets' Swan Song"*

The Tapscott Sessions, Vol. 8. Nimbus NS–2258C. Santa Barbara, 1982–1984. Horace Tapscott (piano).

"Fire Waltz" (1984)
"Little Niles" (1982)
"Crepuscule with Nellie" (1984)
"As a Child"* (1983)

LEADER

Horace Tapscott Quintet. *The Giant Is Awakened.* Flying Dutchman FDS–107. Los Angeles, 1 April 1969. Arthur Blythe (alto saxophone), Horace Tapscott (piano), David Bryant (bass), Walter Savage Jr. (bass), and Everett Brown Jr. (drums). Reissued on *West Coast Hot.* RCA Novus Series '70 3107–2–N. 1991.

"The Giant Is Awakened"*
"For Fats"
"The Dark Tree"*
"Niger's Theme"* (later changed to "Nyja's Theme")

Horace Tapscott. *In New York.* Interplay IP–7724. New York, 5 January

1979. Horace Tapscott (piano), Art Davis (bass), and Roy Haynes (drums).

"Akirfa"
"Lino's Pad"*
"Sketches of Drunken Mary"*
"If You Could See Me Now"

Horace Tapscott. *Autumn Colors.* Bopland K26P–6311. Hollywood, 3 May 1980. Horace Tapscott (piano), David Bryant (bass), and Everett Brown Jr. (drums). Reissued by Venus Records, Inc. TKCZ–79072. 1994.

"Blues for Dee II"*
"Dee Bee's Dance"*
"Autumn Colors"*
"J.O.B."*

At the Crossroads. Nimbus NS–579. Los Angeles, 1980. Horace Tapscott (piano) and Everett Brown Jr. (drums).

"At the Cross Roads"*
"Middle Age Madness"*
"Ballad for Window Lee Black"* (should be "Ballad for Wendell Lee Black")
"Marcellus III"

Horace Tapscott Sextet. *Dial "B" for Barbra.* Nimbus NS–1147. Los Angeles, 1981. Reggie Bullen (trumpet), Gary Bias (soprano saxophone, alto saxophone), Sabir Mateen (tenor saxophone), Horace Tapscott (piano), Roberto Miguel Miranda (bass), Everett Brown, Jr. (drums).

"Lately's Solo"*
"Dial 'B' for Barbra"*
"Dem Folks"* (with Linda Hill)

Horace Tapscott. *Live at Lobero.* Nimbus NS–1369. Santa Barbara, 12 November 1981. Horace Tapscott (piano), Roberto Miranda (bass), Sonship (percussion).

"Sketches of Drunken Mary"*
"Raisha's New-Hip Dance"*
"The Dark Tree"*

Horace Tapscott. *Live at Lobero, Vol. II.* Nimbus NS–1258. Santa Barbara, November 12, 1981. Horace Tapscott (piano), Roberto Miranda (bass), Sonship (percussion).

"Lino's Pad"*
"Close to Freedom"
"St. Michael"

Modern Jazz Piano Forum, Vol. 1. Art Union ART–CD-30. 1990. One selection by the Horace Tapscott Trio. Los Angeles, 12 August 1983. Horace Tapscott (piano), Roberto Miranda (bass), Everett Brown, Jr. (drums).

"Sketches of Drunken Mary"*

Horace Tapscott. *Dissent or Descent.* Nimbus West NS–509C. 1998. Horace Tapscott (piano), Fred Hopkins (bass), Ben Riley (drums). Trio recorded in New York City, 1984. Solo piano recorded in Santa Barbara, 1983–1984.

"As a Child"*
"Sandy and Niles"*
"To the Great House"*
"Spellbound"
"Ballad for Samuel"*
"Ruby, My Dear" (solo piano)
"Chico's Back in Town"* (solo piano)

Horace Tapscott Octet. *Live.* Americana Records AMC-3002. KCRW, Santa Monica, September 17, 1987. Thurman Green (trombone), Gary Bias (alto saxophone), Rastine Calhoun (tenor saxophone), Horace Tapscott (piano), David Bryant (bass), Roberto Miranda (bass), Sonship Theus (drums), Donald Dean (drums).

"Dem Folks"* (with Linda Hill)
"One for Lately"
"Little Africa"

Horace Tapscott. *The Dark Tree, Vol. 1.* hat ART CD 6053. Hollywood, 14–17 December 1989. John Carter (clarinet), Horace Tapscott (piano), Cecil McBee (bass), and Andrew Cyrille (drums). Reissued in *The Dark Tree 1 and 2* on hatOLOGY 2–540. 2000.

"The Dark Tree"*

"Sketches of Drunken Mary"*
"Lino's Pad"*
"One for Lately"

Kimus #4 (sampler). hat ART CD 16004. Hollywood, 15 December 1989. John Carter (clarinet), Horace Tapscott (piano), Cecil McBee (bass), and Andrew Cyrille (drums).

"The Dark Tree"* (3)

Horace Tapscott. *The Dark Tree, Vol. 2*. hat ART CD 6083. Hollywood, 14–17 December 1989. John Carter (clarinet), Horace Tapscott (piano), Cecil McBee (bass), and Andrew Cyrille (drums). Reissued in *The Dark Tree 1 and 2* on hatOLOGY 2–540. 2000.

"Sandy and Niles"*
"Bavarian Mist"
"The Dark Tree"* (2)
"A Dress for Renée"*
"Naya's Theme"* (should be "Nyja's Theme")

Horace Tapscott. *Aiee! The Phantom*. Arabesque Jazz AJ0119. Brooklyn, June 1995. Marcus Belgrave (trumpet), Abraham Burton (alto saxophone), Horace Tapscott (piano), Reggie Workman (bass), and Andrew Cyrille (drums).

"To the Great House"*
"The Goat and Ram Jam"
"*Aiee!* The Phantom"*
"Drunken Mary/Mary on Sunday"*
"Inspiration of Silence"
"Mothership"*

Tapscott Simmons Quartet. *Among Friends*. Jazz Friends Productions JFP 004. 1999. Sonny Simmons (alto saxophone), Horace Tapscott (piano), James Lewis (bass), John Betsch (drums). Recorded live in Longwy, France, July 28, 1995.

"Milestones"
"Body and Soul"
"So What"
"Caravan"

Knitting Factory *What Is Jazz? Festival 1996*. Knitting Factory Works KFW 195. June 1996.
Horace Tapscott Trio on one selection: Tapscott (piano), Ray Drummond (bass), Billy Hart (drums).

"Caravan"

Horace Tapscott. *Thoughts of Dar es Salaam*. Arabesque Jazz AJ0128. New York City, 30 June and 1 July 1996. Horace Tapscott (piano), Ray Drummond (bass), and Billy Hart (drums).

"As a Child"*
"Bibi Mkuu: The Great Black Lady"
"Lullaby in Black"
"Sandy and Niles"*
"Wiletta's Walk"*
"Social Call"
"Oleo"
"Thoughts of Dar es Salaam"*
"Now's the Time"

PAN AFRIKAN PEOPLES ARKESTRA

Flight 17. Nimbus NS–135. Los Angeles, 1978. Horace Tapscott (conductor, piano), Jesse Sharps (bandleader, soprano saxophone, tenor saxophone, bamboo flute), Linda Hill (piano), Adele Sebastian (vocalist, flute), James Andrews (tenor saxophone, bass clarinet), Michael Session (alto saxophone), Kafi Larry Roberts (flute), Herbert Callies (alto clarinet), Red Callender (tuba), Archie Johnson (trombone), Lester Robertson (trombone), Everett Brown Jr. (drums), William Madison (percussion, drums), Louis Spears (cello), David Bryant (bass), and Kamonta Lawrence Polk (bass). Reissued by Nimbus West Records NS–135C. 1997. Personnel on added tracks: Horace Tapscott (conductor, piano), Linda Hill (piano), Adele Sebastian (vocalist, flute), Lester Robertson (trombone), Sabir Mateen (tenor saxophone), Billie Harris (soprano saxophone), John Williams (baritone saxophone), Alan Hines (bass), David Bryant (bass), Roberto Miguel Miranda (bass), Billy Hinton (drums), and Daa'oud Woods (percussion).

"Flight 17" (first movement)
"Breeze"

"Horacio"
"Clarisse"
"Maui"
"Coltrane Medley" (on reissue only)
"Village Dance Revisited" (on reissue only)

The Call. Nimbus NS–246. Los Angeles, 8 April 1978. Horace Tapscott (conductor, piano), Jesse Sharps (bandleader, soprano saxophone, tenor saxophone, bamboo flute), Linda Hill (piano), Adele Sebastian (vocalist, flute), Lester Robertson (trombone), David Bryant (bass), Everett Brown Jr. (drums), Herbert Callies (alto clarinet), James Andrews (tenor saxophone, bass clarinet), Michael Session (alto saxophone), Kafi Larry Roberts (flute, soprano saxophone), Archie Johnson (trombone), Red Callender (tuba, bass), William Madison (percussion, drums), Louis Spears (cello, bass), and Kamonta Lawrence Polk (bass).

"The Call"
"Quagmire Manor at 5 A.M."
"Nakatini Suite"
"Peyote Song No. III"

Live at I.U.C.C. Nimbus NS–357. Los Angeles, February–June 1979. Horace Tapscott (piano), Jesse Sharps (soprano saxophone), Sabir Mateen (tenor saxophone), James Andrews (tenor saxophone), Michael Session (alto saxophone), Kafi Roberts (flute), Herbert Callies (alto clarinet), David Bryant (bass), Alan Hines (bass), Everett Brown Jr. (drums), Adele Sebastian (flute), Billie Harris (soprano saxophone, tenor saxophone), Daa'oud Woods (percussion), Red Callender (tuba), Lester Robertson (trombone), John Williams (baritone saxophone), Aubrey Hart (flute), Roberto Miguel Miranda (bass), Billy Hinton (drums), Linda Hill (piano), Bob Watt (french horn), Desta Walker (tenor saxophone), Mike Daniels (percussion), and Louis Spears (cello, bass).

"Macrame"
"Future Sally's Time"
"Noissessprahss"
"Village Dance"
"L.T.T."*
"Desert Fairy Princess"
"Lift Every Voice"

Billie Harris, *I Want Some Water*. Nimbus West NS–510 C. 1999. Arkestra on one selection recorded live in Los Angeles, 1979. Horace Tapscott (conductor, piano), Billie Harris (soprano saxophone), Sabir Mateen (tenor saxophone), John Williams (baritone saxophone), Lester Robertson (trombone), Adele Sebastian (flute), Aubrey Hart (flute), Alan Hines (bass), Roberto Miranda (bass), Billy Hinton (drums), Daa'oud Woods (percussion).

    "Many Nights Ago"

SIDEMAN, ARRANGER, OR COMPOSER

Chuck Higgins. "Pachuko Hop." Combo 12. Los Angeles, 1952. Chuck Higgins (tenor saxophone), Fred Higgins (baritone saxophone), John Watson (piano), Joe Ursery (drums), Tapscott (arranger).

Peppy Prince and His Orchestra. *Dance Party*. Dooto DL 240. Los Angeles, late 1950s. George Orendorf (trumpet), Dud Stone (trumpet), Joe Kelly (trumpet), Parker Berry (trombone, arranger), Tapscott (trombone), Alfred Caspar (trombone), Chuck Waller (alto saxophone), Milton Hall (alto saxophone), Bill Ellis (tenor saxophone), Jimmie Evans (tenor saxophone), Doug Finis (piano), Russ Weathers (bass), Prince (drums, vocalist), Stan Jamerson (bongos).

    "It Must Have Been a Dream"
    "Peppy's Idea"
    "Medley" ("Solitude," "I Cried for You," "Penthouse Serenade")
    "Sir Galahad"
    "Mean-Po-Gal"
    "Ghost of a Chance"
    "Dance Party"
    "Diane"
    "Jack Pot"

Lou Rawls. *Tobacco Road*. Capitol (S)T 2402. Los Angeles, July–August 1963. Lou Rawls (vocalist), Bobby Bryant (trumpet), Bud Brisbois (trumpet), Bob Rolfe (trumpet), James Dalton Smith (trumpet), Freddie Hill (trumpet), Ollie Mitchell (trumpet), Horace Tapscott (trombone), Lou Blackburn (trombone), Richard Hyde (trombone), Ronald Smith (trombone), Clifford Scott (alto saxophone), Sonny Criss (alto saxophone), Curtis Amy (tenor saxophone), Clifford Solomon (tenor saxophone), Teddy Edwards (tenor saxophone), Jay Migliori (baritone saxophone), Onzy Matthews (piano, arranger, leader), Rene Hall (guitar), Ray Crawford (guitar), Jim Crutcher (bass), and Charles "Chiz" Harris (drums).

"Tobacco Road"
"Cotton Fields"
"Rockin' Chair"
"Stormy Weather"
"Ol' Man River"
"Blues for a Four-String Guitar"
"St. Louis Blues"
"Georgia on My Mind"
"Sentimental Journey"
"Summertime"

Lou Blackburn. *Jazz Frontier.* Imperial IMP.LP 9228. Los Angeles, 1963. Freddie Hill (trumpet), Blackburn (trombone), Horace Tapscott (piano), John Duke (bass), and Leroy Henderson (drums). Reissued in *Perception* by French Sounds Records FSR–CD 307. 1999.

"Harlem Bossa Nova"
"New Frontier"
"Perception"
"Luze Bluze"
"I Cover the Waterfront"
"17 Richmond Park"
"The Clan"
"Scorpio"
"Jazz-a-Nova"
"Stella by Starlight"

Lou Blackburn. *Two-Note Samba.* Imperial IMP.LP 12242. Los Angeles, 1963. Freddie Hill (trumpet), Lou Blackburn (trombone), Horace Tapscott (piano), John Duke (bass), and Leroy Henderson (drums). Reissued in *Perception* by Fresh Sounds Records FSR–CD 307. 1999.

"Manha De Carnival"
"Jean-Bleu"
"Blues for Eurydice"
"Grand Prix"

"Two-Note Samba"
"Song of Delilah"
"Dear Old Stockholm"
"Secret Love"

Curtis Amy. *The Sounds of Broadway/The Sounds of Hollywood*. Palomar G34003. Hollywood, 1965. Warren Gale Jr. (trumpet), Lester Robinson [should be Robertson] (trombone), Curtis Amy (soprano saxophone, tenor saxophone), Horace Tapscott (piano), Eddie Mathias (bass), and Mel Lee (drums). Strings arranged and conducted by Onzy Matthews.

"Goldfinger"
"Get Me to the Church on Time"
"Dear Heart"
"Spoonful of Sugar"
"Love Line"
"Fiddler on the Roof"
"Now I Have Everything"
"Of Human Bondage"
"Sunrise, Sunset"
"Guess Who I Saw Today"

The Sonny Criss Orchestra. *Sonny's Dream (Birth of the New Cool)*. Prestige OJCCD–707–2 (P–7576). Los Angeles, 8 May 1968. Horace Tapscott (conductor, arranger), Conte Condoli (trumpet), Dick Nash (trombone), Criss (soprano saxophone, alto saxophone), David Sherr (alto saxophone), Teddy Edwards (tenor saxophone), Pete Christlieb (baritone saxophone), Ray Draper (tuba), Tommy Flanagan (piano), Al McKibbon (bass), and Everett Brown Jr. (drums).

"Sonny's Dream"*
"Ballad for Samuel"*
"The Black Apostles"*
"The Golden Pearl"*
"Daughter of Cochise"*
"Sandy and Niles"*

William Marshall. *For My People*. Capitol. Never issued. William Marshall (spoken word), Horace Tapscott (conductor, arranger).

Bob Thiele Emergency. *Head Start*. Flying Dutchman FDS-104. Los Angeles, 1969. Bobby Bradford (trumpet), John Carter (tenor saxophone), Horace Tapscott (piano), Tom Williamson (bass), Buzz Freeman (drums) on one selection.

"In the Vineyard"

David T. Walker. *Going Up!* Revue RS 7211. Los Angeles, May 1969. Joe Sample (piano), Horace Tapscott (piano), David T. Walker (guitar), Tracy Wright (bass), Panama Francis (percussion, drums), Richard Waters (drums). Reissued in Japan. PCD-1324. 1996.

"Can I Change My Mind"
"My Baby Loves Me"
"Since You've Been Gone (Baby, Baby, Sweet Baby)"
"I'm Going To Make You Love Me"
"Medley: You Don't Know What Love Is, This Guy's
    In Love With You"
"Stormy"
"Bad Bad Whiskey"
"Going Up"
"Tip Toe Through The Tulips With Me"
"Watch Out, Dynamite"
"Baby I Need Your Loving" (only on CD)

Elaine Brown. *Seize the Time.* Vault 131. Hollywood. Elaine Brown (vocalist) and Horace Tapscott (conductor, piano, arranger).

"Seize the Time"
"The Panther"
"And All Stood By"
"The End of Silence"
"The Meeting" (the Black Panther Party national anthem)
"Very Black Man"
"Take It Away"
"One Time"
"Assassination"
"Poppa's Come Home"

Elaine Brown. *Elaine Brown.* Black Forum BF458L. Hollywood, 1973. Elaine Brown (vocalist), and Horace Tapscott (conductor, arranger).

"No Time"
"Jonathan"
"Can't Go Back"
"All the Young and Fine Men"

"Until We're Free"
"I Know Who You Are"
"Child in the World"
"A Little Baby"
"And We Shall Meet Again"

Billie Harris. *I Want Some Water.* Nimbus West NS 510 C. 1999. Billie Harris (reeds), Horace Tapscott (piano), David Bryant (bass), Everett Brown, Jr. (drums), Daa'oud Woods (percussion), Lorelei (vocalist). Recorded in Los Angeles, 1983.

"Prayer of Happiness"
"I Want Some Water"
"The Advocate"
"Blues for Lupe"
"Many Nights Ago" (see Arkestra listing)
"Why Don't You Listen?"* (see Solo listing)

Michael Session. *'N Session.* ITM Pacific ITMP 970074. Hollywood, 24 March 1990. Steve Smith (trumpet), Jon Williams (trumpet), Michael Session (alto saxophone, tenor saxophone, vocalist), Horace Tapscott (piano), Nate Morgan (piano), Henry Franklin (bass), and Sonship Theus (drums).

"Quagmire Manor at 5 A.M."
"Bavarian Mist"
"Short Stop"
"UMATU"
"No Cash"
"Lately's Solo (Milestones)"
"Maud's Mood"*

Nelly Pouget. *Le Vivre.* Minuit Regards LH 27292. Paris, 18–19 November 1993. Nelly Pouget (soprano saxophone, tenor saxophone), Michel Godard (tuba), Horace Tapscott (piano), Kent Carter (bass), Jean-Francois Jenny-Clark (bass), Andrew Cyrille (drums), and Gerard Siracusa (percussion).

"Le Vivre"
"Minuit Regards"
"Bebe Ange"
"Les Poissons"
"Douceur"

"Humoristique"
"Amour Ange Ange Amour"
"Nina Bebe"
"Variations De Clartes"

Project Blowed. Project Blowed Recordings. Los Angeles, 1994. Freestyle Fellowship (Aceyalone, Self Jupiter, Mikah Nine, and Peace), JMD and the Underground Railroad (Nedra Wheeler [bass], Michael Hunter [trumpet], Randall Willis [tenor saxophone], and JMD [drums]), and Horace Tapscott (piano).

"Hot"

Kamau Daáood. *Leimert Park.* MAMA Foundation MMF 1019. Los Angeles, February–April 1997. Kamau Daáood (spoken word), Michael Session (soprano saxophone, alto saxophone), Randall Willis (tenor saxophone), Phil Vieux (bass clarinet), James Newton (flute), Horace Tapscott (piano), Nate Morgan (piano), Rodney Lee (piano), Karen Briggs (violin), Art Davis (bass), Roberto Miguel Miranda (bass), Osama Afifi (bass), Herb Graham Jr. (drums), Billy Higgins (drums), Willie Jones III (drums), Munyungo Jackson (percussion), Carmen Bradford (vocalist), and Dwight Trible (vocalist).

"Leimert Park"
"Tears"
"Her" (for [Daáood's] wife, Baadia)
"Deep River in Her Voice" (for Billie Holiday)
"Balm of Gilead" (for Billie Holiday and Lester Young)
"Sunbathing in My Tears"
"The Men"
"Liberator of the Spirit" (for John Coltrane)
"World Music"
"Ancestral Echoes"*
"Army of Healers"*
"Art Blakey's Drumsticks"

FILM SOUNDTRACKS

Passing Through. Directed, produced, and edited by Larry Clark. Independent, early 1970s. Score arranged and conducted by Horace Tapscott with the Pan Afrikan Peoples Arkestra.

Sweet Jesus, Preacher Man. With Roger Mosley and Marla Gibbs. Independent, early 1970s. Score arranged and conducted by Horace Tapscott and Linda Hill with the Pan Afrikan Peoples Arkestra.

TV/VIDEO PERFORMANCES

The Store Front series. Solo piano. Sue Booker, producer. Channel 28, KCET.

Afro-American Classics. Solo piano. Michael Wilcots, producer. California State University at Dominguez Hills.

Discography 2:

Music from the Ark

Note: This listing is only of recordings made within the context of the Pan Afrikan Peoples Arkestra, for the most part with other members, and does not include the substantial number of recordings that have been made by members and former members over the years in other settings. The recordings are listed alphabetically by leader; a plus sign (+) indicates an original composition by the leader.

Gary Bias (soprano saxophone, alto saxophone, flute) *East 101.* Nimbus NS–802. Los Angeles, 1981. With David "Eric" Tilman (piano), Rickey Kelly (vibes), John Heard (bass), Roberto Miguel Miranda (bass), Rickey Minor (electric bass), and Fritz Wise (drums).

"Asiki"+
"Dear Violet"+
"Arthur's Vamp"+
"East 101"+
"As Children Play"+

Curtis Clark (piano, clarinet). *Phantasmagoria.* Nimbus NS–3368. Los Angeles, January 1984. With Roberto Miguel Miranda (bass) and Sonship Theus (drums).

"Phantasmagoria"+
"Bouquet"+
"Missing Persons"+
"Thought of One"+

Linda Hill (piano, vocalist). *Lullaby for Linda*. Nimbus NS–791. Los Angeles, 1981. With Sabir Mateen (tenor saxophone, clarinet), Adele Sebastian (flute, vocalist), Aubrey Hart (flute), Fundi Legohn (french horn), Roberto Miguel Miranda (bass), Everett Brown Jr. (drums), Virgilio Figueroa (percussion), and Jugegr Juan Grey (vocalist).

"Leland's Song"+
"The Creator's Musician"
"Lullaby for Linda"+
"Children"+

Rickey Kelly (vibes). *Limited Stops Only*. Nimbus NS–3146. Los Angeles, October 1983. With Dadisi Komolafe (flute), David E. Tillman (piano), James Leary III (bass), and Sherman Ferguson (drums).

"Distant Vibes"+
"Flying Colors"
"Yesterdays"
"Same Shame"
"Dolphin Dance"
"Lush Life"

Dadisi Komolafe (alto saxophone, flute). *Hassan's Walk*. Nimbus NS–3035. Los Angeles, October 1983. With Eric Tillman (piano), Rickey Kelly (vibes), Roberto Miguel Mirando (bass), and Sonship Theus (drums).

"Hassan's Walk"+
"Speak No Evil"
"Calvary"
" 'Round Midnight"

Roberto Miguel Miranda (bass). *The Creator's Musician*. Nimbus NS–468. Los Angeles, 1980.

"Evolution on the Life of Moses"+
"Saint Michael Servant of the Lord"+
"Interpolations"
"Imagined Dance for Solo Bass"+
"Song for String Bass"

Roberto Miguel Miranda (bass, vocalist). *Raphael*. Nimbus NS–1024. Hollywood, July–August 1980. With Virgilio Figueroa-Salidor (conga,

vocalist), George Andujar-Seguidor (conga, cascara, vocalist), Raul
Travieso Rodriquez-Hablador (tumba, vocalist), Andrew Acosta-
Guataca (bell, conga, vocalist), Wynell Montgomery (soprano
saxophone, flute), Vanessa Burch (piano), Alex Cline (conductor,
percussion, drums), Mitchell Sanchez-Itotele (oboe), Wayne Peet
(piano, conductor), Vinny Golia (tenor saxophone, baritone
saxophone), Jeff Littleton (electric bass), Nels Cline (electric guitar),
Louis Raphael Miranda Jr. (drums, percussion), Aviva Rosenbloom
(vocalist), Ben Rosenbloom (piano), Hansonia Caldwell (piano), and
Deborah Miranda (vocalist).

"Bembe"
"A Case in Point"
"Bata"
"Raphael"+
"Faith"+
"Piano Sonata #1"+
"The Creator's Musicians"+
"Prayer #1"+
"Columbia"

Nate Morgan (piano). *Journey into Nigritia.* Nimbus NS–3257. Los
Angeles, 1983. With Dadisi Komolafe (alto saxophone), Jeff Littleton
(bass), and Fritz Wise (drums).

"Mrafu"+
"Morning Prayer"+
"Mother"+
"Journey into Nigritia"+
"He Left Us a Song"+
"Study in C.T."+

Nate Morgan (piano). *Live in Santa Barbara.* Nimbus NS–508C. Santa
Barbara, 1987. With Jeff Littleton (bass), and Fritz Wise (drums).

"All Blues"
"Forest Flower"
"In a Sentimental Mood"
"Night in Tunisia"
"Darius the Bold"+
"Invitation"

Nate Morgan (piano). *Retribution, Reparation*. Nimbus NS–3479. Los Angeles, 1984. With Danny Cortez (trumpet), Jesse Sharps (reeds), Joel Ector (bass), and Fritz Wise (drums).

"U.G.M.A.A.ger"+
"Impulse"+
"Mass Madness"+
"Retribution, Reparation"+
"One Finger Snap"
"Come Sunday"

Adele Sebastian (flute, vocalist). *Desert Fairy Princess*. Nimbus NS–680. Los Angeles, 1981. With Bobby West (piano), Rickey Kelly (vibes), Roberto Miranda (bass), Billy Higgins (drums, gembreh), and Daoude Woods (percussion). Reissued by Nimbus West Records NS-680C. 2000.

"Desert Fairy Princess"
"Belize"
"I Felt Spring"
"Man from Tanganyika"
"Day Dreamer"
"Prayer for the People"

Dwight Trible. *Horace*. Working Class Productions. January 1999. Dwight Trible (vocalist), Kamau Daáood (spoken word), Charles Owens (reeds), John Rangel (piano), Trevor Ware (bass), Billy Higgins (drums), Don Littleton (drums), Daniel Bejerano (drums), Derf Reklaw (percussion).

"A Love Supreme"
"The Statesman"
"Soul Eyes"
"Mothership"*
"Papa Lean Griot" (should be: "PAPA, The Lean Griot")
"Return to the Ethers"

Index

Horace Tapscott (1934–1999) was an accomplished jazz
musician and activist in Los Angeles.

Steven Isoardi teaches at the Oakwood School and
Antioch University in the Los Angeles area. He coedited
Central Avenue Sounds: Jazz in Los Angeles.

Library of Congress Cataloging-in-Publication Data

Tapscott, Horace.
Songs of the Unsung : the musical and social journey of
Horace Tapscott / by Horace Tapscott ; edited by Steven
Isoardi.
p.   cm.
Includes discographies and indexes.
ISBN 0-8223-2531-4 (cloth : alk. paper) —
ISBN 0-8223-2638-8 (pbk. : alk. paper)
1. Tapscott, Horace.   2. Pianists—United States—
Biography.   3. Jazz musicians—United States—
Biography.   4. Afro-American musicians—Biography.
I. Title: Musical and social journey of Horace Tapscott.
II. Isoardi, Steven Louis, 1949–   III. Title.
MI417.TI8 A3 2001
781.65'092—dc21
[B]   00-061752